CARRY THE MOON ACROSS THE SKY

A NOVEL

by Jillian Rose

NEW YORK
Stony Iron Publishing
2018

Copyright © 2018 by Jillian Rose
All rights reserved. This book or any portion thereof may not be reproduced or used in any manner whatsoever without the express written permission of the publisher except for the use of brief quotations in a book review.

Printed in the United States of America

First Printing, 2018

ISBN 978-0-9998847-0-6

Stony Iron Publishing
Brooklyn, NY 11201

www.StonyIronPublishing.com

Sometimes
I wonder

if on the day
you were born

I searched for my way
back into this world.

I can see how
your light could have
shown me the way.

PREFACE

This story is written as fiction. The names are fictional names. The scenes are fictional scenes. But, the story is deeply tied into my truth. Every page comes from my heart. Every word ties together as pieces of my soul.

This is difficult to admit, out loud, and to you, because it is easier to hide behind a mask of storytelling, than bare one's most intimate. But, it would be the height of hypocrisy to strive toward a wholly embodied embracing of truth in expression, and then only share the comfortable bits here.

So, I will tell you first, that I am grateful on the most basic level for the writing process. It has been not only therapeutic and tremendously enjoyable, but life-altering on a deeply spiritual level. And, besides the individually transformative power of expression, I believe the creative process is also tied into a bigger picture. As connected and conscious beings, we touch each other through creation. We transform each other through our creative bravery.

While navigating the deeply transformative process of personal and spiritual development, I often felt alone. I was lucky enough to find exceptional support in certain key characters in my life, but the isolation came in general lack of awareness, both internally and within society as a whole. Before my transformation process began, I didn't even know that such a process existed. And while experiencing the wonders (and the aches) that are sure to come with growth and the opening to conscious love, I felt totally misunderstood by the world at large.

Eventually, I came to understand that I was, in fact, not alone. Instead, I was supported in miraculous ways—ways that I at the time could not even imagine. But, I was still left baffled by the simultaneous secrecy and misrepresentation of the truth of the spiritual journey.

I believe we are drawn to those things that help us to grow. To the people who will open our hearts. The visions that will expand our perspectives. The words that will touch our souls.

We must come together. We must inspire each other. We must share with each other so that we can understand our fear, which thrives off of a shaky relationship with the unknown. We are not alone. We are brave souls, finding the strength and courage to grow through our darkness. And I have come to understand that we brave souls, have one overarching thing in common. The thing that drives it all. We find inspiration in love.

Are you ready to dig your hands deep into your dirt? Believe me when I say, there is a lot of beautiful to be found there.

PART ONE

The Sun

Daylight, full of small dancing particles and the one great turning,
our souls are dancing with you,
without feet, they dance.
Can you see them when I whisper in your ear?

—RUMI

1

There is a candle in your heart, ready to be kindled.
There is a void in your soul, ready to be filled.
You feel it, don't you?

—RUMI

I am going to start at the beginning. Where else would any story start? Thing is, I've had many beginnings. We all do. Each one leads to the next in a tantalizing dance of circumstance and synchronicity. But this beginning? It was different. It was the deck of cards folding in on itself, forming a neat and purposeful pile. It was the leaf that drifted down from the sky into the perfect space between blades of grass. It was the beat of heart echoing tenderly, lacing itself between eons of silence.

It was the beginning that all the other beginnings were made for, and all those to come were molded from. It was the beginning that taught me that there is no stopping a soul determined to awaken through love. Until that night, I couldn't hear its whispers. The world was just too loud. And, that particular night started the same way—born in muffled sound. It intertwined its song with a monotonous and melodious throbbing, sad and soft, that came from my headphones, my heart pumping surges of ache to its quiet rhythm.

The unevenness of the train tracks was made obvious through the not-so-subtle movements of my body, each sway jolting my tense muscles, its rattling steel mingling with my ricocheting thoughts. When I leaned my head back, water pooled beneath my lashes. My dark eyes were ominously awaiting the next phase of release.

Buildings and trees and traffic blurred by. Power lines dipped and arched as if they were in motion. Life's canvas meshed and moved before me, undulating in an impressionist painting of the dusk winter sky, and allowing solace in its numbing and blearing beauty.

I couldn't explain it then, but there was something. Something about what lay ahead that smelled like summer. Something hot and free and alive, while wading through the dead of winter. The future was being painted in real time and I drifted through it, lulled by trance-like visions and urged forward by the mysterious and gentle tug of magnetic pull, each moment delving deeper into the unknown.

I sat this way (drifting forward, swaying sideways, and sitting in place, all at once) until the train's momentum began to slow, about an hour between its starting point and destination. With the change in momentum, the blurred view transformed rapidly into something with more structure; a city of sharp shapes and concrete contours. I could not maintain my trance amongst the distracting detail, so I lifted my head to look around the train car.

The passengers had begun to rouse themselves from their traveling inertia. They made their way toward the still-closed doors with strained postures. They threw bags over their shoulders, tapped their feet and squinted their eyes as if impatient glares would force time forward. I did not stir. I sat milking the last moments of forced respite. The songs in my ears became my metronome, beating to times graces as the train slowed at its own pace. Only when it gave its small and final lurch did I gather my things and make my way toward the platform, looking at the ground as I climbed the stairs.

Penn Station was bustling, as usual. The customarily diverse crowd of weekday commuters was even more-so a patchwork of myriad forms on that night, people running here and there on weekend excursions, alight with that certain sense of possibility that a Saturday evening brings. The air was electric for that reason. I felt it on my cheeks, but where it met me, it sizzled and died, its light escaping like a drop of cool water on a hot pan. None of that energy could permeate my shield, an armor encasing my body in something much denser, and wholly unyielding. Innate and effortless manners of being for everyone else, reflexive actions like smiling, laughing and breathing, were laborious for me. It had only been a week, but it was difficult to remember how these things ever flowed from me without force.

My Aunt Athena once told me that when a dog dies, they take a part of our soul with them. It's not their fault. They are only trying to help. They are so good at holding our space for us while they are here, that our energy becomes a part of them. The problem, once they leave, isn't actually our Swiss cheese soul. It's the fact that we don't know how to fill in the holes with anything other than sadness.

The night before, I slept by Amelia on the bathroom floor. She liked the cool of the tile and the hum of the pipes. She wasn't gone. Not yet. But I already felt as full of holes as a decade old rag.

I swallowed around the lump in my throat. The musty heat that permeated the station made its way into my lungs and laid heavy in my chest. My exhaustion was palpable, the desire to sit down surpassing *want* and quickly approaching *need*. I pulled the headphones out of my ears and maneuvered through the sea of people, grazing shoulders as if I were trying to weave through raindrops. The waiting room in the train station was not where anyone wanted to be; not anyone native to New York, at least. We knew better. But, since one of the side effects of desperation is a shift in priorities, I made my way there without a second thought. There was a chair in the far corner. It looked grungy and overused, but it was the choice with the least populated surrounding space, so I placed my bag on my lap and let my shoulders fall, settling into the uncomfortable seat as comfortably as possible.

The quickly vibrating energy of my nerves clashed with the slowness of my lethargy, a dichotomy that pulled at my insides. Edgy restlessness, when paired with debilitating weariness, is a vexatious combination.

I was sure I looked rather pitiful, hunched over and pale, red eyes glazed over, but I didn't particularly care. I was sure no one else did either. My eyes found a single focus, the space where two walls met sharply with the ceiling above, hoping that I could stare at this space long enough for its to edges blur, its surrounding space to blacken into fuzzy periphery. But the more I tried to will it, the more elusive it became. Thought was taking precedence over numbness. Thought tends to be frustratingly more powerful than most things.

I wanted to get this meeting over with before it even began. My options consisted of a few choices in varying degrees of courtesy and consequence. I could, of course, turn around and go home. "I'm terribly sorry," I'd say, "but because of a circumstance out of my control, I will not be able to keep our appointment this evening. My apologies for any inconvenience this may have caused." And we would reschedule, or not. I could also stay, and go through the motions. Do my duty without any extra effort, answering questions concisely, being sure not to ask any of my own, and as quickly as possible, move on toward my own more pressing matters, regardless of the outcome. Or, I could stay and shove my shaky hands into the pockets of my jacket, attempting to feign my lack of stability with a mask of eagerness and vigor. This, I wasn't sure I could pull off, however. My muscles were too tired to smile.

I let these options percolate as I stared at my chosen spot on the wall, fluctuating between choices as endurance waxed and waned. That unearthly pull that smelled like summer continued to tap me on the shoulder. It was so faint it was almost imperceptible, but it was persistent. I had shoved so many things into periphery that week. It was necessary, but still, it was true. Perhaps, this could not be one of those things.

I checked my phone.

Still no messages. We had never met. Not in person, anyway. He was important. I knew that, and not just because that's what I was told (though that is what I was told), but by the way he presented himself. His emails were short, but sweet, painted with simple confidence and absolute knowledge of his craft. They were somewhat professional, but more so, unrestricted. The casual demeanor was a direct result of the nature of our dynamic, it would seem, being introduced through a mutual friend, even if it was for business purposes.

I met this mutual friend, Jason, at some party a few summers back. We were polar opposites, and maybe that's the reason we got along. Where he was brash, intense, and loud, I was gentle, subtle, and reserved. No one understood the allure, but he was always a good friend to me. Truth is, we balanced each other out. Each of us needed a little bit of the other's natural essence, and each of us saw that the other was far more multifaceted than we let out to the world.

"I have this friend," he said one day, as I sat in the passenger seat of his red Ram truck, watching the highway. "He's a great guy. Really talented. I wonder if he's hiring."

I had been searching for new work for a couple of months. Any leads were appreciated.

"I'll throw him a message tonight," he said.

I was intrigued, but not enough to get ahead of myself. I thanked him with sincerity. He flicked his right hand in the air and shook his head in a *no big deal* kind of way.

"You never know," he said. "Maybe something good can come of it."

I typed up an email that night for this *great* and *talented* stranger named Arun. I assumed the name was Aaron at first, but his email address altered my conjecture. They were totally different names, they just sounded the same. The email included my bare-boned resume, and, as graphic design was a recent career change for me, a portfolio that contained very little outside the realm of student work. I was nervous to send it to him. Embarrassed about my lack of experience. But fear of failure can have a funny way of holding us back from success, and I knew logically that I didn't have much to lose. Except for pride, but that's all relative anyway.

I added a short and sweet line of text thanking him for taking the time, took a deep breath, and sent it. He was gracious enough to respond that same evening, proposing we find a time to meet. A favor to Jason, I'm sure, but appreciated all the same.

With busy schedules and the upcoming holidays, our meeting took a while to come to fruition. I didn't want to be pushy, but weeks had passed since our last correspondence, so I eventually sent him an email.

I'm sure you are very busy, I said, *but I am still very interested in meeting with you, when the time is right.*

I gave myself a metaphorical pat on the back for my bold move, which wasn't as much bold as it was out of character, and waited. A short while later, Arun invited Jason and I to take a trip into the city the following Saturday night. *We wouldn't want this to be all business-y*, he added, calming me with the casual nature of the invitation.

When the day of our meeting rolled around, however, the timing was dishearteningly awful.

Jason couldn't come after all, and I was neck deep in life-circumstance of my own, doing whatever I could to help my best friend Amelia hold onto life. Arun expressed that he was happy to move forward with the plan, just the two of us, so it felt particularly irresponsible to cancel at the last minute. And more importantly, aside from courtesy, there was that particular something else there. The something that smelled of summer. The one that wouldn't let me sink into avoidance. Showing up was the responsible thing to do, of course, but this push—this push came from somewhere much more instinctive. I was blind to its purpose, but I saw its essence like a light in the fog: muted, blurred, but particularly bright against the damp, night sky.

It was something I could not shake.

So, on that night, for that intangible reason, there I sat, on a sticky chair in a train station in Manhattan. I scanned the room for a screen that listed the outgoing train times in running color-coded lists, just in case, though I knew I wouldn't leave. I knew I wouldn't. I just hoped I could make it through the evening with some semblance of poise. That I could find it in myself to take my sadness and tuck it away for a while. Pretending takes a lot of strength.

I checked my phone again, pulling the screen down and letting it jump back up to load the new messages. Cell service in that corner of the station was not ideal. A few new emails showed up in my inbox. The most recent was from Arun, nearly ten minutes before.

I can meet you by Penn Station. En route...

Would he call me, I wondered? I lifted off the chair to put my phone in my back pocket, closed my purse, and got to my feet, shaking off the bleakness that had accumulated on my skin like dust. It would be over before I knew it. I had gotten through worse that week. We all had.

I made my way out toward the crowded station. The congestion was stifling, its stale heat washing over me heavy and hard. I breathed in and out a few times to steady myself, the air loaded with the stories of every passerby filling and then leaving my lungs. It was necessary, breathing consciously that way. The alternative consisted of holding my breath, and everyone else's. And that was just too much to hold.

I stood up straighter, and in that moment, my phone vibrated against me. I reached into my jeans and lifted it from my pocket, staring at the screen for a moment that stretched out across many. If I were watching the scene unfold in a movie, I'd impatiently assume it irrational that the person on the other end hadn't hung up yet. But just as time beats to its own drum in the movies, so it did then. I lifted my finger to answer, and it too passed through time that way, as if any sudden movement could shatter the air on the way there, breaking the moment into a million pieces.

It was Arun. He was late, and he was right on time.

"Hello, Selena," he said.

Something hot rushed through me. I was still for a moment, and then I walked a few quick paces forward, awkwardly, as if the ground were scorching the soles of my feet. It was my name, but no one had ever said it that way before. I repeated it in my mind, but spoke his with my lips, returning the favor.

"Hello, Arun."

It rolled off my tongue like a practiced song. Something escaped from a crevice in my chest, like a few stray champagne bubbles making their way through the neck of the bottle. I swallowed hard.

"Are you still in Penn Station?" he asked.

My heart was in my ears, muting the sounds of the station, but I could still hear every word, every nuance of breath that came from him.

"I am," I admitted, as if guilty of something. "Where would you like to meet?"

"Someplace with some more ambiance," he said. "Or at least some quiet."

There was something about his voice. It was the first time I'd heard it, and I noted its utter uniqueness. It was smooth and eloquent, with a simple sophistication that made it sound like he was from another time. It was soft and commanding. Quick-witted and serious. Penetrating and as light as air. It was this and it was that, all at once, and whatever was in between, I found myself instantly wanting to discover. What was this supposed and ridiculous clarity after only a few short words? Perhaps it was the lack of sleep. It all ran through my head so quickly between our words and I don't know how it fit into such a small space.

"Come out on 7th avenue?" he asked. "Stay on the phone with me so I know who I'm looking for."

"Great," I said, "I'm on my way."

We were quiet as we maneuvered toward our mutual destination.

That unique surge of energy lingered. It came as a surprise, considering minutes before my tank had all but run dry. But, there it was, percolating in my chest, and running both up and down my spine.

I got my bearings in space and looked toward a large stairway that opened up into the night air. I began to walk swiftly, one foot in front of the other, and with the momentum came enough vitality to send me climbing toward the mouth of the station. There was lightness in the air there, especially when compared to the stuffy, stale confines of the station. Crisp, fresh, still, and somehow quiet amongst a sea of tourists and car horns.

My phone was still clasped in my hand and resting on my ear, connecting me through the ethers to this mysterious stranger.

"I'm here," I said.

"I'm mere feet away," he said.

When I looked up, I could have sworn I heard the distinct sound of a *click* as the entire Universe aligned.

2

Respond to every call that excites your spirit.
—RUMI

Our eyes locked as he parted the crowd with effortless grace and gentle command, and walked confidently in my direction. His stride was elegant, muscles expanding and contracting in choreographed movement. His crystal blue eyes were visible even from a distance, and took on an increasingly intricate glimmer as the space between us diminished. They created my focal point, blurring periphery and silencing the sea of people around us. Time teetered on a needlepoint, neither moving forward, nor seeing anything in its wake. The breeze paused as if we stood in some kind of vacuum, my short hair settling in place, laying still in wisps around my face. In that precise moment, every surrounding car and cab and moving piece came to a halt, waiting patiently, nowhere else to be.

Silence. Slowness. Light.

And then, he was there in front of me. The space between us was hardly a space at all compared to moments ago and the rest of life before that. None of that time and distance mattered in that moment, because the *right now* was all that was, as I stood in front of this astonishingly beautiful being that was radiating some sort of *something* that I didn't understand and couldn't try to. It was soft, and it was electric, and it smelled like midnight-wide-awake. His crystal blue eyes held the glint of stars and streetlights, and were close enough then to hold my reflection too.

He lifted his arm toward me and we took each other's hand in a welcoming shake, creating a current, sparking upon contact. The space around us must have been equally touched by the charge, for in that instant, just as quickly as everything had stopped, everything started to move again. Its momentum whirled around me, around us, in a fast-forward symphony of sounds and sights. I held my breath as it took over, hurtling me head-first through time and space while my feet were planted on the ground. I couldn't feel where my skin and the air met. Everything moved as if it were made of one thing, and that thing was me and him and everything.

I knew it was time to speak, but I didn't know how I would find words amidst it all. I continued to look into his eyes, nearly blinded by their light, and uttered with surprising confidence, "It's so nice to finally meet you."

My voice sounded different. It sounded like silk, or honey. It sounded like it came from somewhere else.

"Finally," he said.

And then our hands parted, and I felt the breeze on my neck again. The deep night draped over our shoulders with its cool and gentle fingers, and I noticed the gleam of moonlight on velvet pavement.

What was this?

There was no time to make sense of it, so instead, I stood quietly transfixed in its sublimity; a reality as tangible as floating along the waves in mid-July, and simultaneously, just as dream-like.

"Should we get out of here? Somewhere less crowded," he said, in question and command.

I nodded. He cocked his head to the left, to notify me of which direction we were headed, and he walked, looking back to make sure I followed. I was quickly by his side again. It was a place I already knew I liked being, better than most other places. He moved swiftly, and though my knees were shaking slightly, my feet flitted across the pavement, and I had no trouble keeping up.

Out of the corner of my eye, I looked at him. He wore a black leather jacket, unbuttoned and worn, that hung over his arms and shoulders. The leather cloaked him like the night, contracting and relaxing over him as his arms swung with subtle movement. I noticed his black jeans, which were not too loose, and not too tight. They rested atop black dress shoes, offering a touch of shiny professionalism.

His skin was pale and smooth, his hair soft brown with hints of dusted blonde.

He turned his head toward the street and made his way off the curb, moving with dancer-like grace and impeccable posture. Never did his feet hit the ground harshly, even when shifting from the sidewalk to the street level below. He lifted his arm and strained his neck with the obvious aim of hailing a cab, as they sped past us, three at a time. Midtown was often frustratingly crowded. He, however, did not look frustrated.

"Good thing you're here," he said. "Usually, they pay no attention to me."

He winked as a cab careened from the middle lane and came to an abrupt stop in front of us.

Arun opened the door for me, and I tucked my head to climb in, shifting to the far end of the backseat and composing the grinning lines of my face.

"Hey, man. West 10th and Hudson, please," he said, as he closed the door behind him.

Even in the quiet confines of the back seat there was something strange in that air. A buzzing. It rested between us and it encircled us. I felt it in my hands and in my eyelids and in my shaking knees and in my heart. Could anyone else feel it? The car jerked forward, and Arun cracked his window.

"So," he said, leaning back in his seat and turning toward me. "Tell me."

"What would you like to know?" I responded, with a bit of shake to my voice.

"About yourself. What brings you here?"

I couldn't quite tell him it was the smell of summer. I probably shouldn't bring up the fact that I was magnetized toward the space between us that I instantly understood as warmth in the middle of cold turmoil and light amidst the darkness. I stuck to career.

"Well," I said, looking down at my hands, "I'm trying to figure out my next step."

"Ok," he said. "We should probably go over a few of your last ones then, you know, for reference purposes."

I let out a small laugh. "Right. Ok. Well, I worked as an art therapist for a few years."

"Can I ask what an art therapist does?"

"I worked as a traditional master's level therapist, but I used art in treatment, as an alternate form of expression," I explained. "I've always had an interest in psychology, and I've always had an affinity for art. So, combining them seemed just right."

"Sounds just right," he said, "but I'm supposing it wasn't?"

"It's an incredible field," I said, "but emotionally, it took a toll on me. I worked in inpatient psychiatric units, and a few tough experiences pushed me to explore other options."

"As in, design?"

"Yes. I took online courses and was lucky enough to get a job while I was still in enrolled. At a promotional company."

"And?"

"It may come off as ungrateful," I said.

He cocked his head a degree or two to the side.

"To put it gently," I said, "that place was just not for me."

"That's not ungrateful, Selena. It's reality. What if you didn't put it gently?"

His eyes burned into me. He leaned slightly toward me, his left arm draped over the back of the seat. In any usual interview, I would be more diplomatic. But this didn't feel usual.

"The place was awful. The people, the work, even the office. I had to move on."

"Good. Good." He nodded his head in approval. "So, then what?"

"I worked there for about a year, and then I left to pursue some freelance work. It's been going all right. It's just been tough to maintain without the experience."

"Right. So, what do you enjoy? What kind of things do you want to design?"

I felt my face flush with heat. What did I want to do? Such a basic question, but I wasn't sure. My throat became slick with embarrassment, and the words got caught there. I was usually better in interviews. I guess I wasn't experienced in sort-of-interviews with breathtaking strangers.

"It's ok if you don't know yet," he assured me, as if he could read my thoughts. "Sometimes it's just as important to discover what we don't want."

"Yes. I've gotten pretty good at that," I said.

His blonde eyelashes, that were lighter than his brown hair, closed softly over his blue eyes, and then fluttered up again in a sure and soothing way.

"Can I ask about you?" I inquired, tentatively.

"Of course you can." He paused and squinted and tilted his head forward. I noticed this subtle skill, of adding emphasis of emotion that way, with a stare and a pause and then a breath before the words flowed again. "I'll give you the synopsis, ok?"

"Ok," I said, changing my crossed leg from right to left, and wondering if my nuances gave me away too.

"I don't consider myself a designer, really. I mean, I design, of course. I know how to make things look beautiful. But I think of myself as more of an innovator. A creator of unique solutions, and original ideas and technologies..."

He went on to describe his company, the foundation he built it upon, the clients he worked with, and the type of work they did. He was wildly successful, that was obvious, but that is not what made his monologue so hypnotizing. It was an air of knowingness that permeated his breath; a depth to his passion and drive that ran deeper than I could discover between those short words. I trusted him already. I trusted every word that came from him. Every piece of opinion and advice felt like truth, so obvious in its logic that I couldn't imagine ever seeing things in any other way.

Just as I started to lose his words in my enamored thoughts, the cab came to a halt. He thanked the driver and paid for the ride and I thanked him for his kindness. "Of course," he whispered, his words dancing toward my ears.

We both hopped out and walked a few strides toward a bar on the corner. It appeared well-lit from the outside, but inside things looked different. I'd noticed that about this city. Not many things appeared the same on the outside as they did behind closed doors. The interior was dim and intimate, with flickering lights and high wooden tables. People lined the walls wearing jeans and Converse sneakers, holding bottles of beer and speaking with their company in muffled sound. We found two seats at the end of the bar, near the glow of a soft overhead light.

Arun swung one leg over the stool and straddled it, pulling it closer to the bar as he settled in. I hopped up and crossed my ankles. "I'm going to have a Guinness," Arun told the bartender, without looking at a menu. "What would you like to drink?"

"I'll have the same," I said, keeping my usual indecisiveness out of the equation, and a few minutes later, two frothy stouts were placed in front of us.

"To moving forward," he said.

"To moving forward."

I didn't start smiling then, but only because I already was. It felt so easy that I hadn't even noticed. I guess remembering how to smile is like riding a bike. My muscles remembered what happiness looked like.

We talked then about the room we were in, about the beer we were drinking, about the small little flowerpot-shaped candle holders that held the flickering lights in front of us. We didn't talk about the way our legs were turned in toward one another, since there was no room between the high stools and the bar. I didn't mention how it felt to bring our faces close, to speak something into his ear when my words got lost in the sounds of the crowd.

"I just feel ready to *live*, you know? In a different way than I have," I explained. "I don't know. Suddenly, not taking the risk felt a lot riskier than actually taking it."

"Our work lives are symbolic," he said. "What do we settle for? What do we strive for? How much control do we want over our destiny?"

I shook my head and tucked my hair behind my ear.

"Lack of foresight into what is to come next is daunting," I said, "but freeing, too. As if every possibility is laid before me."

"As it always is," he responded with a slight shrug.

"Right," I said. "Why is it so easy to forget that?"

"Maybe there's comfort in thinking there is some kind of order," he said. "Some kind of script to follow."

"You don't think there is?" I asked. "Any order, I mean?"

"I don't know," he said. "I do believe that we are creators of our circumstances."

"Yes, of course," I said. "But..." I thought for a moment. "Can't there be some kind of order and still room for endless possibility?"

"I don't see why not," he smiled, our thoughts aggregating like building blocks. "So, what do you think makes the unknown so daunting?"

"Fear runs its own scripts sometimes," I said, far more honestly than expected. It seemed a vulnerable answer. It seemed there was quickly a new language there, where words were laced with expansiveness and non-words were understood.

"You know what they say." He stopped for a moment to readjust his position on the stool, leaning in slightly. "How we do anything is how we do everything."

I sat quietly then, allowing my eyes to wander above his. I surely had not lived a life of risk and adventure in the past without fear making decisions for me, sometimes peeking its head in, and sometimes threatening to swallow me whole. But, what I believed and how I behaved were not the same thing. I knew how I saw the world, and it seemed it was just like he did. Maybe I was just learning to live it in this way; in the way I believed it. And maybe, that moment was the most present and alive I had felt in a very long time.

He got to the bottom of his glass, and I sipped away at my glass half full.

"So, can we bring up your work online?" He asked.

"We can."

"Good. I have an idea. If you're up to it."

"Sure," I responded without question, and then asked, only because it seemed I should, "What are you thinking?"

"Would you feel comfortable stopping by my place? It's not very far from here. This way, we can peruse your work, and I can hand some files over to you that I'd like you to check out. Some things you can learn from."

"Sure," I responded again.

"I was at a business dinner before this," he said, "so I don't have anything with me."

I loved to hear his voice, but explanation was unnecessary. I trusted his lead as we headed out of our nook and back onto the busy streets.

"It's only about a 10-minute walk. Shall we forego the car?"

"Yes," I smiled, "It's a beautiful night." And we walked. I tightened the belt around my jacket and exhaled. It was in fact a beautiful night, but I could still see my breath on the air. It hung before me for a moment before becoming one with the city, dancing in the light, and evaporating into the black sky. I thought of Amelia. I could almost hear her quick pitter-patter across the pavement as I pictured her marble eyes, wise as the sky with a glint like the stars. I thought the ache would be impossible to hide, but it lingered beneath my skin, shadowed by the light I was otherwise being doused in. I let it burn for a moment, and then I carefully tucked it away again. Any discomfort that normally permeated my moment to moment struggled to find steady ground, shriveling upon contact and falling through my cracks.

"Here we are," he said, as he pulled a heavy, bronze pocket clip from his black pants, and brought the front door key between his fingers. "Hope you saved some energy. I like to take the stairs."

I laughed inside, and nodded toward him. I had saved none, but somehow, some had found me.

"No elevator, ever?" I asked.

"Whenever I can avoid it," he said, looking back at me. I didn't ask him why, but he offered it up. "Control," he shrugged. "I have more of it this way."

His apartment was on the 5th floor of a charming building in downtown Manhattan, surrounded on all sides by culture, art, diversity, and an air of mysterious excitement. I nodded as we climbed past the 3rd floor. "We could all use a little more of that."

We were silent the rest of the way. I watched him climb as gracefully as I would have imagined while my heart pounded from the ascent. He opened his door with a decisive click, and I forced my breath to even, stepping with lightness into a long hallway. The entire apartment was under a blanket of darkness until he took his phone in his hand and turned on dim, golden lights with a few taps of his finger. The light cascaded softly over the space, touching everything with its muted glow.

The hallway led into an open room with a large window decorating the furthest wall and overlooking the downtown skyline. Unlike most New York apartments, the space was not confining. The living room was warm and airy, with contemporary décor and the marked touch of an artist's hand. A black leather couch, purposefully worn, sat with a massive black and white painting above. A wooden grooved coffee table rested in front atop an irregularly shaped black rug. There were pops of color too, but they came from life: trees, plants and flowers, in every corner, and on every sill.

There was too much to take in upon first glance, but my awareness homed in on the details as if it were snapping photographs that I could flip through later. Lining the walls were artifacts and works of art and science, small statues and old pages, and things I loved and things I didn't understand. Every piece, every detail, appeared to sit where it was with purpose, filling the room with reason and intrigue.

"What an incredible place to call home," I said.

"I'm one of those people with New York in my blood," he said. "I think it's the greatest place in the world. Now, would you like a glass of wine?" He collected two glasses that hung from a rack above the kitchen table.

"If you plan on opening a bottle?"

"If you want some, then I plan on it," he stated simply, as he cocked his head to the side, and one of his eyes caught the light.

"Well then, I'd love one. Thank you," I said, that now familiar heat rising from my core.

"You say *thank you* a lot," he stated, definitively. "More than most. In my experience, at least."

I never understood the lack of desire to express gratitude. I lived on the other end of the spectrum, where I experienced discomfort when taking anything from anyone. I guess that end wasn't extraordinarily healthy either.

"I think it was something worthy of thanks," I said.

"People expect a lot," he responded, "and then forget to be grateful for it." He scanned the wine rack, both with his eyes and with his floating hand, and then, seemingly changing his mind in an instant, opened the refrigerator instead. "Nevertheless, you do not have to thank me for every little thing. Or anything at all, for that matter." He smiled then. He chose a chilled bottle of white and held it up. "Good?"

"Good."

He poured two glasses of chardonnay that smelled of flowers and crisp morning air and happiness. I rarely drank white wine. I loved deep and velvety Cabernets that effortlessly warmed me with their fruity spice. On that night, however, I was appreciative of something bright. Something to combat the rising heat and dry mouth.

Arun went to gather his files, and I sat on the couch, situating myself, altering my position to simulate casualness. I was hyper aware of every bit of myself; every nuance of moving muscle, every rush of heart beat, every tenseness and every softening of my face. I was terrifically nervous to open my portfolio in front of him. I perhaps had never been more nervous to show anyone, anything. I felt the prickling heat of a sweat breaking. I wondered if he'd notice and the wondering made it worse.

He floated back from his room and landed on the couch next to me, sitting more closely than expected. He appeared to have none of the same issues as I did. No irrationally extreme facial muscle awareness or sweat breaking under his shirt. I could tell by the way he smelled. He was as fresh as the chardonnay, but far more perfect. There is no better way to describe it. It was its own essence. I filled myself with it quietly.

"Let's have a look, shall we?" He opened his computer, the newest MacBook Pro, and motioned for me to pull up my portfolio. I directed my shaking hand to the keyboard, fumbling to type in the address, backspacing over typos, and then allowing the cursor to move forward again, exposing me through mediocre pieces of creation.

His pointer finger slowly moved across the trackpad as he made his way down the page that housed my small compilation of accomplishments. I sat quietly, watching him scan and discreetly wringing my hands as I waited. He ran through each piece with extreme focus. Where he saw fault, he softly narrowed his eyes, as if his glare tried to give it life where I didn't know how. And, where he saw something beautiful, I watched him lighten ever so slightly. It was as perceptible as the way the air changes when a bird flies overhead, and it was just as lovely.

He was very kind in his criticism, but he was honest. I feared his overarching reactions of disgust were hidden beneath his kind words of encouragement, but intuitively, I trusted his transparency more than that. I had always lived a creative life. I don't know why I felt so confined in this particular world. So creatively muted and afraid of failure.

"Let's do this," he said, decisively. "I'll send you some files this week. Some work I've done in the past. You can noodle around with them a little, get a feel for some aspects of the programs that may be a bit more advanced than you're used to. And then, we'll move forward from there."

"That sounds wonderful. Thank you," I said instinctively, going slightly crimson.

He smiled. "Consider it a mentoring program. I'd like to help you get some footing here. Build a great portfolio. You've definitely got potential, which is the first necessary quality. Let's see where it can take you."

"It would be an honor to have a mentor such as yourself," I smiled back.

"You sound like a robot," he said, straining his face to hold feigned seriousness.

I blurted out a sharp, quick laugh, then settled myself and whispered honestly, "this made me nervous."

"Don't be. It's done and settled," he said. "Now, onto more important things."

He fixed his eyes to mine as he leaned slowly back. It was a moment I was sure I would play on a reel, over and over, long after it passed. His arm draped purposefully over the arm of the couch, confident grace radiating from every nuance of breath and a sideways smile painting itself elegantly across his face. I sat in front of him totally vulnerable, feeling not just looked at, but seen. His eyes burrowed into me. They were the color of the sky. Pools of transient wonder, of which I felt I could see to the bottom.

"Do you ever meditate?" He asked, seemingly out of nowhere, softly and ironically shaking me from my reverie.

"Meditate?" I asked. "I try to every day."

There was gentle confidence to my honesty, too. It wasn't always that way, but it was then.

"Everyday?" He gave a small laugh: the surprised and impressed kind, not the judgmental one. "I didn't expect that."

My shoulders rose and fell in a small, friendly shrug. "Well, yes, usually. That is the goal, at least. Why do you ask?"

"Curiosity," he said. "I've been trying it out."

"And, what do you think?" I asked.

"I'm intrigued, at least. Tell me about it. Tell me about you."

"Well, I worked with a teacher for the last, hmm, has to be seven years or so now," I said. "I adore her."

"That's a long time," he said. "In what way do you work together?"

"I've always taken group classes," I said. "I love the class space. Many invaluable and life-changing lessons. Lately, however, I've been trying my hand at dedicating myself more intensively to an independent practice, as well."

"What kind of practice?"

"I've always found it harder to truly commit outside of a group, and it seems it is time," I said. "A deeper delving."

"In what way?" he asked, digging deeper too.

I thought for a moment. "Using the tools I have learned to focus on further awareness and growth. Learning to trust my own voice and intuition in it all. I want to embrace life differently. Differently than I have in the past."

I stopped, and he leaned in closer.

"Go on," he said, burning me with his gaze. "What do you want to embrace?"

"A life of conscious awareness, I guess would be the best way to explain it. Bringing my spiritual practices down into my physical life. My meditation is a pretty active one. Energy work. Not so much about quieting the mind, but more about looking at thoughts and emotions, plucking out irrational reactions and beliefs, clearing and shifting, learning to flow with life and..." I suddenly felt I was talking too much, perhaps about something that wasn't making enough sense. These things sometimes seemed magical when spoken aloud, though not always in the way I meant them to. It was very real to me. Sturdily transformative. Ethereal without the abracadabra.

"It's hard to explain concisely," I said, apologetically.

"Well, then you don't have to explain it concisely," he said. "Am I being too invasive?"

"No, not at all," I said, because he wasn't. "It's quite refreshing, actually."

These weren't things I expressed often to others, but I felt safe expressing them to him.

He portrayed his understanding with a small nod.

"Anyway," I said, "it's changed things for me, as far as perspective goes, but I still have a long way to go when it comes to living it. I just can't shake it, you know? The idea that there is something so much bigger than we are, but somehow, is still *what* we are. And that we all have a lot more power than we give ourselves credit for."

"Power over what?" he asked.

"Ourselves. Our lives. Our world. Tough things will happen in life, of course, but there's just too much beauty to forget how miraculous it all is. How vast and eternal we are. It doesn't have to be so *hard*. That's a part I'm still learning..." I looked down when I said it. We both went quiet for a moment. He saw me shift into something like sadness. I hoped he didn't think it was his fault. It wasn't. I just remembered for a moment, that's all. The fact that it was only for a moment was the only thing that *was* his fault. If it wasn't for him, I would have been swimming in sadness all night.

"And what about you?" I asked, soothing the moment, for both our sakes.

"We all need a break, you know? From being up in our heads all the time."

I agreed with a shake of mine.

"I have so much trouble sitting still long enough," he admitted. "But hey, I guess that's why they call it a practice."

He leaned forward and closed his computer, looking off into someplace beyond the room and then directly back to me.

"Have you ever had a panic attack, Selena?" he asked, as abruptly as it seems but without tension in his face.

"I have," I responded, just as matter-of-factly. "Many, unfortunately," I laughed. "Have you?"

He looked slightly relieved. It's always nice to be in good company.

"Sure," he said. "It all moves pretty quickly up there." He tapped on his forehead. "It's easy to lose your hold on it sometimes."

"Maybe it's a worthy trade-off?" I asked. "A fast-moving mind would be a terrible thing to waste."

"Maybe," he smirked. "Until we find a way to have it all."

"You never know," I said, leaning back on the couch and noticing a softening of my muscles. He watched my eyes with his as he got up, and I was reminded of the leftover heat stuck under my blazer.

He went to get his phone that he had left on a small table by the hall, gliding across the floor, shoulders pushed back without effort. It was as if I had always known these intricacies. As if they were already a part of my neural passageways, weaved into me with wonder but without surprise. His bluntness may have appeared jarring to some, but not to me. There was a unique genuineness in it. A certain unsullied charm. I adored the delving he did, inquiring curiously into the things that I was comprised of. Things many others didn't care to know. I was immersed in him, in every word he spoke, and in the sensation he created in my core.

I wondered what life felt like to him then. If it was filled with something shadowy. If it was filled with something like mine.

"Seems we can learn a lot from each other, Selena."

And before I could respond, his phone rang.

"I'll be just a minute," he said.

I nodded and got up too, making my way back to the hallway that we had initially entered, and pushed open the bathroom door. I flipped the switch and the room flooded with light. It was harsher in its fluorescence than any other I had seen that night. I squinted for a moment, but adjusted. Light can be blinding if we aren't prepared for it.

I turned on the faucet and let the cool water move over my skin, my reflection looking back at me from the mirror. It was me, but it wasn't really. I was there in body, but a reflection is closer to mirage than to the tangible. I liked that. I liked that I was able to see myself from that perspective; to look at myself from a distance.

I had short dark hair, dyed black, cut in purposefully choppy pieces that framed my face. My skin was Italian skin, which to me meant extraordinarily pale in the winter, and just as golden tan in the summer. It was milky white then, contrasting starkly against my dark features. I had a small frame, and I was draped in some sort of uneventful, business-casual type attire that I threw together in the daze that was my afternoon: a black fitted blazer and black V-neck t-shirt.

All I had seen that past week was sadness; grieving eyes and transparent skin. But, in that moment, I saw the curves of my face and I let myself fall over them without familiarity. I noticed the shapes I saw before me, the intricacies of the peaks and the valleys of face and fabric, the sharp yet graceful geometry of my short hair framing my cheeks. And I noticed a glow. It was one I had not seen in a while. A soul, slightly alight. It resided beneath the skin that housed the body that brought me to that very place. The place where Arun was.

I watched her take her hand and place it on her heart. I felt myself there.

The midnight blue hand towel that hung by the sink had that lingering scent of perfection on it. I took it in my hands and nested them in it for a moment, removing whatever was left of the cool water, and then made my way back into the living room.

"A buddy of mine," Arun said, looking up when I returned, "his band is playing at this place a few blocks from here. I had told him I'd stop by."

I looked at the time. It had moved more quickly than I imagined. "I hope I haven't held you up," I said with concern, as I made my way over to organize my things. "I really should get going anyway."

It's a funny thing, how quickly things can change, feelings can transform, life and perspectives can realign. A lump sat in my throat as I zipped up my bag, but this time it wasn't out of dread of travel. This time, I didn't want to walk in the opposite direction of wherever he was.

"Not at all," he said. "Actually, do you have any big plans tonight?"

I looked up, straight-faced to hide the rest. "Plans? No, not really."

"You should join us," he said.

I swallowed around something and it collided with the delight. I could only navigate the evening without that dichotomy for so long.

"I wouldn't want to impose on your night," I said.

"Nonsense," he said. "Come with us. It will be fun."

It was selfish to stay. I knew that. But the current of the percolating ecstasy was more powerful than logic. A remedy for the guilt that would have been heavy enough to take my breath from me.

I had missed breathing that way. Could I leave yet, even if I tried?

"I can come for a little while," I said, in compromise.

Just a little while.

We got our things together, made our way down the stairs, and headed to a bar that was only a few blocks from Arun's apartment. In New York, nothing is too far away. Every spot is precisely the center. Everything is within reach. Cities are so innately narcissistic. It's part of their charm.

The bar was an old, run-down, two-story masterpiece. There was movement and sound amidst the darkness, and there was just enough blue-hued light for me to be able to make it out. Arun directed me through the denseness of people and palaver, and led us up a tight, cement staircase toward the second floor. The band was setting up in the far corner.

"Hey, man! You made it!"

A tall, broad man with a long beard and large hands gave Arun an embrace that was at once strongly masculine and gently affectionate. To elicit both of these things at once is rather captivating, and I liked what was immediately present between him and Arun: obvious altruism and effortless camaraderie.

"Selena, meet Chase."

I reached out my hand. "Pleasure."

"Pleasure is all mine," Chase responded kindly. "How do you know this guy?"

"Work stuff," I smiled. "We only just met tonight." It sounded very much like a lie.

"Selena is a talented designer," Arun specified, far too generously.

"Aspiring designer," I said in quick clarification. "Arun is helping me out."

"Ah. Well, he's a good guy to have on your side," Chase said to me, and then averted his eyes to Arun.

"Seriously man, I don't know what to say."

"Hardly a thing," Arun said, and then changing the subject, turned to me.

"Let's go get a drink while we wait for these guys to go on."

Chase gave Arun a small salute, gave me a glad-to-meet-you nod of the head, and we walked toward the bar. I got swept up in the surrounding energy, but the crowd didn't overwhelm me as it had before in the stuffy train station. It seemed, instead, to add to my vitality.

This *before* was such a short while ago, but it must have been a different lifetime.

"Did you get him the gig?" I asked over the crowd.

He shrugged, his modesty warming me. "He's a good friend." He squeezed his way in toward the crowded bar then, and I waited on the periphery just a foot or so behind him. The distance was small, but I still felt far away, so I looked at my thoughts for a few moments without him seeing them. Each one was like a song, their melodies crooning with increased vigor. Musings were dancing through my head that seemed silly in their grandeur, so they had to be kept tucked away. They tried to tell me what this was. They tried to tell me it was everything.

Arun turned around then, holding two beers, and handed me one. It was my third drink of the night, so I resolved to sip it slowly so as not to affect my composure, or whatever was left of it. He stood so close to me, pressed by the increasing crowd, that I could feel the heat of his skin. I was enveloped in his warm glow; his aura of amber and midnight blue. I felt my own insides react and harmonize with it. I felt the hot pulses that ignite like flames; the ones that start in your chest and flicker outward and down. Attraction made palpable.

"Is your boyfriend supportive of your new career?" he asked.

"My boyfriend?" I was taken off guard. Chase's band had just started playing, so I wasn't sure if I heard him over the rhythmic and sanguine sounds.

He shook his head and spoke a little louder. "Is he supportive?"

"I don't have a boyfriend anymore," I said. "We broke up," I calculated quickly in my head, "a while ago now."

"Why?" He asked as bluntly and beautifully as ever, and for that reason, I didn't even have to think about it. I made something complicated into something simple, like algebra equations or Cliffs Notes.

"I have very high emotional standards," I said.

"As you should," he said.

We were quiet for a moment then, looking toward each other and letting the words reach past our ears. He must have seen gratitude rush over me. It must have done something to the color of my cheeks.

"You are very beautiful," he said.

I took a sip of my drink to hide my extravagant smile, as if he could not see right through.

"Am I allowed to thank you?" I asked.

"You just did."

And he took a sip of his.

3

The wound is the place where the light enters you.

—RUMI

The darkest moments are often illuminated by the Divine; an abstract quality of light that permeates the deepest reaches of painful breath, and reminds us of the parallel intensity of ecstasy.

If this is a truth, it is a truth with or without our agreement. But what is it that makes us aware of such a truth? What makes it become our reality? What is it that allows us to appreciate this Divine illumination, this magic, in times of pain?

When touched by one of these moments, the biggest regret would be from seeing this miracle through the eyes of the non-believer; boxing up a sparkling moment into compact descriptors of coincidence, happenstance, or irony. There is always within us, sometimes buried deep below layers of conscious awareness, an ability to open to the vast recognition that some things are crafted by a beauty beyond the scope of cerebral comprehension. That these synchronistic moments may not be understood in the usual way because they are not created in the usual way. That they are instead, and with elegant perfection, painted by a greater hand. That this miraculous occurrence, in all of its ethereal glory, will leave us changed.

Life presents us with many opportunities to realize its grandeur. Our choice of how we perceive our situations and our surroundings are dependent upon many things. We may, of course, view the events of our lives with any lens we choose, though consciously removing the appreciation of miracles can deprive us of the joy, wonder, and awe that can only be accessed in reaction to the extraordinary. Even to someone who doesn't subscribe to the notion of divine order or in fate or in the existence of any of these intangible glimmers of reality, there are moments in life that undeniably have a distinct sense of enchantment to them; a certain lightness or magic that, at least for a little while, can instill in one the illuminating belief that anything is possible.

During times of darkness, it seems that we are more readily able to access awareness of the miraculous. Look at the artists, the poets, the healers, the creators—look at their creativity and awareness of something *more* in times of pain. That is not to say that pain is the only path to enlightenment, but it is undeniable that such a state often elicits transformation, forcing an otherwise difficult to access ability of the brain to look at things with a changed perspective, and with a depth that is unique to the usual monotony of thought that our society most often evokes. It is a strange irony, perhaps, but in our moments of greatest darkness, we seem to be open to the most incoming light. Like a dark room with the shades pulled down, in opening our door to the afternoon sun, light will come flooding the interior like a dam has broken, instantly creating a golden glow where before there had only been blackness.

This light is consistently present, internally and simultaneously comprising the vast ethers of our surroundings, no matter our current physical circumstance. Even if it is at times hard to discern, there is always more than sufficient shine available to illuminate our souls. And, this light can come in many forms. It can be a literal glow, of course, but it can also be viewed as a state. A state of lightness, of joy, of peace. A state of completeness, and a removal of the veil of separateness that causes our suffering. It is an aid in our ability to see: further, deeper, and without pain. The distinction between this miraculous flooding of our corridors not only in times of joy, but in times of darkness, comes in our ability to notice it. With eyes clenched shut, we are holding all the darkness in place. With hearts contracted, we are not allowing any of the beautiful in.

And, there lies one truth most of us can agree on: there is a lot of beautiful.

In that moment, I was flooded by the miraculous. Maybe it was because there was so much darkness to contrast with it. Maybe it was because my heart was touched and started to open at just the right time. Maybe it was because I was breathing deeper, and my eyes were wide without sleep. Maybe it was the music and the drinks and the smoky light and the laughter. Whatever it was, I was standing awed by my moment, with my feet on the ground in a space that felt like the sky. My darkness was so flooded that I was even more blinded by its alternative. The light was so glaring that it allowed me to see with something beyond my eyes for the first time in my life. My soul was leading the way, and it was beating to the pulse of my heart, and the pulse of my heart was beating to his.

Sometimes, this world makes the heart swell. Perhaps the *sometimes* is simply when we notice. We are forever swimming in miracles and I was awed by the one that had brushed against my heart. His glow sang to me, and in those moments, I noticed every bit of magic. It seemed there was nothing that was out of its reach.

I looked over at him then. How quickly he became that—a him—the rest need names to set them apart. We leaned against the wall, and I watched all the light dancing around us. It was saturated with stories, but moving to our rhythm, and my pores were emitting some kind of magic into its colorful mix, making me an integral part of its aliveness.

Arun may have felt my eyes on him, because he turned toward me, too.

"Your life is about the change, Selena."

It was a surety beyond what anyone should be able to promise, a clear premonition without any tangible substance, but I believed him. Whatever he meant, it felt true. The lights flashed and danced and blurred before us, undulating in the foggy, mystical interior, mixing together and pulling apart in such a beautiful way that it made me want to cry. I smiled into his eyes and saw all of it and myself reflected in them.

"It already has," I whispered into the air, though the words sounded voluminous because at that moment the music stopped and I felt a shake. It was like waking up from the most beautiful of dreams, still bleary-eyed and not quite sure where I was or where I had been. I pulled my phone out of my pocket and checked the time. It was late. Later than I imagined.

"I really should go," I said.

"Now?"

Even if I caught the next train, I wouldn't be home until after 1 o'clock in the morning. Reality peeked its head out of the misty light, and blurred my vision.

"The next train is in less than 30 minutes. I have to try to catch it."

There was a slight tremble in my voice. Very slight. But he caught it.

"Ok, then you'll catch it," he said. "Come with me."

Arun took my wrist in his hand, and led me down the stairs, weaving through the smoky crowd until we were back out into the cool, open air. We were in a car before I knew it, moving through the city night. Streetlights moved like fireflies but the moon hung still. He insisted on accompanying me to the station. He would not take no for an answer, and I didn't argue much. I wondered if I would ever see him again. I wanted to spend as many moments next to him as I could.

I was quiet as we moved forward. There was a small lump in my throat where the reality continued to creep in, reminding me where I was headed and what awaited me there. It was stocked with the sadness and anxiety that had been submerged for the last few hours beneath layers of lightness. It was taking me away from him—the only part of it that felt like peace.

"Selena?"

"Yes?" I responded with failed attempt at nonchalance.

"Is everything ok?"

I shrugged a small shrug, and noticed the exhaustion beginning to return.

"I'm very tired," I said. "It's been a long week."

He nodded his head, aware that I was leaving something out. I felt his gaze on me, burning through my layers as I watched my feet vibrate with the dark floor of the car.

"Do you want to see something?" I asked tentatively.

"I do," he responded.

The night had begun in sadness, and even when I was too swept up in him to notice, it painted my background. It couldn't be avoided any longer. It wouldn't be right. I took my phone in my hand and flipped through a few recent photographs. I landed on one that made me feel adoringly melancholy, and turned the screen toward him.

"This is Amelia," I smiled sadly. "My dog. My family's dog." She laid upon a bed made of pillows, her blonde curly hair and big black nose squished up against the cushion, her sweetness frozen in time.

"She's beautiful," he responded.

I nodded with shaking tenderness. "She's been very sick," I said, and the smile vanished.

"Oh," he frowned, looking down at the photograph that was oozing with her delightful charm. Amelia hid her pain much better than I did.

"Amelia is with my Mom. I live with my sister, not far away, and the two of us have been taking turns staying with them the last few days. Caring for her has become pretty intensive. None of us could do it on our own."

"I'm so sorry to hear that," he said. "That must be very difficult for all of you."

"Thanks. She's family, you know? A lot of people don't get that."

He shook his head in understanding.

I smiled then again, but it was small and weak. "Anyway," I said, shaking something away, so as not to rub off my heavy on him, "precious looking, isn't she?"

I put my phone away as the cab came to a rolling stop in front of Penn Station.

"I'll walk you in," he said with gentleness.

I would have told him it was no big deal; that I could find my own way. But still, I was not ready for him to leave. Moments were slipping out of my grasp more quickly than they usually did. The second hand had a life of its own. An arrangement beyond the rules of time and space.

The train, on the other hand, was scheduled to leave in 5 minutes, and following time's usual rules, it was already waiting in the station.

"That was a lot of fun," he said, as we walked down the stairs toward the train doors that had opened into the city just hours before, and were now ready to close me back in.

"A lot of fun," I agreed, as we stopped in front of them.

We looked at each other for a moment. I didn't know if we should join hands in a professional shake, or embrace each other with warm lips. We did neither.

"I'll be in touch, with those files and such," he said, and I thanked him one more time for good measure. I gave him a small wave and then made my way over the gap between the land his feet lay on and the land that it didn't. I found a seat, and watched him walk away, gliding up the stairs with leather crinkling and bunching and releasing and a stride that was his own.

And then he was gone.

I was in a haze of thought and emotion as the train pulled out of the station. I meditated on the quiet darkness outside of the window, watching the soft blur of passing life under the cover of night. It felt good to sit comfortably on the double seat that I had to myself, curled into my warm coat, lulled by the movement and recent memories.

What had just happened? Who was this mysterious Him that just infiltrated my life, changing the way my blood cells moved in my body, the route of the nerve connections hopping the fissures between each nuance of self? I felt different for these reasons, my physicality lighter and more graceful than it had been. It was a strong contrast to the extreme tenseness I had felt before the night had begun, but it was something more than that.

Something was shifting. Something had opened. I felt my solid ground quaking, cracks forming and being instantly filled by something that felt more alive—more fertile—where seeds could be planted that before would crumble under the weight of my foundation.

I could see myself in the window, and as it had in Arun's mirror, my reflection was alien. There was something different behind my eyes. A veil had been lifted. A film wiped clean, allowing me to see more clearly. For a short while that night, I came into focus. All facets of myself clicked into place, and I was peering at the afterglow.

I needed to find that place again. It was where I belonged.

As I contemplated this and the recalibration that was undulating in my chest, I wondered: what power is it that creates this? What is it that allows such a powerful reaction to another human being, a being just as fragile and broken and magical and intricate as I or anyone else? What made this different? Perhaps, we are not all the same. Perhaps there are certain people who just vibrate differently; that emit a frequency so unique that not all can notice it, like a duck whistle just out of our range of hearing. Was this my reaction to a different frequency? Did anyone who came in contact with Arun notice this light, or did I only notice it because it was within my range? Maybe this is just what happens when certain lights combine; a glow living inside each that oozes out at just the right time.

Maybe, I recognized it because it was the same as mine.

And then, embarrassment prickled on my cheeks. There was also the possibility that it was all in my head. An imaginary interchange crafted through the lens of my heightened emotional climate. It was a scary thought—one that made me feel unstable.

The train slowly came to a halt, much sooner than I thought it would. I had been lost in a reverie that again had no regard for time. I shook myself with it, and got up. I took a very deep breath and walked toward the air, and with each grounding step, the ethereal fell away. It slipped through my fingers like quicksilver, mercury moving and reflecting the lights in the sky until it was one with it once again.

The air was more biting there, where I lived, just a short walk from the ocean. The wind was hitting my face in whipping gusts, and I could smell coming snow. I moved quickly away from the train station with my head down, my neck contracted as far as it could burrow into my coat, my hands in my pockets and my shoulders tightened up around my ears. I got in another cab, tired now of the myriad modes of transportation. It was warm inside the car, but it smelled stale, and as we moved forward, I held my breath. The staleness begged to make its way into my lungs, but my insides said no. They just had a taste of ambrosia, and it made them suddenly and extraordinarily aware of every surrounding poison.

I gave the driver his fare and a tip, breathed out a *thank you* with the little air I had left, and dove out of the backseat to inhale the heavy, clean cold. I made my way to the front door of my mother's house and fumbled through my bag for my keys, wary to go inside. I knew it wouldn't smell stale, and I knew it wouldn't smell of ambrosia. It would have that particular smell of dread. It would smell like sadness, and that scent is one that tends to linger, heavy and unforgiving.

My mother lived in a house down the block from the beach that, under normal circumstances, was light and airy. You could feel the ocean on the breeze at night and, if you looked out the right window, you could see a sliver of sparkling water during the day. It wasn't a large home, but it was bright, with skylights, clean white walls, and enough fond memories to overflow the space. I grew up in that house. It would always be my home, even though I was living elsewhere since the summer before.

The house was dark when I walked in. Not even a night light lit the downstairs hallway. I walked upstairs on my toes so as not to disturb anyone. My mom was sitting on the couch, Amelia sleeping between her feet on a cushion on the floor. The television was on, but I could tell my mother wasn't watching it. She looked up at me as I edged closer, and she looked so tired. I felt worried about her in the way you worry about someone you love more than anything in the world. I wished I could give her some of that night's breath—a short reprieve in a time of sadness.

"Selena," she whispered. "You're home late." She said it gently, with exhaustion but without accusation.

"I'm so sorry, Mom. I'm so sorry. Are you guys ok?"

"It's fine. We're hanging in," she said.

"I'll sit with her. Go get some rest," I said. "Madeline will be here in the morning?"

"Yes," she said. "First thing."

"I don't know where the time went tonight," I mumbled as I removed my coat.

"What happened? How did it go?" she asked. She was always present with me, even in her preoccupation.

"It went well," I said, "I'll tell you about it later. I'm just sorry to be back so late. It was selfish."

"You have been amazing with her, Selena. Stop apologizing. We managed just fine."

"Please try to get some rest," I repeated, this time through a yawn. "I'm here now."

She moved over slowly so as not to disturb Amelia and made room for me on the couch. I curled up next to her, the night's events too quickly becoming a memory. My chest tightened and my head was so heavy I could not help but to lay it against the back of the couch. My mother drifted off in moments and I wrestled through bleary wakefulness, eyes burning with sleep, struggling to pry magnetized lids away from one another until deep slumber won my battle too. Two hours later, we heard a whimper, and we were up again with throbbing heads and tired eyes. Our discomfort was irrelevant, however. Her pain was all that mattered.

Amelia was an angel beyond description: kind, wise, gentle, fun-loving, and as sweet as can be. For the past thirteen years, she was by my side, and for that, everything was more beautiful. There was so much laughter because of her existence in our lives. So much joy. We loved to run on the beach together. She was faster than me, but she would never let herself get too far ahead. When our distance became too great she would stop short, all four paws hitting the sand at once as it catapulted around her in all directions, and then turn around and look at me, smiling and shaking her tail so rapidly that her whole body moved with it. When I laughed, she laughed with me. When I cried, she kissed the tears off of my cheeks. When I slept, she was beside me, dreaming of whatever things angels dream of.

Her paws smelled like buttered-popcorn sometimes. I never understood why. I just knew it smelled like happiness.

And then, everything was different. It happened suddenly. It was about a week prior that Madeline shook me from sleep, so early in the morning that the first glimpse of deep purple sunrise had not yet appeared in the sky.

"Wake up, Lena," she said, with dark urgency. "Something is wrong with Amelia."

I was up so quickly I was lightheaded, rummaging through my closet blindly for a pair of sweatpants. We got to our Mother's house in minutes, speeding down the empty, early-morning streets.

"She tried to get up," my mother explained, "but she just couldn't move. Like she was weighed down by something heavy."

In a panic, Amelia fumbled forward and yelped in pain, her back legs obviously and completely unresponsive. From there, it was a downward spiral, her health deteriorating rapidly. Her nerves were shooting irrational impulses through her body, limbs twitching and jaw tight where her smile used to be. She could not walk, and she could not rest. She would try to pull herself around by her front legs, but after minutes, succumb to disappointment and exhaustion. She was in a perpetual state of fear, and she was experiencing consistent pain, even with all of the medication we lovingly forced down her throat.

To make matters worse, she lost the ability to control her bladder. We took turns squeezing urine from her, three times a day. If we didn't press hard enough we couldn't alleviate her fully, but we hated putting so much pressure on her already pained and fragile body. She acquired a severe urinary tract infection since she wasn't being flushed properly, and the medication was not combating it quickly enough to ease the symptoms. More pain, more discomfort. She was always covered in urine, seeping out of her and the diaper she wore. We tried to keep her as clean as we could, but it was impossible to keep up, and impossible to do so without causing her more discomfort. It wasn't the smell that bothered us. It wasn't the fact that every time we lifted her stiff body from the floor we too were doused in it. We just hated it for her. We hated that we couldn't help her find any normalcy.

We tried everything in that short period of time. Everything helped a little, but nothing helped enough. We were told we needed to give the treatments some time. That nothing would work overnight. But she was miserable. We all cried, all the time. The tears just didn't stop. We cried when she cried. We cried when we saw her in pain. We cried from fear. We cried when we considered the unfathomable threat of loss. And then, secretly, I cried with the beginnings of realization.

This reality was at first unimaginable for me. I could see on the faces of my mother and Madeline that it was the same way for them. I understood death, but not like that. Not by my hand. Not my best friend. Every time the thought arrived, I pushed it away, shoving it deeper into denial's depths. But soon, it got too heavy. I felt the fear transforming into something that was like grief. I was at a turning point, and I needed guidance.

"Hello?" Athena said, on the other end of the phone.

"It's Lena," I said, meekly.

Aunt Athena was wildly intelligent, funny, and remarkably kind; an exquisitely special person who simply shined brighter than the average. She instilled strength in me when I needed it most, swooping in with her passionate and unarguable solutions. She had this unique way of initiating tough love in the gentlest and most beneficent way. When she heard the shaking of my voice, I didn't need to explain much for an imparting of her wisdom.

"What do you think Amelia would want?" she asked me.

Anxiety pulsed through me and showed up as indecision. "I don't know," I stuttered. "I don't know."

"Well, I know that you love her more than anything," she said.

"I do," I said. "More than anything."

"You love her with a forever love, don't you Lena?" she asked. "One that stays with you regardless of circumstance and separation."

"I do. I love her no matter what," I confirmed through tears.

"This kind of love," she said, "It exists regardless of her place in this reality. Beyond the confines of time and space. Regardless if she is of this earth, or of someplace more vast. Do you understand what I mean?"

I whimpered softly, the enormity of the conversation ripping at my heartstrings.

"I love her unconditionally," I sniffed, without second thought. "Yes. Forever. No matter what."

"What does she want, Lena?" she asked again. "What would she ask you for with words if she could speak them?"

Tears weighed heavily from my bottom lashes until they catapulted down, my heart pounding in my throat and my lips quivering. I thought about Amelia's eyes. I thought about what they said to me then when I looked into them.

"She doesn't want to be here anymore," I whispered through a cracking throat. "She's done. She's nearly begging."

The tears poured out of me as if something had collapsed. There was silence on the other end as Aunt Athena allowed my emotions to transfer from the inside to the out.

The knowing hit me hard. It hit me deep, where only the strongest emotions can reach and rattle, but with the unique benevolence that comes with clarity. That's a thing I've noticed about truth: it can hurt like hell, but rarely feels confining in the way falsity does. It doesn't sit in your chest like denial. It's too certain. In its reality, there is something comforting. Something renewing in its discovery. It cleared enough space in my fogged head to hear Aunt Athena's words more clearly.

"It's the most selfless thing you could ever do, to give her what she wants, rather than keeping her here because you aren't ready to let her go. Dogs have a way of accepting things that we find difficult. She is not afraid of death. She will welcome it, and with it, there will be no more pain."

"You're right," I choked, through streaming tears. "You're right."

"She'll never be far away, Lena," she promised.

When denial becomes more harmful than truth, we have to wade through some pain to find the kindness. I knew that somehow, as the one in the family who was always looked upon as weak and afraid, I would have to be the one to sit my mom and my sister down in truthful discussion. I would have to be the one to speak this, so that we could all find that same clarity together. As strange as it would feel to hold that responsibility, one that I could never have imagined being strong enough to hold, I knew I had no choice.

That is what I held that night I met Arun. That is what, for a few hours, he saved me from. From the cascading realizations of the night before. Soon, I would talk to my mother and Madeline and we would make a heart-wrenching decision. But that night, I only held it. I held it, and I let Arun, at least for a little while, hold me too. It felt so good to be cradled in his light.

My mother and I stroked Amelia's coat until daybreak, and the next day, we all held each other through truth's tears.

4

*The garden of love is green without limit and yields
many fruits other than sorrow or joy.
Love is beyond either condition:
without spring, without autumn, it is always fresh.*

—RUMI

It was a sunny day when she left us, but we could not see it through the tears.

When the time came, it was really Amelia who made the final decision. She knew so much. So many things that we didn't. She decided she would stop taking that medicine. All of it. She just looked at us with those deep black eyes, her curly, flopping ears shaping her beautiful face, and we couldn't force it any longer. She was ready to stop treading that water. I understood then, but I don't think I would have been courageous enough to do the same.

We watched the clock that day as if we could slow time's passing with our fearful glares. How could those moments be the last? I wished I could stop focusing on what was to come, and for even a few short moments, be fully there with her. I tried. I really tried. The tears were just so powerful. I sat on the ground next to the couch where she laid. It was cold. I leaned my cheek against the arm of the couch, and touched the tip of my nose to hers. It was slightly damp and warmer than the air. I was focused on the rhythm. When she breathed out, I breathed in.

When the vet arrived, my mother held Amelia in her arms. It felt right for her to be the one. Madeline and I sat close, the uncontrollable dampness blurring our vision and making our chests heave. We each held a paw. They were warm between our hands, their billowing softness full of life. There was so much life that it was hard to believe that soon there would be no more.

Amelia exhaled deeply, and something shifted. We watched her muscles begin to relax, her eyes begin to calm. For the first time in a week, there was no shaking, no tenseness, no rigidity. She exhaled it all out. It was a miracle, for sure. Just not the type to keep her there. We all understood then. Her freedom was coming soon, and with it, she saw peace.

She was so wise, our precious Amelia. No one knew unconditional love like she did. No one gave it like she did, lived it like she did, embodied it like she did. It was her eyes and her heart and every wispy curl of blonde hair. And then, it was her soul. Something told me it still sang with me. I didn't know how I could ever thank her, for all of it, for everything except to try my best, every day, to be more like she was. To think about her loving wisdom with every step I took.

That day was very painful, and I was sure the ones to follow would be a blur of grief and memories, but I didn't see Amelia as gone. I felt her. I felt her warmth with every beat of my heart. I imagined her vital again, soaring above me, wanting to tell us how happy she was, and how lovely it felt to be free. I missed her with a depth and an ache that was beyond description, but this knowingness, this belief in something more, was comforting. It cushioned the dreadful blow and gave me something beautiful to hold. Ending her life was a kindness. The ultimate kindness. With that decision, I saw a strength within myself that I didn't know I had. It made me sure of something I wasn't sure of before: that there was more to this than simply accepting an end.

My family was grieving differently. They saw this loss as nothing but blackness. They were gripped with fear and their eyes were shut tight, contracted by grief's incessant grasp. They only saw dark there. Normally,

I turned to them for support with panic in my throat and a stuttering heart. This time, it was different. There was that light of hope behind my eyes. This belief beyond the blackness. As muffled as it was in sadness, they must have seen that strength that came with my faith. They must have seen something, because this time, they turned to me.

I was always looked upon as fragile. People, ever since I was a little girl, tended to tiptoe around me. I was nervous, small, breakable in their eyes. And out of love and caring, they were careful with me. Change was always tough growing up. And there was always fear. I feared being alone, I feared my body, I feared illness and pain. Fear was always, and frustratingly, a dominant force in my life. A consequence of living in this fearful state so often was the corresponding anxiety, at first erupting in accordance to specific fears, but as I got older, generalizing and leading to ebbs and flows of panic and depression. Of course I looked fragile when my eyes hung purple with the exhaustion of mental turmoil. I get it. I don't blame anyone for seeing me that way. Sometimes, I looked at myself that way, too. The thing, though, that many people didn't see, was the tenacity that came with it. Living with that fear was what made me a hell of a lot stronger than I got credit for. Amongst any of the angst, I kept on moving. It wasn't fun or comfortable, but I was still moving, and that had to count for something.

Experiencing such deep and painful emotions at a young age did something for me that was pretty unparalleled when it came to maturation. Though I was a bit "behind" the curve when it came to a lot of things in life that society would deem appropriate, such as career advancement and the like, I was always on a full-speed-ahead growth trajectory when it came to my emotional and spiritual growth.

People described me as an "Old Soul" even when I was very young. They said that I had a consistent look of concentration in my eyes, as if my thoughts were focused on something far away. I always preferred to sit at the adult table, listening to their tales and their laughter, rather than eat pizza and drink soda with the kids who forget to wash their hands before dinner. I sometimes spoke with a vocabulary beyond my years, and it always frustrated me when that was met with laughter or adoration. I wasn't trying to be funny, or unique, or acquire any attention. I was just being myself.

I supposed I was just different, and I wasn't quite sure if that was a good thing. Like most children, I had trouble coming to terms with this understanding of my uniqueness. If I couldn't fit in with the kids or the adults acting like myself, maybe there was something wrong with me. Something that I needed to change, or rather, something that I needed to hide. And that's when I built my mask.

I never stopped thinking, creating, and imagining, but when I was amongst people, aside from select family confidants, I simply went through the motions. I learned to quietly fit in. I learned to be myself but not show all of myself, because even when I did, no one seemed to understand me anyway. As I grew up, I had a lot of friends, but there were few people I was completely genuine around. It was a bit lonely at times, but luckily, I liked being alone. I got used to feeling separate.

I always knew, however, that there had to be more. More when it came to life. More when it came to connectedness. Something stronger, greater, more powerful. Something more whole. I always looked toward the sky toward this something, even when the light was blinding, squinting my eyes as the sun rose over the enkindled water. I watched the clouds move in their mystery, while simultaneously wondering why I couldn't just be fully and heartily satisfied with where I was on the ground, even if just for a little while.

It's no surprise, I suppose, that I was born on a full moon. And, named after one too. I adored the magic and mystery. If only I could learn to live up to my name, I often thought, perhaps I too could embrace some of that lightness.

This enigmatic belief in *more* was a monotonous burning in my heart. It always kept me moving away from situations, people, and circumstances that didn't feel just right. I worried that this behavior stemmed from a lack of gratitude. From an inability to appreciate the gifts that were laid before me. In my heart, however, I knew that was not the case. There was so much to be grateful for, and I was grateful for all of it. There was just something about the sky and its secrets.

And then I met Arun. The sensation of separateness that had been carried through to my entire adult life had been temporarily crumbled. I can't explain why, but for a few short hours that night, I was not alone. I was met in the middle of some space in the ethers where separateness did not exist and words were not needed. It was that very feeling that I had always searched for without realizing what it was I was really seeking. The seed of desire planted deep in my insides, never tended to out of fear of failure.

Arun's appearance in my life, paired with Amelia's simultaneous departure, created a combination of internal forces that was emotionally momentous, chiseling at my mask and creating fissures in spaces that were once impermeable. Suddenly, my belief in this intangible *more* did something beyond creating isolation, loneliness, sadness, or guilt. I saw more in Amelia, and I saw more in Arun. Suddenly, through both my terrific grief and my intense captivation, I felt something that I could only describe as connection. To them, of course, but also to something greater. It was as if everything intangible that I had ever leaned on in faith was proving itself to me at once.

So where did it leave me? What had changed? Physically, she was gone, and in a different way, so was he. But that day, I felt her everywhere. *Everywhere.* That day, she threw me into a full immersion spiritual growth spurt. My faith kept me vital. It gave me the strength to hold Madeline's hand when she felt particularly afraid, and the words to speak to my mother when she felt particularly lonely. And so, I told them what I saw when my eyes were closed in meditation and I was so close to Amelia that I could smell her popcorn paws, or when I drifted to sleep and in my mind's eye she told me everything would be ok. I told them I felt her. I told them that I knew that she was there with them, too.

As for Arun, I looked upon our meeting with gratitude. To say only that, however, would be an understatement. It would be taking the sky out of the equation, a sky that Amelia was now a part of and of which

I was pretty sure, even through the sleekness of his black leather exterior, Arun was made from. I knew meeting him was a pinnacle experience; one that was momentous beyond my understanding. It was a moment of joy in the passing of my eternity, somehow reminding me who I was. I felt with absolute clarity the profound awareness that everything I had been through up until that point led me to that very moment. It helped me, at least on that night, to navigate the rough waters my family and I were swimming in. But still, it was something bigger than that. I was too distracted to contemplate its enormity as I swam in grief's waters those days, but it crossed my mind the way a cat moves quietly from one room to the other late at night. It crossed my mind with subtlety and mystery, obscured but always present.

That night, as I sat with my mom and Madeline, quietly navigating our thoughts and our grief, I received a text message.

I had a really good time the other night.

It was a dark night when she left us, but somehow, I still found some light.

5

And you?
When will you begin that long journey into yourself?
—RUMI

I woke up a few days later to a shining sun, and then moments later, a burning chest. I always found it intriguing, those first few moments of waking, before life came into conscious focus. It is perhaps only in those brief sleepy-eyed moments, when the sun comes through the curtains and the dust in the air dances its way around the room in its crisp morning light, that we are most able to see beauty. When we forget, ever so briefly, the circumstances that threatened to keep us from sleep the night before, and that ricocheted in our brains as the day inched on, threatening to steal our peace and replace it with fear.

After those few brief moments, it hits us, and we remember what pained us when we laid our heads down. I looked to where Amelia would have been sleeping right next to the bed, nearest to where I was, allowing us both to feel safe as we drifted to sleep. The memories of loss surged through me like a wave breaking through its dam, held at bay overnight and then flooding my capillaries and flowing over into the rest of my skin and bone.

Following the initial deluge, the surging waters calmed into a monotonous, lulling tide. The pain lapped against my insides, and in their rhythm, there was another stirring. It started beneath my rib cage and grew in intensity until it became a warm glow; a lit candle flickering gently as it swayed to a nearby exhale. It was full of the beginnings of hope, and its company warmed me.

I remembered that connection to something bigger. Something more. Something beyond myself and the small confines of an illusionary loneliness.

These feelings, emotions, and levels of awareness met within me, swirling around each other, vying for space. It overwhelmed me, squeezing a tear from my eye which rolled down my cheek sideways and hit the pillow where my head rested. I pulled the quilt down.

The chill was immediate, so I grabbed a sweatshirt and stuffed my feet into a pair of slippers, stretched deeply, and made my way out of the room. It was a bright winter day, and the light shook the tired from me. My mother was up drinking her morning coffee, and I put on some water for tea.

"So, you never told me about your night with Arun," she inquired, after some small talk about the weather, in full avoidance of the only thing that was on her mind.

I considered how much I wanted to say. When things feel beyond words, trying to explain them is futile, taking something away from the magic with descriptors that can't capture their essence. I felt frustrated when my truth appeared as a dramatic exaggeration. It reminded me of being laughed at for using a big word as a child, and then wishing I hadn't said anything at all. The desire to justify myself and my words always felt terribly ungrounded.

"He's an exceptional person. There's a lot I can learn from him," I said, simply, and honestly.

"Is he hiring?"

I laughed to myself. I had completely forgotten the initial purpose of the meeting.

"He's really just extending a hand right now, which is very kind, considering he was under no obligation to do so."

"Yes," she agreed. "Very kind."

"It was strange," I said, as I sprinkled loose chamomile flowers into the hot water on the stove.

"Strange?" she asked.

"The night was nice," I said. "We looked over some work. Grabbed some drinks. It was usual in that sense, I guess. The strange part came in my reaction to it. To him."

"Hmm," she said, as she looked out toward the sky. "How so?"

"It was as if I'd known him...for a long time," I said, more to myself at that point, than to her.

She was distracted. And I felt I had said enough, anyway.

"Do you want to do a little shopping today?" I asked. I thought the outside air would do us both some good, and we spent the day floating through a sea of shoppers, their bags in one hand and coffees in another. We almost looked like we belonged. Our small and occasional smiles may have been painted on, and our chests may have been tight, but there is a certain relief that comes with facing a painful inevitability. We were able to move in a different way; different than trudging through fear of the unknown on two and a half hours of sleep.

We arrived back home when the sky was just starting to take on its lavender hue, smelling like winter and blanketing all it touched with quiet. Light was beginning to linger in the sky, stretching itself toward brighter days, but darkness still fell early. We jumped into our sweatpants and fuzzy socks and hopped onto the couch, and somehow, we were exactly where we were supposed to be.

"Hot chocolate?" I asked.

"Yes," smiled Mom, and we sipped at its warm and velvety sweetness until she fell asleep on the couch pillow. I sat with my feet curled under me, the television quietly flashing against the back wall. I hadn't brought up Arun again. I was surprised I was able to resist, because he hadn't left the down-reaching corridors of my mind all day. Would I hear from him again? Would he remember his kind promise that he made with soft words and bright eyes to "be in touch?" I inhaled and I could almost smell his Midnight-wide-awake, as if his cologne had rubbed off on my cheeks. That now familiar surge ran through me. *I had a really good time last night.* I responded in agreement, but the conversation ended there. Even if he was just being polite, the message was unexpected, and more friendly than professional. In the very least, I had crossed his mind, and these thoughts filled me with that thing that causes a smile to happen whether it is consciously permitted or not.

I flipped off the television, placed my mug into the sink and turned on the faucet. The mug filled quickly with cool water and then overflowed, the contents cloudy at first and then purifying as it cascaded over the smooth, ceramic edge. I watched, mesmerized by its erratic rhythm, and then turned off the faucet and made my way to the bedroom. I'd probably head back home tomorrow. Madeline already had. I just needed a little more time. My mom needed it too.

I grabbed my computer and hopped into bed, feigning nonchalance in purpose. The new emails loaded, and there, below three layers of spam, was his name. I hovered over it, relishing in the surprise and what it did to my fingertips. They were poised to bring it into view and tingling with potential.

Hey Selena. Sorry for the delay. Things have been a bit busy on this end. I have most of the relevant stuff I want to send over to you at the office. I'll be there bright and early in the morning. Didn't want to leave you hanging.

Hope you have a good rest-o-the-evening.

I exhaled. I imagined he closed the message with a wink and a sideways smile. I'd never know if that was true, but my imaginings were good enough. I deleted and re-wrote my response several times, wondering if my words would weigh more to him the way his did to me. If they were arranged just right, maybe there was more of a chance.

I thanked him. I told him there was no rush. I told him I was looking forward to it. I didn't tell him how much.

I was sure I wouldn't hear from him again that night, but I wasn't ready to sleep. I was racing with words and thoughts and potential; an exquisite relief laced with enchantment. It was a state that wasn't meant to be wasted, so I lit a candle and shut the lights.

A streaming station played meditative music as I removed my shoes and placed my feet gently on the ground. I sat upright, in a regal way, though my shoulders hung comfortably. The light of the candle danced on the walls, bathing my space in its warmth and moving to the hypnotic sounds of the music. I rested my hands on my lap, safely vulnerable with my palms turned up to the sky, and softly closed my eyes. I took a deep breath in through my nose and held it for a few seconds before exhaling slowly through parted lips. The space was mine, but it was also everyone else's. I adored that connectedness. A place where anything could be explored, created, seen, or cleansed. Where I could find my deepest peace and wade through my deepest fears.

It took some time to work through the onslaught of thought, but eventually, I felt more grounded, able to sense not only the smoothness of the wooden floor beneath my feet, but also the connection to something beyond it. I watched as I created paths for energy to move through, to release, to shift, carefully trusting in my ability to clear away what no longer belonged within me. Allowing it to gracefully make its way out of my space and into the vastness of the universe.

As I became more present, visions appeared in my mind's eye. I saw a ball of white light, floating in the middle of black nothingness. It was a small, concise ball of pure illumination; an iridescent pearl that spun and glimmered and moved as if it were ballroom dancing, slowly, deliberately, and majestically. It danced alone, unabashed, until a partner rolled in with the deep chroma of a marble of hematite. It was velvety rich in color, black with a glimmer of silver-grey. They danced in step, creating a beautiful rhythm, undulating and encircling each other in elegant form. Beams of light shone from them, entrancingly reaching out in every direction. They were few at first, and they multiplied exponentially, forming a grid of pure light that seemed to go on forever, with these two yin yang balls at its center.

It was soothing there. It was like watching the star-drenched sky.

Until a clatter. A car door. A noise from the night. The cool beneath my feet. The cushion where I sat. The heartbeat in my chest. My fingers in their place in space. I moved them, slowly, one after the other. Everything that was dancing before my eyelids evaporated like mist. I filled myself in with a deep breath and with the gentleness and gratitude that I felt, letting it seep into every ounce of my being.

The light of the candle was still painting the ceiling with its glow. I blew out the flame, turned off the music, and laid my head on the pillow. I fell asleep in seconds.

~

Hey hey,
We are going to do three things:

The next morning, Arun proceeded to list the importance of updating my resume, getting some spec work, and enhancing my skills in select design programs. He attached a few large files that would take a while to download, so I let them gradually make their way to me in the background as I read through the email multiple times.

...Remember: don't be intimidated by this stuff. It may seem like a lot, but not to worry—we simply start with the basics. I'm sure you'll be editing and flying around it all in no time.

I visualized his eyes rolling over the screen and his adept fingers tapping upon each key. I could picture the subtle concentration in his face, the muscles in his arms tensing and releasing with each word he created on screen, his blue eyes reflecting the light in a way all their own.

My response was genuine (as if, with him, there was any other way).

I really can't express how much I appreciate this. It means a lot to have some direction, and it's not every day you meet someone that is willing to take the time, especially for someone they hardly know. So again, as I'm sure comes as no surprise, I wanted to thank you.

I then fumbled to respond to his bulleted list, feeling inept without an opinion, too inexperienced to even know what I liked, and what I didn't, what I wanted, and what I wanted to avoid. But that's what he was helping me to do; pushing me to grow and understand, to gain experience and create a voice for myself. I sent whatever I could put together, and he responded back within minutes.

Call it karma, kiddo.
Noodle around with these files, and let me know how it goes. And please, let me know if I can help in any way. To be fair, they are even confusing to me at times.
As an aside, I've attached a picture of this antique, glass Buddhist statue that I am dangerously close to obtaining. Thought you might be into it.
-A

I clicked on the image of a blue-hued, thick glass sculpture. It was the head of Buddha statue, hollow on the inside but filled to the brim with something majestic and otherworldly. I liked that he liked it, and I liked that he knew I would too.

Why dangerously close? Your apartment is going to be the ultimate Zen space. I'll have to get you some crystals to add to the ambiance.

If I was at home, I would then have looked over at my copper statuette of Ganesha sitting by a large chunk of unpolished amethyst and a string of multi-colored mantra beads. I loved all of it. All of the ethereal magic it stood for.

A bit of time passed then, and instead of staring at the computer, I got myself up and dressed and ready to head back to my apartment. I was looking forward to some normalcy and routine; a day of mundane tidying and errands.

I gave my mom a kiss on the cheek, followed by a long and heartfelt hug. It was intimidating, leaving her comforting presence, but I had to do it eventually.

Madeline had been spending most of her time at her boyfriend's place, so when I got back to the apartment, everything was exactly as I'd left it. A mug sat in the sink, which over a week ago held hot tea. A towel that I had used after my last shower hung, now bone dry, over the top of the bathroom door. Time froze there. It was as if everything around me lived in the *before*, and I was floating in my *after*. I washed the mug and threw the towel in the hamper, and then I checked my email again.

Nothing. I wondered if my response was too forward. Just playful banter, of course, but, maybe he found that his help and his friendliness was giving me the wrong idea. He was sending me work, discussing business, and any other interesting tidbits were just a part of his charm. My response didn't need to be so astonishingly unprofessional.

I was picking at my nails as irrationality proliferated like a rising wave until it crashed and I felt even more ridiculous. He couldn't possibly care as much as I did about any of this, and especially not enough to read that much into my short and unimportant words.

So, I shook it off.

I dried the mug and placed it in the cabinet. I collected the towel and some other items from the hamper and put them in the washing machine. I sat on the couch, and then got up again. I went over to the refrigerator, and stared at bare shelves. I grabbed a banana from the counter and brought it over to the couch, closed my laptop, and ate my fruit.

It was lonely there. My chest was tight with it. A piece of hair lay across my black leggings. I picked it off to drop it to the ground, but I stopped myself. It was hers. I put it into the pocket of my sweatshirt instead. I didn't know what I would do with it once the sweatshirt went into the laundry, but I couldn't just throw it down haphazardly, this part of her that I could still hold.

I looked over at the clock. It read 11:11 a.m. Maybe it was the symmetry. Or the fortuity. Whatever it was, there was a comforting auspiciousness there that roused me.

If it wasn't so cold, I would have loved to be outside, walking under the warmth of the sun. Winter is beautiful, but confining. Sometimes I liked the forced quiet, finding comfort inside without the associated guilt. On that day, I was too restless to enjoy it. I decided on yoga.

There was a class at the nearby studio that started at 11:30, so I moved quickly, changed into leggings and sneakers, and threw my cell phone and car keys into my bag. I headed for the door and stopped in the threshold, considering for a moment. It would take no time at all to grab my phone out of my bag and check my email one more time. But I decided against it.

I spent the next hour rotating between downward facing dog and child's pose, trying to clear my thoughts that would not stop cascading through my consciousness and all the while trying not to try. At least I worked up a sweat.

∼

I showered the stickiness from my skin when I got home, taking my time and using enough hot water to generate a sauna out of my small bathroom. I dressed again, dried my hair, and made a to-do list of things I didn't have time for the week prior. Welcomed things that kept me occupied. Madeline stopped home for an hour or so, grabbed some clothes, and went back to her boyfriend's house. She was dealing that way, I was dealing this way. We all have our ways.

Come evening, I lit some candles, curled my feet up under myself and into the couch cushions, and ate dinner alone. I switched the television on and then quickly switched it off. The flashing screen and commercials were jarring. I put on some melodic music instead. After I ate, I made a cup of chamomile tea, and while I let it cool to a comfortable temperature, I checked my email again.

And there is was. This time, I opened it as quickly as my heart accelerated: with no skip of a beat.

I'm bidding on the statue! As un-Zen as it sounds, these other bidders have nothing on me.

Dangerously. Close.

I spoke to Jason today. He asked me how things went. I thought about telling him 'terribly' just to mess with him a little.

I did have a really good time with you though.

So...I was wondering if you wanted to hang out again, this time, say, over Japanese food? I wouldn't want anything to be weird, with me helping you out and all. That obviously wouldn't change either way.

-A

I read it, and then read it again. It's funny how much more words mean when they are coming from someone you care to hear them from. Most words are made of air: valuable, though usually unappreciated, taken for granted when we breathe them in. His were made of flowers. They bloomed before me and smelled of life and I could read them over and over as if they were the most beautiful and interesting things in the world. I let each word merge with the next to create their short and sweet story, and allowing space between the lines where the hope sat. Where the story could be longer. Where the details would lie. Cell by cell I was filled.

I walked over to the window, aiming to scatter the energy before it came bursting out of me. The sky was velvet. The moon was full. I ran my fingers through my hair and bathed in its translucence.

My intoxication may have appeared frivolous, but I knew it wasn't. I knew that this was important. As important as that moonlight. I could not explain it any other way.

He wanted to see me again, *this time, say, over Japanese food.* It wasn't business. It was pleasure. And it felt damn good already.

Hanging out over Japanese food sounds great, I said. *No weirdness necessary.*

6

What you seek is seeking you.

—RUMI

We made a plan for the following weekend, and as time has that funny way about it, our meeting that was set for what felt like a far-off future became very suddenly present tense.

I took my time getting ready, rustling through a closet of clothes that didn't seem just right, carefully smoothing and then messing my hair. I wondered what we would talk about. Although conversation had flowed so effortlessly last time, would there be enough to say the second time around?

I chose a casual, yet attractively fitting, black, long-sleeved dress, and a pair of ankle-high boots. Unaware of our destination, I needed to find something that could fit appropriately in any setting, and this particular choice was understated while still hugging my skin in just the right way. I applied enough makeup to enhance my features, adding a subtle glow to my winter skin and a deepening to my eyes, and polished myself with a lightly perfumed lotion. I took a deep breath that splintered on the way out. There was just something about him. Something about his ironically rugged smoothness and playful sophistication. There was a level of perfection to it all, and it made me extraordinarily aware of my insecurities. Arun had a certain power over me, that was for sure, but its discomfort was intriguing. It did something to me. It pushed me toward higher ground.

I was overcome by nervous excitement as I left the house. When I got on the train, I found a corner seat by the window and nestled my headphones in my ears. Although everything else had changed, the movement and the music cradled me in its rhythm much like it did the last time. I let myself fall into it, my chest rising and falling with its gentle pulse. Life is filled with so many moments, we so often forget to appreciate them. This was a moment I was glad to be in, and I didn't need time and distance to prove it to me. There was something dreamlike about moving toward a night that would be filled with him. Maybe it was the awareness that made it feel that way; that made it feel like I was a part of something bigger.

Arun texted me as the train pulled into the station. He shared with me the coordinates for a mysterious downtown location, and had called me a car. I made my way through the crowded station and into the air while the rumblings of nervousness still bubbled under my skin, but I didn't fight them. I let them flow through me and then vanish into the air that felt as much a part of me as my own beating heart. I had visited that city countless times, but this time felt different. I felt far away and vulnerable. Not unsafe, but wide open. I became more and more aware of my distance from Arun, or lack thereof. I imagined there was an invisible thread connecting us, that expanded and contracted as we danced about in our separate lives, the gap between us closing with every passing moment as the car sped on

We pulled over to a corner, and I peered out of the window, noticing the street light wash over the sidewalk. It was golden against the new night and interrupted by an inky shape that stretched toward me. Since the brightest lights create the most elegant of shadows, at the end of it stood Arun. We smiled toward each other as our eyes met. Met with a decisive click. The thread tugged at me like a heart string as I got out to meet him.

He looked the same, but different. His dress shoes were swapped out for a more casual pair of black boots, which met a pair of black jeans at his ankles. We matched in our darkness against the warm light. He wore the same leather jacket, and it fit him just as softly, expertly contouring itself to his strong but delicate frame.

"Hello, Selena," he said.

And just like that, I wasn't far away anymore.

"This way," he said, gesturing me to follow, and we walked half a block toward an entrance a few steps below ground level. The door was covered in graffiti, without any markings to disclose what laid beyond it. He pulled it open it with some effort, and then ushered me down a long, concrete stairway. An obvious red hue emitted from a doorway at the bottom, and when we turned into the room, our skin turned red too. The entire place was made of concrete, and the walls were doused in pictures and markings, the graffiti making its way from the outside in. There was a small bar in the corner, and a cluster of tables crammed together that took up the rest of the floor space. A man with a piercing that ran from his eyebrow to his left nostril ushered us to our seats. He was covered in tattoos and his black hair was shaved on both sides, but only on the sides. The rest fell over his shoulders like a scarf made of shadows. Every person that worked there looked that way. A way of their own.

We sat in the far corner. It was a tight seat, but it gave me a nice view of the place. I'd never been anywhere quite like it.

"I hope you like sake?"

"Yes," I said. He ordered something chilled and unfiltered. I wasn't sure what that meant, but it sounded delicious. He added an order of wasabi-infused octopus, looking toward me for approval.

"Sure, yeah, sounds great," I said. His unique taste intrigued me, and his decisiveness was eloquent, making whatever he chose feel like the only choice there was.

"Don't let this place fool you," he said. "You are about to taste one of the best cups of sake you've ever had."

"I don't doubt it," I said, looking around at the people and the art and feeling safe in the darkness coated in warm red.

"So," he smiled, "tell me about life since I last saw you."

I quieted for a moment.

"Life has been interesting," I replied, "as it always is." I took my napkin and placed it on my lap. "And how about you?" I deflected. Life had been Amelia. I couldn't bring up such heaviness before our drinks even arrived.

He wouldn't have it, ignoring my question completely. "Interesting how?"

"Oh, you know, a lot of family stuff. Changes. Been keeping busy."

"Right." He narrowed his eyes slightly. "Amelia. How is she doing?"

Our seats weren't yet warm, and already he burrowed into me.

"You remembered her name," I responded in gentle appreciation.

"Of course. So, how is she?"

I took a deep breath and looked down at our still empty plates. I couldn't avoid this direct question. "She passed away this week," I said, in a whisper. "We had to put her down."

"Oh God, Selena, I am so sorry."

"Thank you," I shrugged sadly. "It was really, really awful. But she isn't suffering anymore. When you love someone as much as we love her, that's really what matters."

I elaborated a bit more and he listened intently, shaking his head when necessary, fastened to my gaze when I needed a little extra support. I was consoled in his kindness, able to speak about the loss in such a way that didn't bring me to tears, telling him parts of my story rather than drowning in it. The deep light bathed everything around me and I saw a glimmer of it reflected in his eyes. They were lasers in that light, embedding truth into me and eradicating whatever pain they could make their way to.

"I can only imagine how difficult that must have been. How's your family?"

"Having a tough time, but we have each other, so that counts for a lot. Have you ever had to make that kind of decision?"

"No, I haven't, but I can empathize. I've lost some amazing pets." He stopped. "Do you want to hear about them?"

"Yes, of course I do."

I sensed he was afraid to speak his story while I was in the midst of my grief, but that was not my reality. Instead, it was comforting. I wanted to hear his story. I wanted to hear all of them. He spoke about his beloved childhood dog, and his sweet hamster, recently deceased, and just as he had held my space, I held his. I watched softness drape itself over him, compassion lacing his words and his stare. He looked beautiful there, in his sentimental reverie. A side of him that I had not yet seen.

The food and drink arrived, breaking our empathetic trance, and we watched as the server place our appetizer plate and a carafe between us.

"Thank you," said Arun, nodding his head as the server walked off, and taking it upon himself to lift the carafe and serve me a small cup of the milky white liquid.

"It is customary," he said, "to pour your companion's glass."

"And so, it is equally customary," I said, bringing my hand to the carafe before the liquid reached his own, "for me to pour yours as well."

He smiled and waited, and then lifted it towards me. "To Amelia," he said, clinking my glass against his in the middle.

"To Amelia."

The sake was ambrosial. It was fuller and sweeter than any I had ever tried, and it coated my tongue with its decadent smoothness.

"This is delicious," I stated emphatically.

"And wait until you try this," he said, plucking a piece of octopus between his chopsticks and placing it in front of me.

I was a pescatarian, meaning I ate seafood, but no other meat. It felt hypocritical in ways, but I looked upon it as a positive step on an unfolding journey. As guilt-laden as I felt to see that octopus laying there in front of us, I took it to my mouth with gratitude, both for its sustenance and for the company I shared it with. It would be impossible to deny its uniquely delicious taste and texture, both savory and sweet.

"Right?" he asked.

I shook my head in agreement as I put another piece in my mouth and washed it down with a slow sip.

"I love this city," I said, looking around our space again. I was so immersed in him, that it was easy to forget my surroundings. "So many hidden gems."

"Have you ever considered a move here?"

"Sure," I said. "I love New York. But the beach is so much a part of me. I have a deep love for my hometown, I admit. It's hard to imagine being away from it."

"I don't blame you. Must have been amazing to grow up by the ocean. I've got to get out to the beach more often."

I wanted to tell him he could visit anytime, but I stopped myself.

"The city does something to you though," he said, eyes alight. "It's like no other place in the world. I think everyone should try it, even if just for a little while."

"We are lucky to live in such amazing places. Not everyone can say that they love where they are from. But it would be really good for me to branch out a little, you know? To take a leap. Try something new."

"I have the perfect solution for you," he shrugged.

I laughed. I didn't at all doubt he in fact had the perfect one. "What's that?"

"You strive to have a home in both. A beach house, a city apartment, and a place upstate too, because if we are dreaming big, we might as well go all the way."

"Such grand aspirations," I smiled, moving my fingers through my hair. "Maybe I should find a new job first."

"Just call it a *someday*."

"A someday," I repeated. I liked the way it sounded.

Every worry I had about the flow of our conversation was wholly unnecessary. There was no effort. His graceful words floated into the air and approached me with gentility. I took them, mulled them around for a while, and returned them with parallel ease.

"By the way," he said. "we aren't eating dinner here."

"We aren't?" I asked, as I looked down at our almost empty carafe and our chopsticks laid poised on napkins.

"Where would the adventure be if we sat here all night? Simply an appetizer. You're overdressed for this place anyway."

He said it with a smirk, but I still blushed accordingly. He retrieved the check from the server, which laid on a cracked black metal tray. I motioned toward my wallet and he stopped me with a stern sideways glance.

"You were kind enough to accompany me for underground octopus. This one's on me."

I let out another small laugh.

I loved it there. I loved the walls and the people and the darkness, and that we were underground together in its cement cocoon. I loved sharing food out of a mutual plate, our chopsticks occasionally aiming for the same place at the same time and hitting against each other with the faintest tap of wood to wood.

"Ready?"

We made our way back toward ground level and traveled a short distance to our second destination, where a well-dressed woman took my coat from me, removing it from my shoulders one arm at a time. I thanked her, and looked up at the high ceilings and vast landscape of the interior. People sat talking quietly over glasses of white wine and plates adorned with delicate and colorful cuisine, also Japanese, but plated more elegantly and against a grander backdrop. There was a massive replica of a tree in the center of the dining room, its roots twisting up toward the sky in beautiful abstract rhythm.

Arun directed me to the sushi bar, aside the kitchen that was enveloped in a glass enclosure from floor to ceiling, where the chefs worked at their art with absolute focus.

"This is beautiful," I said, awed and unable to hide it, marveling at an unfolding experience that seemed purposefully designed. Though both were spectacular in their own way, the grandeur of that location was appreciated all the more because of its contrast to the last.

We sat down, and he ordered an ensemble of things for us to share, some of which I had never before tasted.

"What else would you like?" he asked, as we moved our attention over the elaborate menu.

"You seem to know what you're doing," I said, trusting his taste with no desire to interfere. I watched him move his magic wand over everything that he touched while we sat in view of the glass-enclosed kitchen, our seats at the sushi bar leaving nothing between us but air.

We ate, and we drank, and everything was so delicious that I was sure to take it in with reverence. The wine started to warm us, and he pulled his chair toward mine. Our knees hovered inches from each other, and I could not only hear his words, but I could feel them on my cheeks. We talked. We talked and we talked. We talked about everything. Our fears and our desires. Where we wanted to go, and how we wanted to get there. What we knew and what we didn't and what we wanted to find out. We spoke about our past loves, what they had been like, why they ended. We talked about life and what was missing and what was beautiful.

He looked at life differently than most people. He saw people. He saw situations beyond their surfaces. He looked at the whys and the hows, while navigating his own, and he did so with grace. He was so unique in his openness and honesty. He exuded both confidence and vulnerability simultaneously in a way I had never seen. In the space we created, there was only me and him and a murmur of other life in the background, washing over us with its calming lull. Periphery was muted, blurred, black and white. His features were sharp, eyes as blue as the sky.

"So, what else can you tell me about yourself?" he asked.

"Hmm," I said. "What do you want to know?"

"Three things," he said. "Name three things you like."

"Anything?" I asked.

"Anything. First things that come to mind. I'll go first." He thought for a moment.

"Paella, Nine Inch Nails, and magnets."

"Eclectic," I said. "Magnets?"

"They have always fascinated me," he said. "That invisible pull, you know? But no stalling. Your turn."

"Ok, ok," I said, taking a moment to think as well. "Ok." I sat up straighter.

"Painting, herbal tea, and stones," I said, definitively.

"Stones?" he asked. "As in, like, rocks?"

"More like gemstones. And crystals" I said. "Amethyst and hematite are my favorites. It's incredible, you know? These beautiful things, formed in in the earth."

"Incredible, indeed," he said, with a smile in his eyes. "You'll have to teach me more about your rocks over Paella one day."

I agreed with an amused nod.

"So, have you dated anyone else seriously since your ex?" he asked, changing the subject rather abruptly.

"Not really," I said.

"Why not?"

"I don't know. I just needed some time, I guess. The last guy I was seeing was really great. I just wasn't ready."

"Tell me about him," he said. "What made him great?"

"His name is Justin," I said, with no fear of being straightforward. The lack of appropriateness in discussing other relationships on a first date was extraneous there. "He's very kind and we got along well, but I just wasn't ready for anything serious, I guess. And then Amelia got sick, and you know how it is..."

"This was very recent, then?" he asked.

"It was," I said.

"And now, here you are," he said.

"And now, here I am," I smiled.

He raised his glass in cheers. "To Justin," he said, in a playfully sarcastic way. "I hope he is having as much fun as we are tonight."

I gave him a sideways look, pretending to chastise him but unable to control the smile that never stopped pulling at the corners of my mouth.

"To tonight," I said, revising the cheers, then connecting my wine glass to his with a clank.

I watched his glass meet his mouth, and I watched his slow swallow. He placed it down and I heard its small clink against the polished wood counter. He took both hands and placed them on his thighs, pushing up his shoulders slightly, and then he reached across me, grabbing a piece of sushi between his fingers and skimming my hand with his. A voltaic pulse ran through my body, alighting my nerve endings.

The attraction was so intense it was palpable. I wanted to get closer to him with every breath. I wanted him to touch me, more, and again. His hands looked strong and kind. I imagined them in my hair, lingering by my temples, making their way down my neck. And his lips. I could almost feel them pressed against mine, soft and warm. They were glistening slightly with the lingering scent of wine, and his words slid off of them like silk against silk.

It was one of those rare nights. A night of blurred magic. The kind you wished would slow down. The kind you savor every moment of, but still feel you aren't savoring quite enough, because you are so immersed that you forget to pay attention. We sat in that restaurant for hours. Probably for longer than we were welcome. We didn't notice until we looked up and saw that we were the last ones there. Time slid by like his silken words. I could not grab it, so I watched it charmingly ebb away.

After a lingering hug, I walked away down a flat path that felt like an uphill trek. A trudging against attracting magnetic poles. My heart floated home in reverie, but my body swam against his rushing tide.

That night, even my dreams couldn't touch my reality.

7

The minute I heard my first love story,
I started looking for you, not knowing how blind that was.
Lovers don't finally meet somewhere.
They're in each other all along.

—RUMI

When I woke the next morning, something had changed. The foggy-eyed ignorance leading to a stabbing moment of rushing remembrance that had been my waking state for weeks was replaced by subtle elation.

I had caught the last train out at what I had considered a respectable hour. I had peeled myself away from him, that I will admit. As much as I would have liked nothing more than to spend as much time as possible soaking in the periphery of his aura, I told myself that it was healthier that way. Healthier to leave a little mystery, even though I was moving forward full-speed-ahead in all manners that he could not see. In most circumstances, this structured belief system I created might make sense, but with him, I wasn't sure. My reaction to him was a strange phenomenon, one that I could not explain and of which rules did not seem to apply. It felt as if I had known him for a very long time. Much longer than those few short meetings allowed. Our connection was obviously unique. I knew it, but I could not explain it. The molecules floating between us just vibrated differently, and through that connection to him, I felt more connected to everything else.

After that night, life quickly became split into two parts: time spent with him, and time spent without him (in which I was thinking about him). There was no middle ground. There was only this and that. And it seemed time became simply what passed like a blur between life at its fullest.

"Meet me at my place?" he asked the following night, his hum reverberating through the phone. "I want to cook for you."

I was even more nervous than the first time, or the second, each moment adding to its momentum. I let the clock move, filling the hours with half-hearted work and daydreams until it was time to go. Because of the sporadic train times, I arrived to Penn Station a bit early, which was better than being late. With my extra time, I decided to navigate the subway system. I rode for 25 minutes with headphones in my ears and more daydreaming, missed my stop, and ended up in Brooklyn. By the time I got back up to him, I was winded and late after all. I buzzed his apartment with trepidation and, noticing my dry mouth, took a sip out of my water bottle before climbing the stairs. Only when I reached the 5th floor did I remember there was in fact an elevator in the building. But, if the stairs were good enough for him, they were good enough for me.

I knocked on his door, quickly fixing the way my coat and my hair was hanging. He opened it and smiled a hello in my direction. My knees were shaking slightly as I walked through the threshold of the dimly lit hallway, the interior illuminated by lamps and bulbs rather than the overhead fixtures. I had a seat on his white kitchen stool, and willed my knees to still.

"How was your trip?" He asked.

His black converse sneakers were thrown in the corner as he walked around barefoot in his low-cut black jeans.

"It was fine," I said honestly, but leaving out the details. "Sorry I'm a little late."

"Not at all," he said. "Perfect timing. This stuff needs some time to marinate."

"What's on the menu?" I asked. "It smells amazing."

"I hope you like mussels?"

"Yes," I said. "Can I help?"

"Yes," he mirrored, shaking his head and handing me a bottle of Cabernet. "By opening this."

He directed my gaze to the corkscrew laying on the table nearby. I took both in my hands and clumsily removed the deep red foil wrapped around the top of the bottle.

"Otherwise, we are all under control," he added, as he finished cutting pieces of yellow squash with a large knife, making a rhythmic sound as it met flatly with the cutting board. "Tell me about your day."

"Well," I said. It was mostly spent in daydreams, but I'd leave that part out. "I've started a new project."

"Anything good?" he asked.

"Branding and some marketing stuff for a yoga studio," I said.

"Look at you," he said. "Full speed ahead. And merging interests while you're at it."

I laughed. "I don't know about that," I said. "One step at a time."

"Well, feel free to bounce some ideas off of me," he said, as he dropped the squash into the pan and it let out a loud and satisfying sizzle, flavorful vapor erupting around him, and then subsiding into pleasing wisps.

I smiled toward him, suddenly and wholly distracted. The succulent wafting of garlic and basil and thyme mingled in the air, and I watched him from where I sat. His back was turned to me, his right arm raised to stir what was in the sizzling pan, and his other gently lowering the flame, standing almost on his toes in poised and purposeful ease.

He glided toward the cutting board, and grasped a handful of herbs in his hand. "I've been growing my own," he said, moving in a choreographed dance at one with the savory steam. "Can you smell it? So much more fragrant this way."

"It's lovely," I said.

Leaning toward the stove, he sprinkled the ingredients over the pan and they cascaded down into the misty heat. I watched his shoulders rise in deep inhale.

He looked absolutely beautiful in that moment and it flooded me. I watched him from there, and I loved him.

I was sure of it. I was as sure as I have ever been of anything, and then even more sure than that. There was no doubt. There was no gripping, no push or pull, no fear or irrational longing. There was just clarity, gentle and wholly full of aliveness. It was an ambrosia, washing over me, rushing peacefully through every crevice. It sparkled on my skin and rippled through the rest of me with its vital essence, waking up dormant parts of me where joy was easy and where muscles were tender with inertia.

The emotion coated me in its unique and quiet grandeur, filling my eyes with the beginnings of tears, but I had to keep my composure, or else risk a crumbling of the molecules between us like dominoes. As pure as that feeling was, I understood I was alone in it, unable to imagine anyone else feeling as sure as I was in that moment, after so short a time. When he turned around, I looked down, so as to not give myself away.

"What are you thinking about?" he asked, as he placed two empty wine glasses on the table to be filled. I could feel his gaze on me as the red liquid cascaded from the bottle, splashing elegantly against the curve of the glass.

"Just taking it all in," I smiled. "I like watching you work."

"It's hardly work if you enjoy it," he said. He wiped his hands on a dish towel that hung by the sink and took the glass by its stem, clanking it against mine and swallowing slowly. "Things don't have to be difficult just because they are worth having."

I nodded my head in agreement, sitting there with him in that moment, the easiest thing in the world.

"And I think that goes for most things," he said.

I waited for him to elaborate, but he didn't.

"Like what?" I prompted.

"Well, take relationships, for example. Too often, they become strenuous. Doused in tediousness, you know? And then what's the point?"

"Yes." I thought for a moment.

"If something is right, even the tough spots can be graceful," I said.

"Right," he smiled, and then he let it fade, shaking his head slowly and looking somewhere beyond me. He stayed there for a few moments and then brought his eyes back down. "I mean, there is nothing wrong with getting your hands dirty, especially for someone you care about. But there's a limit."

"Maybe there's a difference," I said. "Between handing yourself over... and opening yourself up. You know, being able to merge with someone while still holding your own space."

"Maybe that's it," he said. "Balance. But I wonder..."

He gave the mussels a stir.

"Do you think there is always one person who cares more than the other? Or do you believe that we are meant to find an equal? I mean, is that even possible? I wonder because without that, how can there be any balance at all?"

I chuckled with surprise, but only inside of myself, where he could not see. I wondered if he read my thoughts, curiosity and nervousness mingling in my stomach.

"I know what I believe is possible," I said, somewhat cautiously, "and what I believe the ideal to be, though it doesn't always turn out that way."

"What do you believe is possible?"

I thought for a minute, or maybe for just a few seconds that seemed longer.

"I think, when it comes to love, there is always enough, and there is never enough. You can't be afraid of a little paradox."

He was quiet for a while then also.

"Tell me what you mean."

"I don't think love, true and actual love, can be quantified. I've been on both ends of that spectrum: I've loved more, and I've been loved more, whatever it is that *more* means, and all were equally beautiful in their own ways..."

I hesitated for a moment, wary that I was saying too much.

"Go on," he said, leaning in with intrigue.

"I do believe, however, equally requited love would simultaneously be as beautiful and the most beautiful of all. That's part of the paradox. Does that make any sense?"

"It does." He stood up and cocked his head very slightly to the side. "It does. I never looked at it that way."

"In what way did you look at it?" I asked.

"With less of a positive spin," he smiled. "And as more of a carefully calculated algorithm. You know, the science of attraction and all that. That maybe it even comes down to something as logical as biology. But as for equality in emotion? It never seemed logical to me, you know? For two people to feel exactly the same way. More about finding balance in imbalance to create something that works, I guess."

I focused my eyes on him as the corners of my mouth turned slightly downward. There were experiences there. A hardness. It made me feel sad.

He shook his head. "Well, that's at least how I used to think. I'm not sure how I feel now. Life is funny that way. Experiences have a way of messing with our carefully constructed views. A particular type of wisdom that comes with a combination of age, interest, and circumstance, I suppose."

He was ironic in expression then, at once as outright as ever and simultaneously reserved. He was expressing in words whatever snippets ran through his mind, but leaving out the details.

"Have you ever felt it?" I asked. "That balance?"

"I don't think so. I've been on both sides also. My last relationship fluctuated between the two. No even ground. An incessant and subconscious struggle for emotional dominance."

"No one ever comes out on top," I said softly.

"Maybe some of us just need to learn the hard way," he shrugged. "You know what they say about pain. A good teacher."

I nodded in compassionate understanding, noting his increased vulnerability.

"How long ago was your last relationship?" I asked.

"It ended a few months ago," he said matter-of-factly, albeit with obviously feigned nonchalance. I could tell by the way he shrugged his shoulders, and where he put his eyes.

I was surprised. When we talked about past relationships over dinner the other night, I hadn't realized that his last ending was so fresh. I felt a slight sinking feeling, both in compassion for him, and in realization that he may have been in a more complicated and fragile place emotionally than I had thought. There I was, falling for him in a matter of days, and as he flitted around the kitchen, he probably thought of her with a lump in his throat. An all-too-familiar feeling for most of us.

"That must be very hard," I said.

"Such is life," he smiled as he retrieved square, white plates from above the stove. "And so far, it's been a pretty good one at that."

He dipped his metal spoon into the simmering and buttery vegetables and served each of us a steaming heap. Its smell of sweet garlic had the certain quality unique to home cooking in its care and devotion. We made our way over to his couch and set our plates and glasses down on his grooved wooden table. He lit two candles and placed them on either side of our settings.

"Let's see if this is any good," he said, changing the subject for the both of us, using his fingers to pry open a mussel that was doused in a light broth.

I followed suit and nodded in appreciation, letting any insecurities fall slightly below consciousness as I focused on the light of the candles that reflected warmly on the mussel shells. We watched a documentary as we ate, a smart depiction of a street artist that had us in a space of intellectual ping-pong, removing us from our previously emotionally charged exchange. We bounced from depth to lightness in conversation with such ease that it seemed there was no transitional in-between.

We sat not far from each other on the couch, and that nervousness and excitement of new closeness hung in the air. It was thick with something like hopeful anticipation, but I think it was much more like awareness.

Once we were done eating, we both leaned back, our legs barely touching at the knee. I was no longer shaking. The wine was smooth and elegant, augmenting my newfound relaxation, and by the time the movie ended, I was pressed into the couch cushion, my shoes by his on the ground, and my legs curled underneath me. The two flames danced on our faces, blushing our cheeks and mingling with the dreamlike atmosphere, and he turned to me.

"I can't figure you out," he said with piercing eyes that reflected the light. "I'm usually pretty good at this, but I can't figure you out."

"What do you mean?" I asked with surprise. "What do you want to know?"

"I'm not sure." He stopped, shifting on the cushion and leaning towards me, eyes slightly narrowed. "I can't tell how you feel."

"Well," I said slowly. "I've been cautious, I guess. I can't quite figure you out either."

"You know, Selena," he said, his voice deep and slow, "I don't like games."

"Neither do I," I said, suddenly flushed. "I'm not playing any games."

"So why are you being so careful?" he asked.

"I'm not sure," I said honestly, but then thought for a moment.

Perhaps it was because I was so high already. Perhaps it was because if I went any higher, my heart would shatter into a million pieces if it fell.

"I..." I said, trailing off, apprehensive of what words I should allow to seep out.

"I like you," he said, with the most straightforward and elegant simplicity. "Actually," he corrected himself, and I listened on the metaphorical edge of my seat, holding onto his last words, and hoping he wouldn't change them.

"Actually," he said, "I'm pretty fucking into you."

And then I realized that sometimes change isn't a bad thing. I sat very still. The words and the darkness and the lingering scent that mingled in the quiet room was mystifying. His eyes burned into me.

"I was into you since the moment I first saw you," he said. "It was something about you. And then, you spoke. You didn't have to say much but I was sure of it. You are different somehow."

The intricacies of these words ran through me, hot and fast. I let myself drink them in. I wanted to lean toward him and pour myself into him. I wanted to touch his mouth and run my now electric fingers through every strand of his hair. I wanted to tell him that he was the most beautiful person in the world. That since the moment I saw him, my heart beat differently. That every moment before that was *then*, and this *now* quickly became all that was.

I wanted to tell him that at first site, it was for me too… whatever you'd like to call it.

But all I said was, "It felt different to me too."

I was afraid. I was so afraid of giving too much and frightening him away. I couldn't explain exactly why, but I felt it. He seemed fragile. Emotionally brittle. Like it was one thing for him to express it but another for him to receive it. That it might be too heavy for his delicate shoulders. It wasn't the truth that I was afraid of speaking, but that he wouldn't be able to catch it. That it would pummel through the air and fall through his hands, hitting the ground at his feet like cement.

"Let's just be upfront, ok?" he said. "We want to call each other? We do it. We want to hang out? We say so."

"How refreshing," I exhaled.

"And, you know" he said, his head cocked to the side, a small, gentle smile painting itself across his face, "someday, I will kiss you."

I blushed, heat coursing through me and showing up on my cheeks. He leaned back, seemingly satisfied with my reaction, and took a long sip of Cabernet.

I thought it strange that he hadn't kissed me yet. Strange, and lovely. The anticipation was peaceful and electric at the same time. I've never before felt such a pull. Such an intense and organic attraction. It's difficult to imagine the sensation of kissing someone for the first time. The way someone's lips mesh against yours is always surprising in its newness of sensation and experience. And then, after a few times, you can't imagine it any other way. But you know when there's some kind of enchantment there. It's something beyond the physical. It's the way someone moves and tastes and lingers. An energetic reaction. An intangible relating. I had a strong feeling ours would be an aligning of something spectacular.

  I took another sip and tasted the deep and elegant sweetness on my lips, longing to know if his tasted the same. He watched me roll my tongue over them and moved closer. We were nearly touching, but not quite, until he took his fingertips and brushed them almost imperceptibly across the top of my hand.

  He turned toward me and looked into my eyes, and everything around me became blurred periphery.

  "It's late," he said. "Why don't you stay here tonight?"

  My gaze dropped slightly in consideration of nonsensical and self-imposed rules.

  "Don't worry about the *shoulds*, Selena." He took a strand of my short hair and placed it behind my ear. "There are no rules here. I just don't want you to leave yet."

  I didn't want to leave yet, either, and I told him so. And just like that, it was settled.

  He took my hand in his, and lifted me gently from the couch. He stopped there for a minute, gauging my reaction, gave me a soft smile, and then led me slowly to his bedroom, our bare feet not making a sound against the cool, wood-paned floor. He dropped my hand, and walked past the bed, where he rustled through his closet, and pulled out a large t-shirt for me to wear. I removed my tank top, and then discreetly pulled the t-shirt over myself before removing whatever else I had on underneath. I stood there, then, in his shirt that smelled like his midnight-wide-awake, and my lace underwear, feeling comfortably vulnerable. He looked at me and then pulled his shirt over his head, only breaking his gaze when it came into his line of vision.

  I liked seeing his skin, more of it than I had yet to see. He was pale and smooth, thin and toned. I inhaled him as he shut off the lights, and I watched him through the static and fizzing darkness as he made his way to the bed.

I followed.

He pulled the covers up over us to the shoulders, and once enveloped, I felt myself burning for him. It was so hot, the way it burned under my skin, that I wondered if he could feel it oozing out, radiating off of me. We were turned toward each other, slightly curled in perfect mirrored pose. He put his arm over my shoulder, and we laid there for a moment, face to face in the dark. I couldn't make out all of his features, but I could see his outline and the slight shine of his blue eyes. He took his hand and ran it through my hair, softly, slowly. His touch sent shock waves through me, each brush of fingertip to skin waking up the surrounding nerves and creating ripples through my entire body. I started to ache for him. It was so soon. It was so new. But I didn't know how to resist him. I took a breath and he was in every cell of my body. It was as if there was nothing between us. Not even the air.

His face came close to me, and the moments leading there were slow and delicate. When our lips touched, there was softness, unparalleled, and a perfectly unique warmth, as if we were melting into each other, two parts of a delicate whole. We lit up our dark cocoon, slowly at first, appreciating every wisp of skin to skin, and then growing in passionate embrace. His mouth fit against mine like there should have never been any space between them. Fit as if they were created as one and then separated just long enough so that we could fully appreciate their flawless reunion. With this kiss came the awe of perfection. There was nothing to be changed, nothing to be conscious of but the natural interchange of mine to his and his to mine. Could we possibility be gifted such grandeur and bliss without reason? I swam in what I was sure was miraculous purpose, and it made my eyes water.

Soon, we became pure passion. Our hands spoke our desires. We were grabbing at each other, pulling each other closer, wrapping limbs around limbs. I was losing myself in him, giving myself to him, finding myself in him. Every nerve ending was alive, hyper-aware of every touch of his mouth against my neck, his firm grip of my skin, his hips rubbing up against mine. His readiness was obvious and throbbing through his clothes, growing in strength, vigor, and need with every pulse.

He rolled me over and pinned me down, hands on each side of me, arms elongated, straddling my torso and clenching my hips between his knees. He looked at me with a savage look that didn't frighten me, staring into my eyes for a few brief moments, until he took his piercing glare down my body. I felt it wash over my neck and my chest like hot silk, piercing at any composure I had left, throwing me into a burning of which there was no return. He took the weight off of his hands and slid them onto me. He took the lace and slid it down my legs.

"It's so soon," I whispered.

But it felt like I had waited a lifetime for that moment.

It felt like I had waited an eternity.

"I just want to make you feel good." He said it in a low growl; a seductive whisper that made my every defense crumble like sharp glass turning to soft and shimmering dust.

He put his mouth to me, where the lace had been, and my body convulsed, writhing in its space on his bed made of clouds. His tongue was warm and soft. It moved against me, intoxicating me with its rhythm. With closed eyes, I floated in bliss, arching my back to meet the heavens that were descending upon me. I let him have me. I handed myself over and I watched myself tumbling out of everything I was before, falling into the sky that held me.

I unfolded around him in cascading ecstasy.

8

*Lover, tell the night that your day
will never end in its arms.
The religion of Love is a sea without a shore
where lovers drown without a sigh,
without a cry.*

—RUMI

I left the next morning in his t-shirt after a late and slow breakfast of ginger tea and poached eggs. I floated home in a state of bliss.

Bliss. It was one of the two predominant states I lived in for the next month.

I had never felt so joyous. So excited and alive. So driven and inspired. I was limitless. Eternal and expansive and vast and made of stars and ocean waves and laughter. Everything was brighter and alight with possibility. *This is life at its most beautiful*, I thought. *This is happiness.*

We spent time together every few evenings, embracing and exploring his city, my beach, and each other. Our meetings were filled with enchantment; pinnacles of experience in which a sense of time was lost, and a complete immersion in exquisiteness of the present moment came without effort. I noticed through love's high that this immersion creates a particular type of euphoria; one of which must be the very essence of peak experience. It carried with it an element of steadfast awareness, and elicited an effortless sense of peace. It evoked a fluent happiness in a language I never spoke before. Perhaps it was soul speak.

It seemed we had it all. Intellectually, we inspired each other toward consistent immersion in obscure and thought-provoking banter. We learned from each other. We discussed science and spirituality and the Universe. We agreed on most things and disagreed on most things. We came at things from different angles, me from the ethereal, him from the methodical, but somehow, we always understood each other's vantage point. It was an easy irony. One my mind expanded around. We gifted each other an entirely unique but parallel perspective that allowed our consciousness to flourish with twice as much space. We had a delightful lightness to our interaction, and simultaneously, a depth of caring that was obvious, though unspoken.

Emotionally, I was filled. With him, I could be my unabridged self, but it wasn't in a comfortable way. It was in a soul-driven and emotionally quenching way. The relationship pushed me. From him, everything caused my soul to enlighten. He shook me out, allowing cobwebs and old stories to fall out like dust. Every moment became a memory that I used as a piece of saved-up joy, allowing me to live our moments over and over and over again as if they were clips from my favorite movie or chapters from my favorite book. I cared about him deeply, but it filled me quietly. Love was alive in every cell. It expanded not in a straight line, but like a plant or a snowflake. It was as exponential as life itself, each bit of light shining upon countless others and each of those bringing life to just as many to follow, on and on for eternity.

Physically, I had never experienced such intensity. As in most aspects of his life, Arun was dominant in our sexual relationship. I would succumb to his power happily, pleadingly, over and over again. We melded together effortlessly; he thrust his strength into me with vigorous passion, softening his approach where he met my gentleness. His touch was electric. I couldn't get enough of it. I wanted him always and everywhere. He spoke to me, demanded things of me. "That's a good girl," he would croon, as I wrapped myself around him, swallowing him hungrily. And he'd throw himself into me and I'd moan as if it hurt but we both knew it didn't. I'd hear him in my dreams when I slept at night and if he wasn't by me when I woke, I'd close my eyes again and imagine he was.

When we were not together, I lived both in daydreams and a brighter reality. Life was thriving in so many ways. I was more ambitiously working toward my goals, enjoying time with friends and family, and delving into my spirituality in a deeper and much more all-encompassing way. I lived more often in a state of ease, life flowing gracefully from one moment to the next, and in that space, I was more able to embrace spiritual principles I had been abstractly practicing for so long. The depression and anxiety I had struggled with for a lifetime had lost their grip there. I felt less separate. Less uncomfortable in my own skin. I stopped thinking so much about *how* I would embrace life joys. How I would escape the consistent state of unease and introspection about my place in this life. I stopped thinking so much about how to be happy. I just felt it. I didn't have to try.

Bliss. That was one of the states I floated in that month. It took up almost all of my time.

Almost.

The place that was not bliss would come without warning. It would happen when I was washing dishes or blow drying my hair or when I was outside and a cloud floated unexpectedly in front of the sun. It would come over me so quickly and with such force that it would take my breath. It would tell me stories; scary stories that were dark and alone.

As can ironically happen when we hold a shining constellation in our hands, I felt terribly afraid of losing it. If life was given meaning in this love, then what would happen if it was to be taken away?

The more blissful I felt, the stronger the fear was when it hit. The more I allowed myself to open my heart and yield my soul, the rawer my fear bruises became. And after that first month of predominant joy, the fear to bliss balance started to shift. I wondered if these two states were mutually exclusive. Could you only have as much of one as the space the other left?

Somewhere along the way, I started to notice some inconsistencies in Arun's behavior. They were subtle at first, but I was so in-tune to his breath that I could recognize even the smallest shift in rhythm. There was perhaps a day without a phone call, a delayed answer to a text message, a Friday night that he had other plans. As time unfolded, my fear started bubbling up more often, inflamed with even the slightest hint of discord. It abated when I spoke to him again, and he gave me the perfect reason for not calling. Or when I saw him again, and he held me, reassuring, in his arms. In stark contrast to the grounded life I was living in our joy, I shamefully became controlled by our tides. Swept up in its warm lulls and its chilling currents.

One Sunday morning, a few weeks later, we were laying on the couch, lazily watching a movie, his arms wrapped around me from behind. I had been seeing less of him, and when we were together, he fell asleep more quickly at night, ending our evening without the usual immersive conversation and passionate embrace. Sometimes, he had places to be in the morning, and I would find myself hurrying to show myself out. I couldn't understand why he hadn't wanted to touch me, needed to touch me, in the way I needed him, when prior, we could not keep away from each other. I could not relate to this. There was never a moment that I did not want to feel my skin against his. Never a time that I wasn't burning for him.

The rapidly shifting balance was more obvious in contrast to the elation. I started to feel tense more often than not, my chest tight with worry and my heart contracted. I hoped that I was only imagining these shifts out of fear. That these things were stories I told myself. That they didn't have to mean destruction.

We laid there on the couch, the television flashing its muted light into the sunlit room, and I turned around to kiss him. I placed my hand in his hair and lingered on his lips. I lingered long enough to turn around and wrap my arms around his neck, and let him feel all the hot emotion rushing through my fingertips. He responded, and took me firmly in his grasp, rolling me on top of him, driving his tongue deep into my mouth where I could taste his savory sweetness. I made my way down his torso and then down further, taking him even deeper into my mouth and into my throat. I heard his pleased and heavy exhale. I swallowed him slowly and vibrated against him with a slow moan, feeling pleasure in how engorged he was. He hadn't even touched me, and I was already drenched with desire. I moved rhythmically, hungrily for some time, until he took me by the shoulders and pulled me up toward him. He removed any clothing between us and firmly thrust himself into me with a sharp groan. I was so ready for him, but still, it shocked me. He came at me hard, almost violently. He slammed himself into me, eyes on fire, their flames looking angry this time.

I took his head in my hands and looked at him, right in the eyes, forcing him to look back. I lost control, craving his response. I gripped his skin with my hands, grabbing all of him that I could and I let my eyes give me away. There was no stopping the deluge. Love poured out of me and crashed into him. It washed over us, encircling us in its waves. I felt him contract against it. His movement became increasingly intense, rough with physicality, eyes burning with something that was not the same as mine. They were closing him off, blocking everything that was radiating from every inch of me. His forehead tightened and he grunted loudly, making one last push, until he came hard and beads of sweat seeped from his shoulder blades. Not seconds later, he pulled himself out of me. I was still dripping with him, looking for my next breath, and he was up off the couch, grabbing his pants and walking briskly toward the sink, where he poured himself a glass of water.

I laid there, naked and soaked in sex. I laid there alone.

I watched him from a distance, a weight laying heavily on my chest, and then rose slowly, eyes to the ground. I could not look at him for fear he would read my mind. Watch my thoughts unfold as a story in fast-forward. A story that he was not supposed to see. I feared too that I would read his. See some truth that would hurt too much to hold. I found my clothes, one piece at a time strewn across the floor. We were quiet as we dressed.

"I should go." I said it with a small voice. It was one that I had not heard from myself in a while. I cleared my throat and spoke louder. "I have some things I need to do."

"Yeah, ok," he said, pushing words out of his mouth seemingly out of obligation. "Let me know when you're home safe."

He always said that when I left. Usually, it was phrased kindly as he looked into my eyes with his arms wrapped around me. This time, he sat down on the couch and opened his laptop, looking down in the same way I did.

"I'll talk to you later," I mumbled, the words getting caught in a throat which only minutes before was filled by him.

Wary of shattering the tense air, I tiptoed over to the couch and gave him a soft kiss on the cheek. I was tight and uncomfortable. I felt like my insides were being wrung out to dry. All of the emotion I was feeling had nowhere to go, so it bounced around my space in a panic, oozing out of me and choking me with an overwhelming vibration that I could not house. He looked up only for a moment, and I turned away in the next, making my way to the door and turning the knob slowly. I hoped he would call out to me. He didn't, so I walked out into the fluorescent hallway, stepping cautiously, feeling every inch of tile beneath my black leather boots, as if landing too roughly would crumble the ground behind me.

I focused on these external things: my steps and the air. It helped me to keep moving and away from a rash alternative that could flood me without proof or substance. That vicious mix of fear and crippling disappointment was usually laced with irrationality, and could only show up as pain.

Just like that, my bright new world was dimmed. What did this mean? What was he thinking? It was so sudden. Was it possible that it was as bad as I feared, or was I catastrophizing something out of nothing? Since when did I let another person, especially a man I had met only a couple of months before, control my happiness? My entire sense of self? I couldn't possibly be that dependent. Could I? I definitely never had been before. I tried to conceptualize what had happened, tried to will myself to stop jumping to conclusions and allowing my imagination to run away with me in such a treacherous way. But I couldn't think straight. Every nerve and brain cell felt as if it were short-circuiting. Ideas and emotions and feelings and fears ricocheted violently, threatening to take over.

I texted him when I got home to let him know I arrived safely. He didn't respond, and the next couple of days, I didn't hear from him either. I spent a lot of time with my phone nearby, fighting surges of fearful realization.

I was obviously contracted, slow and tight and quiet. I was distracted almost to the point of inertia. My thoughts burned me. I could feel them singe where they touched below my skin. They lingered there, smoky and dark, but I did not allow them to reach the brim of my insides. Pain exists in the flooding. It is felt when the dam breaks. Once that happens, it can drown us. There were still far too many other things keeping me afloat, so I just let it singe me. Simmer and slither around my hope.

On the evening of the third day, after many hours of work, a hot shower, and a dinner of pasta and vegetables reheated on the stove, my phone rang. I forced myself to still long enough to swallow whatever food was sitting idly in my mouth, and my shoulders released slightly, as if they knew something that I didn't.

Hello Lena, he said. *What's doin'?*

Words, words, words. Words and their meanings and meaninglessness. It had been quiet without his around.

Relaxing, I responded simply, leaving all the rest between the lines. It was only about five percent true, but still true. *What about you?*

I want to try out this new recipe, he said. *Pretty healthy and all that. Right up your alley.*

What is it? I asked.

A surprise, he said. *My place tomorrow?*

Tomorrow night? I asked apprehensively, buying time between my thoughts.

Actually, he said. I tensed. *Actually, are you free a little earlier? Expecting some good weather. Maybe a walk in the park first.*

I lightened with the subtle provocation of hope. I would say yes, right? That wasn't really a question. The real questions came separately, and there were many of them.

I would go. I would go and figure out the rest later.

Yeah, Ok, I said. *That sounds good.*

I was on a roller coaster. It was an erratic ride of fluctuating emotion. I was lightheaded. I closed my eyes tight, and emotion squeezed out of their corners. In the blackness in front of me danced a bubble, its colors mingling in the day's afternoon light. I watched it behind closed lids, swirling in its gentle kaleidoscope so naturally, flowing with the air's undulations. I opened my eyes before it could land on hard ground. I wanted it to stay whole and beautiful forever.

Maybe this was salvageable. Maybe it wasn't. But why did I let one experience, one interaction, paint my entire picture? I hadn't even spoken to him about any of it yet. I didn't know how he felt, and I was sure he hadn't realized the extent of the effect our last meeting had on me. It felt so childlike, all of it, letting my emotions run rampant that way. I would discuss it with him, and whatever the response, at least there wouldn't be any more questions.

I sat down and forced myself to still, finding my meditation space, though it was a bit shallow and restless. I desperately needed to ground myself, rid myself of the stories I had running on loop which allowed my emotion to take over. Whatever this was, it was. This grappling and guessing would do no good. I had completely shifted myself out of conscious awareness, allowing first negativity to take hold, and then ripping myself out of it so fast I was giddy and unstable. I was disappointed in myself, and even that was frustrating. I was gripping and pushing and pulling, leaving no room for grace. I sat in meditation long enough to start breathing deeply again. Long enough to remember. I focused on the obsessive emotional loop, removing one piece of it at a time. It was arduous, but when I felt impatient, I removed that too.

Eventually, my breathing became more even and reached a deeper space in my lungs. I chiseled away at the weight on my chest and the lump in my throat until they were only recognizable, but not overwhelming. And then I had more room for some of the softer things, like happy anticipation, and a touch of joy. In one day's time, I would again be next to him, and the excitement now had more room in my chest without making my head dizzy in its quarrel for dominance.

The next day, I had trouble focusing on much of anything else. I wanted to feel excited. I wanted to feel the buzzing. And I wanted that to be ok. I had to stop being so hard on myself. There was palpable relief in that space. Perhaps, after that evening, I would understand. Perhaps all of that negativity had been crafted in my mind, and soon, everything would fall back into place.

But come late afternoon, I still had not heard from him. I wasn't sure what time our meeting was planned for. He was usually more specific and open in his communication. Though I reminded myself that there was yet no logical reason for alarm, fear was gradually creeping its way back in. I could feel it in my throat before I felt it anywhere else. I decided to take a long, hot shower, and prepare for the evening anyway, pushing worse-case scenarios out of my head. I got dressed, and undressed, and dressed again. I applied my make-up slowly and carefully, frivolously grabbing on to unimportant details as if they were going to decide my fate. I avoided contacting him. I was avoiding it because of the lump that was growing in my throat.

Come 6 o'clock, I became anxious. Though not a strenuous trip, it was also not a short one, and it was one that had to be planned if I was to make it before dinnertime. There was no reason I shouldn't take initiative to solidify our plans. It only felt uncomfortable because I had never had to before. I gathered the prowess to send him a message, feigning nonchalance with alacrity, when really, it caused a brisk sweat to break out on the back of my neck.

What time?

I stared at my phone then. I stared at the screen, and my message, and the blinking cursor mocking me in the send box. It was the same screen that just yesterday held the words that brought me joy. Now, there were no words at all but my own, empty and alone. I stared at the screen for what felt like an eternity. I stared at it, and then put it down, and then minutes later, picked it up again. I did this, over and over. It must have been hours, dangling in a space of tense longing that was completely void of my control, until the answer arrived. It just was not the one I was hoping for.

I can't, Lena.
I'm sorry.

He was gone.

I knew that he was gone, and there was no need for me to verify it. I knew this was more than a cancelled plan or a late night at work. I knew because of the way it *felt*. It felt as if he inflicted a physical blow to my already fragile chest.

The pain that I had held back for days, the pain that was covered up by the things that were as comforting and expansive as hope, the pain that I intuitively knew was going to flood me soon enough, flooded me then. It came over me like a tidal wave.

I walked into my bedroom, slowly, my feet scraping against the ground, and shut the door. I leaned against it, my back sliding down the panels until I sat flat on the ground with my knees to my chest. I was too numb to cry. I stared at the wall where the moonlight was chiseling into the darkness in a sharp geometric pattern and let the stabbing hurt wash over me. I let myself feel every intricacy of it, seeping its way in like a black cloud and filling my lungs with its smoke. It rang in my ears and pounded at my chest. It blurred my eyes until they burned, forcing the ache out of dehydrated spaces and letting it cascade down my face like sandpaper.

This reaction was so seemingly irrational in its catastrophic nature, that even in experiencing it, I couldn't understand it. I had never hurt that much in reaction to any singular action by any other person. I knew it was something bigger. That it meant something beyond my comprehension. Something that was a fundamental part of all I was and all I was meant to be, breaking to pieces. An integral part of the patchwork of my life, stripped from its constitution.

My chest was ripping in two. I was in a vortex of something more powerful than myself. All I could do was sit there, frozen in the eye of its spinning black tornado, watching everything that was mine get sucked into its abyss.

I let myself go dark.

9

When I am with you, we stay up all night.
When you're not here, I can't go to sleep.
Praise God for those two insomnias!
And the difference between them.

—RUMI

My every waking moment was him, and my every dream was him. Never had I felt such love. And never had I lost such light. However fleeting. However unrequited.

I was quiet. I spent a lot of time staring into the sky. I moved slowly. I ate little. I tossed and turned when I slept. I cried often. I was grieving the loss of a life that was so fleeting, but still became all there was. It did not feel like depression. I knew depression. I was bubbling over with pain but I was not empty. I was filled with a unique longing that kept me in a place that was not void and was not vibrant. It was an emotional purgatory. It was a sad, creative fire. It didn't let me rest on either side. It didn't let me rest at all.

I was quiet, but I wrote poetry. I stared at the sky, and then I painted it. I moved slowly, with a book in hand, and read of love and loss and beautiful things that made my heart ache. I ate little but I filled myself with meditation, sitting for long periods at a time in a space beyond myself. I let the pain pour out of me. I let it land everywhere else, but it was as if it had an innate ability to multiply more quickly than could be released.

Every part of me that was left empty upon its absence filled again quickly, like an uncovered bowl under water. I fluctuated through emotions in such rapid succession that I couldn't grab onto any of them. The contrast from the joy I had felt was so acute that the sadness, filled with deep, deep yearning, was even darker in comparison. It was complicated. Suffused with every intricacy. And it just did not lessen as time went on.

Every time I felt like I was breathing again, he would appear. I would see him through third eye, feel him in my stone chest, and my hope would flutter. As high as I let myself get, that's how far I had to fall back again. Every time. But he never fully went away. He lingered there like a leaf rustled from its branch by the breeze. Right before it was about to hit the ground, a soft gust would send it floating again into the air in front of me.

Amongst it all, I didn't regret a thing. Even while wading through the pain, I wouldn't have wished it away. The pain was a testament to my experience. I felt it that strongly because I was blessed to experience a joy that was even more powerful. I was sure that, in one way or another, Arun would change the world, and for whatever it was worth, he had already, and irrevocably, changed mine. I would never be the same. His light, however fleeting in my life, was an unceasing inspiration.

But I had questions. So many questions. What had happened? Was it all just a game to him, after all? Anyone would tell me I was crazy to think he ever cared. And maybe I was crazy. But that didn't mean I was wrong. Something got in the way of our thriving, but it was more complicated, the experience much larger, than I could understand. I couldn't help but to be laced with compassion for him. He didn't owe me anything, really. I knew that. The only promise he had broken was his word to remain straightforward, one he had shattered in his silent disappearance.

Love isn't about possession. That seems obvious, but it isn't to many of us, especially when we are in the throes of an intense emotional reaction such as heartbreak. We cannot fault someone for being where they are, even if where they are isn't where we want them to be. And Arun was unique. I knew that, and I would not fault him for it, or for being exactly who he was. I couldn't. But still, there was something about the whole experience that was beyond even that. Something that helped me to rise above the usual resentful and irate reactions. Something that allowed me to put my love first, even if it was unrequited. Even if it was trampled on. Not out of naivety. Not out of weakness. But out of something much stronger. The perspective was just too vast for my small eyes to see. In my pain, I held onto a strong determination to unlock its secrets. I wanted to know why. I wanted to know what it was about being next to him that made me feel like I was one with the sunrise sky. I wanted to know what it was about being away from him that made me understand the blackness of night, but through it, cry from joy at the sight of the stars.

What was happening to me was nowhere near normal. This was not heartbreak alone. This was something else.

It went on this way for weeks. I pictured our short story, and I felt that as much as I appreciated all of it, I didn't appreciate it nearly enough. What I wouldn't give to walk down the street with him away from his apartment at twilight again, and watch our words steaming up in the cold air. To have his arms wrapped around me as we slept, feeling his heat against mine. To again see that certain smile of his, my favorite one, the crooked smile without crafting or confining that made me feel that I had known his soul for a lifetime. I dreamed of so many things in that abbreviated space of joy. I saw a future that was nothing short of magic, and I cringed in frustration with the realization of my ignorance.

I had to build a new vision, but nothing seemed to shine as brightly. I continued to move with the world as best I could. I had to keep moving. I had to shake off the excess weight. I had to learn to create space for myself amongst the immense darkness that was following me, merging with every exhale. Again, I felt separate from others, but this time, with an even greater disparity. I had experienced a light that felt extraordinarily misunderstood, even by myself. How could I ever be anything but alone in that? I floated through life with my secret.

People must be placed on our path for a reason. They must. Every experience changes us, helps us to grow, be it through joy or pain, grace or frustration, ease or struggle. Some of these relationships last a lifetime. I was lucky to have some that I was sure would sustain. Others are meant to be fleeting; a blip in our vast reality. I thought about Amelia, and the momentous effect she had on my very core after a short thirteen years of life together. Arun, who had changed the very way my heart beats after only a few short days. I had not let go of Amelia, but I accepted that she had to go. I understood that our story on this earth may have turned a page, but that we would always be together. Obviously, the situation with Arun was quite different, but in some ways, the grief was similar. It was loss. It was loneliness and it was pain. I couldn't accept that he was gone. He still walked this earth. He still breathed in the same air as I did, and looked up at the same sky. He weaved through life as I did, and our paths came close together and then ebbed far apart, but we were navigating the same map, floating through the same particles of light and dark.

10

As you start to walk on the way, the way appears.

—RUMI

The darkness fell after a day of quiet and intense introspection in April. I was at home alone, curled up on the couch with the television turned off, the lights turned low, the book I was pretending to read thrown to the side. There were tears in my eyes as I laid with my phone by my face, resisting the urge to speak to the only person I wanted to speak to. On that night, I was more immersed in sadness than I had allowed myself in a while. Maybe it was the weather. Maybe it was the emotional exhaustion. Whatever it was, I laid there, rolling over considerations and ruminating in an endless search for clarity. The more I tried to force it, however, the more I found myself in the center of a deep fog of which I could not see any periphery.

I was lonely, but I didn't want to be around anyone. I had been working from home most of the time, and had spent my other hours filled with no one but myself. I didn't want to face people. I had no desire for small talk. Usually, I enjoyed my alone time, but I had taken it to an extreme. There is a difference between enjoying time with yourself, and shutting off the rest of humanity. There was only one person I wanted to be next to then. I was craving his presence above all else. Positively longing for it. I imagined his lips against mine, his hands grasping my hips, his voice low and kind. I wanted all of it. I wanted to reach out.

I wanted to. But I wouldn't.

And then my phone sounded.

The disappointment flooded me, as usual. It was never him anymore, but I always hoped it would be. Every single time I heard that familiar alert, I begged the Universe for the gift of his words. This time, it was Justin. I was surprised, and at least that chipped away at some of the pounding disappointment. I had not heard from him in months.

We had fun when we were dating. It didn't end because it wasn't enjoyable. It was a timing thing. With everything I was processing in my own life, I'm sure our shaky connectedness was a consequence of my preoccupation. And, upon meeting Arun, everything fell to the wayside anyway. It wouldn't be fair to compare, and all considered, I definitely wasn't being fair in pretending I gave it a fair shot. Justin was extraordinarily kind and strikingly attractive. He was dark-skinned and muscular, and his eyes were deep and soft and wise. He was gentle, and quiet at times. He was the type of person who would do anything for anyone without question and without expecting reciprocation. He liked me. People thought I was crazy to walk away from it, but that was nothing new.

Hey Selena, been a while. What are you up to tonight? Want to join us for some drinks and dancing? We'll be close to your place.

It was late, almost 11:00, and I laid there, contemplating how I would word my refusal. I picked up my phone to begin typing my apologies, but for some reason, I stayed there, frozen for a moment, unable to form an excuse. I felt an odd prickling on the back of my neck. A wave of indecisiveness. A discomforting push from somewhere in my gut. I looked down at myself, sprawled on the couch, my sweatpants ripped and hanging unattractively, my oversized t-shirt wrapped around my torso, caught up between my body and the cushions, and I winced.

Gnawing myself out of the shape I had created within the couch cushion, I roused myself from my sad reverie, finding first a seated position, and then, slowly, my footing. I felt lightheaded upon rising, but it only lasted a moment or two. I went over to the mirror. I didn't like how I looked. *Too many days of this*, I thought. It was enough.

I moved in the way one rips off a band aid: quickly, with some discomfort, but no time for thought. I made my way to my closet and chose a short dress and high heels to adorn myself in. The dress was very short, and the heels were very high. I washed my face and applied black eyeliner and two quick wisps of blush. I brushed my teeth and smeared my lips to glistening with deep-hued gloss. I sprayed myself with fruity and flowery perfume. I threw a few belongings in my bag, and before I knew it, I was walking swiftly through the chilly spring night, away from my home, and toward the hope of breathing in some life. I walked as if I was on a mission. I walked with vengeance. I walked with each stiletto hitting the hard ground in a victorious rhythm.

And just like that, I was angry.

I was angry for feeling that way for so long. I was angry that Arun was taking from me my independence and my joy. I was angry that he vanished without a word, and I was angry that he didn't care. I was angry at his lack of regard, and I was angry that it meant so much to me. In some strange way, I thought that by leaving my tear-soaked couch, I was taking a stand. I pretended I was taking a stand against him, but really, I was just standing for myself. Standing up strongly on high heels and balancing with a bruised heart.

I walked a few blocks toward my destination, and opened the heavy door that led to a crowded and musty bar. The man at the door asked me for my ID and I showed him my picture and name and age, and felt silly, because I didn't even know who that person was anymore. He shook his head *yes* and allowed me entry. I scanned the crowd for the man that I knew. I had some trouble spotting him amongst the sea of dancing and drink-spilling, but I made my way further inward, and caught his eye. He saw me and he smiled. It was genuine; a welcoming and gracefully honest type of smile. A big smile, and it made me smile back. Mine was genuine too. I hadn't done that in a while, so I took note of it, and moved forward.

When I made it to the space that Justin and his friends occupied, I was greeted with a warm embrace and more friendly grins. He was surprised to see me. Happy to see me. And, to my surprise, I was almost glad to be there. I saw his eyes light up as I made my way closer, and I felt none of the gripping need for deciphering or hoping that I had felt for some time. When I was within arms' reach, he took my hand and spun me around, and whispered in my ear "let's get you a drink." Before I knew it, he was whisking me away, and placing his hand in one of my hands and a beer in the other. I felt safe there. It was hard not to. My shyness dissipated into the dense air.

We danced all night. We danced, and we laughed, and it was uncomplicated. For a short while, I allowed myself not to forget, but to place my pain in a small space, and shove it down into myself where it couldn't visibly interfere. Where the sting couldn't affect my rhythm. I smiled, and I let myself. I drank more than I should have, but I didn't care. I drank first with my newfound anger, and then I drank because it felt good. Because it was fun. The night made me feel light. It took me away from my thoughts. Even though I knew it was temporary, I let myself enjoy it. It was the first relief from purgatory that I had felt in weeks. My first relief from the heavy weight of depth.

At around 3:00 o'clock in the morning, I started to feel exceptionally tired, and we made our way off of the dance floor. Justin led me by the hand again, and we found a quiet space in the corner, where he wrapped his arm softly around my waist.

"I'm so happy you came," he said.

It was nice to know he meant it. It was nice that I didn't have to worry about him disappearing into the dense crowd. I was sure he wouldn't.

"I'm happy I came too," I said. "I haven't been getting out much."

He looked at me. He looked at me in the way someone does when they want to kiss you, but they aren't quite sure if they should. I became apprehensive and averted my eyes, but I was going to let him. I was going to let him put his lips on mine. I knew what they felt like, but I knew they would feel foreign again. I had tasted someone else's in between. I looked back up bravely then, and as his warm eyes spoke to me, I felt a buzzing from my purse. *Who could this be*, I thought, *at this late hour?*

I was protecting myself from the possibility of crushing disappointment, but really, for some reason that I could not explain, I knew who it was. I just knew.

"Sorry," I said, as I rustled through my purse, breaking our moment in a quick and crushing way. "My phone."

I found it quickly and eyed the message as privately as I could, not because anyone else would care to see it, but because when something is that important, it has to be handled with care. I looked at it, unblinking.

The message read: *I never meant for it to be this way.*

My face blanched and Justin looked at me with concern. I saw it soften his edges, and he extended it without words. I could not be touched there, however, because I suddenly did not exist outside of a new center. I was probably dangerous to anyone that tried to penetrate the fiery aura that encased me. I had to protect him from myself.

"I'm sorry," I said, already walking away from the crowd and making my way toward a front window. "I'll be right back." There was no time to explain. There was no space for anything else. And all of the events of the evening slipped away, just like that. I was sobered. I forgot about my aching feet. I separated from the kind and sexy man standing not far from me, who just moments ago I would have shared a soft kiss with. Undeniably, that didn't matter anymore. Nothing else mattered.

With shaking hands, I went to type a response, but his next message came before I had the chance.

...do you hate me?

And of the little I knew, this was one thing I was sure of.

I could never hate you, I said.

And that was it. I said goodnight to Justin and walked home. I removed my heels and fell asleep in Arun's t-shirt that didn't smell like him anymore, but I imagined it did, and that was enough.

11

A mountain keeps an echo deep inside.
That's how I hold your voice.

—RUMI

The next morning, I slid into a pair of warm boots and led myself toward the sand. Spring mornings by the beach still held a chill, and sometimes, even a frost, but on that day, the cold air was complimented by a sun that sat low and large in the sky.

Salt air wafted on the light, painting a muted scene of soft blue and gold across the ground. The ocean was calm and it sang deeply. A bird flew over its depths, swirling in the waking sky with the same gentleness as the clouds. When the wind changed direction, it flowed with it, and as the sky changed colors, it did not falter. It did not press, or push, or pulse. It flowed through the sky, soaring upon the air and kissed by the light with peaceful surrender. I stood mesmerized, the warm light thawing my wind-beaten face.

It amazed me, what such a simple act from Arun could inspire. There was still that same raw longing. That same poetic reaction to every one of his words and belief that every expression, even the most ordinary, was laced with more than its veneer. Even through all of the pain and frustration, he was still my greatest relief. A few short words here and there, however, would not change the absoluteness of our dissipation.

I had held my words back the night before, because anything else would have sullied the moment. One too poignant for questions and details. But, still, I had so many questions. An insatiably curious ego that gripped onto every intricacy, trying to connect solid meaning to a truth that was like a melody. A song that undulated between here and there with no regard for time or space. I wished to control a situation that could not, or should not, be controlled, but I was still so immersed in that space that I could not yet see beyond it; where the bigger picture was painted, where the grander story was told. There was something vast right at my fingertips. Something more expansive than my squinting eyes were allowing me to see. It went on forever, but in that moment, to me, it was an invisible eternity.

I knew it was time for a change. A new way of breathing. A loosening of my shoulders and a releasing of my fists. With all of my energy sucked into a rigid center, I'd sit exhaustively in my own ignorance.

The bird landed on the sand, casting his long shadow amongst millions of fine grains. I made my way back home, pulled off my layers, and made a cup of tea.

If only I could see him again.

Time continued to unfold. The chill hung on only slightly, grabbing on to the curls of ocean waves and the deepest insides of tree barks until even those began to thaw. And soon, the warmth arrived in full bloom, alive with its floral scents on the breeze and life erupting from earth and sky.

There is nothing quite as restorative as that first bit of abiding warmth on your cheeks, carrying with it an air of possibility and inspiration. So I began to dip myself back into the world I had disconnected from. I dedicated myself more diligently to my meditation practice again, both independently and in a class space; a fourteen-month immersion program, my most committed decision yet, in which we tenaciously devoted ourselves to reaching our own depths and heights through advanced energy work. I also started a new job at an advertising agency. It wasn't a terribly exciting position, but it got me back into a routine, and it was a good way to get my feet wet in the corporate world.

The pain was still there, but the faster pace was a welcomed relief from its monotony.

And then, there was Justin. He called me often after that night we had together, and for a while, I kept my distance. I was far too distracted to focus on our interaction, and I didn't want to be leading or unfair, so I had plenty of excuses as to why I couldn't see him when an invitation arose. But, his friendship was important to me. He was one of the people I started to let in. One who I found I could resonate with, and since that was rare, I truly didn't want him to stop calling. I just wasn't ready for anything more than a casual interaction. And, I told him so.

But he didn't give up. He wasn't obtrusive, but he was consistent. I knew spending time with him would not be the end of the world. Actually, it would probably be really good for me. He was fun to be around and obviously respectful of my boundaries, and even if he had something beyond friendship in mind, his patience was admirable.

"I am not going to stop trying," he said one night over the phone, after a half hour conversation about our favorite books. "Someday, you'll let me take you out."

"Someday," I said decisively. "I promise."

"Tomorrow night," he said. "Italian."

I hesitated. I had not heard from Arun again. That was the reality. The longing and all the rest was emotional hogwash. I was holding on to such a thin string of hope that I was afraid it would snap with the slightest movement. But I needed distraction. And Justin needed Italian food.

"Ok," I said. "Let's do it."

He smiled. I couldn't see it. I could just tell.

"Great," he said. "That's great. That place on Main Street? Or do you want to head into the city?"

"Main Street," I said, sensing my own abruptness. "Let's stay around here, you know, in case I get out of work late."

Either he didn't notice, or he played it off like the gentleman he was, but he agreed wholeheartedly.

"I'll pick you up at 8."

Already, it was easier. No wondering, no fear or confusion. And the next night, it was even easier than that. We had fun. We enjoyed learning about each other. Conversation may not have been as intangibly captivating, laced with a poetic reaction to every one of each other's words in the way I had become accustomed to, but it was graceful. Kind and comfortable. The night was truly not as jarring as expected. Actually, it was kind of the opposite. So, we started doing it more often.

I had gotten used to the lump in my chest that was the exact weight of Arun, so I was learning to notice it while still keeping the rise and fall of my chest even around Justin. I knew it wasn't a terribly healthy state, but I also knew it would be a process. The early stages of healing. I just had to keep moving forward until my striving became something more genuine. And, Justin was incredible. I mean, I could not say one negative thing about him. His kindness was quite extraordinary. He was smart, and funny, and dashingly handsome. He was so different than Arun. Where Arun was dominant and electric, he was subtle and reserved. Where Arun was bold, he was gentle. Where Arun was thin and lean, he was muscular and masculine, with a chiseled jaw and strong shoulders. And where Arun was always leaving, he was always there.

He was forthcoming about his caring for me, and he never faltered. Not once. Maybe it didn't have to be a bolt of lightning. Maybe what I needed was a warm wave rolling over the shore, encircling my ankles. The kind that reflected the deep hues of late day.

I was decidedly honest with Justin from the beginning, and I never stopped being honest with him. Months passed, and still, I could not commit to him beyond our casual interactions. I told him that I cared for another, though I didn't tell him how much. It seemed unnecessary, as it was slipping further and further into the past anyway.

"I am immersed in some kind of spiritual growth process because of it all," I said. "I would elaborate on it, but I don't even fully understand it myself."

Even then, I had really only begun to realize the extent of that truth. The shifts that Arun had caused in me remained somewhere outside of comprehension, and I was feeling its growth aches in different ways as time passed. At first, there was the magic. The ethereal that shook me at the core and raised me higher than I had ever been. Then came the repeated blows to the chest. The ripping pain that grounded me right before I flew too high. And then, a new space. Some sort of growth trajectory. An exercise in consciousness. A training session in how to hold pain and keep moving forward anyway.

I didn't explain *all* of this to Justin, of course, but I did tell him I was going through something obscure. That I needed time to open up to other possibilities. As much as he didn't enjoy that, he accepted it, and gracefully allowed me the space I needed, while still being there with me whenever I acquiesced to his support. As heavy as things were, and as little sense as it made to get close to anyone else at that time, something kept me there. It may have been selfish, but I didn't want him to be out of my life completely. As time went on, it became increasingly impossible to ignore: the more I opened to it, the more fun life was becoming with him around.

We started to explore life together, sharing in the enjoyment of small adventures. It was exciting, and natural, and as we moved deeper into spring, I became aware of a blossoming within myself. Something breaking out of the darkness that had taken hold. The longing and desire were still present, but there were also seeds of joy that, with enough nurturing, were starting to sprout, little by little, one by one. It made me more buoyant, and as I rose, I wondered—what would happen when the chain that held my anchor ran out of space? I knew I could only move so far from Arun without feeling the tug that would keep me from fully surfacing.

Still, Justin was patient, his compassion allowing me to thaw. Though we had not yet fully committed to each other, as I started to give him more in return, I could sense his rising confidence in what we could be. I was starting to feel it too, but it would seem only fair, I suppose, that as I continued to test his patience, I would eventually be tested too.

Just a few days before the last weekend in May, I was on the phone with Justin when I heard it. The text message alert. I shifted to speakerphone for a moment, so that I could see the message without breaking conversation.

Hello, Selena.

I felt the rush from core to limb. A jolt from my electric counterpart. I closed my eyes and held them there, where I could better appreciate the sensation.

"Selena?" Justin said, sensing my distraction. "Everything ok?"

"Fine," I said, shaking off the preoccupation. We spoke a while longer, making plans for the weekend, and when the conversation ended, I sat silently, allowing the erratic vibrations to settle to softness.

Hello, Arun, I said, the now-familiar bubbles rising and bursting and reforming in my chest.

How are you? he asked.

I'm well, I said, and whatever was between those lines stayed tucked away.

It's been a while, he said.

I took a deep breath. *It has.*

There's this restaurant I want to try, he said.

A minute or two passed as I waited, wondering if there would be more. Wondering where this was headed.

Which? I asked.

It doesn't really matter, he said. *Let's go. Together.*

I froze. A lump quickly accumulated in my throat. I felt the words fill me up and then pour over. I didn't have enough space for them, even in their simplicity, and I had trouble finding any of my own through the clutter of emotion and longing. Time stopped moving there, but the earth continued to spin, and he noticed the lapse in space as I formulated a response.

No? he asked, shaking me out of my unmovable state.

I held the phone lightly between my fingers, my hands shaking slightly, my eyes concentrated on a far-off space.

I would like to. But, I can't.

You'd like to... he reflected back. *That's not enough?*

A question, deserving of an answer. Was that enough? Desire at times does not coincide with morality, but morality is at times only a story. The philosophy ran through my head but there was no time now for an internal debate. I'd have to think about it later.

It's not that simple, I said.

My eyes would be to the ground if we were face to face. He would see my cheeks turning pale and my lips trembling.

Honestly, he said. *What is simpler than that?*

I was almost embarrassed by my lack of resentment. Any of the desire that I had kept hidden behind skin and rib started again to pulse. I was a plant leaning toward his light as if he was my source of life. Any confidence I had in my ability to grow away from him was dashed in an instant. It was that quick. Laughable, really. The desire grew in intensity as each moment passed, and I was overwhelmed by the strangest sensation of luring enchantment; a large horseshoe magnet hovering in front of my chest, pulling me into its field with such strength I had to focus on grounding my feet so as not to be swept off of them.

This pull was not desire alone. It could not be confined to descriptors of chemistry or hormones releasing and ricocheting through my synapses. This pull came from my soul. I was sure of it.

But did that mean that I shouldn't resist it?

Selena, he said. *I know it's been a while. I know. But, this isn't about dinner. We have to talk. Don't we?*

Of course we needed to talk. A rushing relief came with his candor. A placing of this intangible necessity into shared reality.

We do, I said.

Ok, he agreed. *Tomorrow night?*

I wrote my response but I left it there, unsent. Seconds, minutes. Time passed quickly and not at all. I had made a promise to myself that I was focused on healing. I had made a promise to the kind man that I was spending time with that I was focused on healing. And there I was, ripping off my scab, letting my raw flesh again hit the air, risking a deepening of my scars and the possibility of new wounds. But, it was undeniable. There was not an ounce of me, not a cell in my body that wished to resist this invitation. My soul was calling so loudly that it rang in my ears. What had always been a quiet voice, whispering in wisdom and intuitive nudging, found something to feed its strength, allowing it to break free from my rational mind and demand I pay attention to the only thing that mattered.

Time passed quickly, and it didn't pass at all. I looked up at the clock. It read 11:11.

Sometimes, we are pulled from somewhere beyond our earthly ego reasoning. Beyond our mental body clutter and emotional gripping. Sometimes, we are pulled from somewhere *else*. An intangible draw that brings us to the edge of reality, imparting us with the courage to dive headfirst into the unknown that lies just beyond our fearful vantage points. Perhaps it is here: in this jump, in this faith, that we find the answers. Perhaps it is here that we birth miracles, and it is from here that we live them. Perhaps.

But even still, the guilt poured over me like wet paint.

Tomorrow night, I confirmed.

12

*Goodbyes are only for those who love with their eyes.
Because for those who love with heart and soul
there is no such thing as separation.*

—RUMI

The next night was warm. I let it caress my cheeks and weave through every strand of hair with its lightness as I made my way toward Manhattan. I could feel him in it, gently laying himself on the breeze that made its way in circles around me.

I told myself in calculated contemplation that I should see him again, just one more time, in order to allow myself to move forward. That I needed to ascertain his intentions, understand more clearly his thoughts, so that I could live my life without this confusion blurring my vision. And, though that was all true, these reasons were merely periphery. Distant truths that were like cloudy wisps my ego tried to solidify. The reality was, I could not wait to see him again. The longing broke free of its enclosure and flooded my insides. I could almost smell his aroma of bright night as I pictured his smile, his icy blue eyes, the way his leather jacket draped over his shoulders. My chest hummed gratefully.

I made my way to his apartment, moving through space deliberately and with awareness. I noticed the train rattling beneath my feet, the feel of my pocketbook weighing gently on my shoulder. I felt the energy of the crowds, and as quickly as everything moved around me, the simple act of noticing seemed to slow things down. I softly smiled at people as they passed by, noticing their place in the surrounding space while holding my own, appreciating their stories, and mine, and how we became one somewhere in between. It was my silent reverie of awareness and gratitude.

We all have a story, I thought. All of us. Mine is a story of wonder and laughter, and joy and pain. Of love and depth, and fear and magic. And so is everyone else's. We all live our story differently, but these constants are always true. We are infinitely connected to all that is the flow of life around us in such an integral way that we are in fact co-creators of it. We don't only learn from nature's tides and seasons. We *are* nature's tides and seasons.

I wanted to trust the flow of my life like water trusts its cascading over stone and sand, rising in wave and crashing on shore. To move forward in time and timelessness in that way, everything unfolding both as it should and as it is created. Where, paradoxically, nothing is out of our reach, and whatever is out of reach is accepted. Forward flowing anyway. That's what I wanted. But that would take time.

When I arrived at Arun's address, I made my way up the stairs slowly, so as not to lose my breath. So as not to lose focus. Months of waiting, of longing, of angst in the elusiveness of the unknown was soon to come to an end, and it was not to be taken lightly.

Or, maybe, it was. Maybe it was to be taken as lightly as that water cascading over stone.

Either way, I raised my finger to the doorbell, and my heart fluttered in nervous anticipation. A deep breath steadied me, and a few more tricked my body into easing my pounding heart. By the time the door opened, I was ready. I had to be. And the moment our eyes met again, everything stilled.

Time stopped in that moment, and simultaneously, it was like no time had passed at all. It came with an exhale, long and slow. It reached in and smoothed out pain's jagged edges. It ran through my body and coaxed each piece of me with a soothing touch, removing the clutter that comes with pain.

We could not, for moments, look anywhere but each other's eyes. And then, just as quickly, we both looked away. We almost said too much.

"I've missed you," he said, as we stood with space between us, but less than there had been in months. His words surprised me but danced into my ears just as they always had. If only he knew how much they meant to me.

"I've missed you too."

And then, just like that, relief. Amongst all the questions, it felt bizarrely simple. Strangely uncomplicated. My shoulders fell without forcing them down, and my breath was even without urging it to find rhythm.

"Tell me," he said as we walked through the familiar hallway. "What's new?"

I told him about the easy things first, like work and my excitement over the coming summer. He told me about the same things, just differently. He smelled the same. He looked the same. I took him in with just the same admiration. But a stacked-up past of experiences was there now. It hid, curled up in the darkest corner. I told it to stay there for a little while.

"Some fresh air?" he asked.

Day was quickly transforming into soft dusk, and we walked east toward the water as the sun nestled itself into the horizon. The late light was soothing, and laid itself across Arun's face in a gentle and beautiful way. I didn't know how I would react to that night. To being close to him again. But whatever I had imagined didn't touch the reality. I was not nervous in that moment. I was, somehow beyond my comprehension, curious but not begging for answers. Instead, I was peacefully lavishing in my own consciousness. Wholly present and gliding through time joyfully and at ease.

Was it denial? After all of the heavy emotion of the past few months, was I only intoxicated by his skin that again was only inches from mine? We walked quietly for a while, watching the last of the fire-orange reflections on the water until everything was doused in navy blue. I let these questions waft through the background of my mind as Arun stopped and turned toward the deep sky, placing his hands on the metal rail that separated us from the water. He looked so gentle. So beautifully innocent. My chest expanded. It needed more space as I allowed myself to calibrate closer to the truth.

I was there again, dipped deeply into peak experience. It only took his presence. It only took him. And it was as elegant as the evening sky. Together, we looked out at the moving water. It was a unique moment in my vast eternity. One that reminded me what beauty is.

Perhaps the moment itself doesn't lift us up. Perhaps the moment simply opens us up enough to allow it. Allow us to find contact with our most natural state, and float there for a while, without the usual human distraction. In that moment, I found that space I had lost; the space where I was utterly, fully, and incontrovertibly my Self.

I was so immersed there that it seemed nothing could break that state. That nothing could ever take it away from me. I almost believed for a moment, drunk on my soul's high, that I had discovered how to hold onto magic. But those intangible things can be so elusive, and our demons are skilled in the art of defense.

Arun turned toward me.

"Beautiful, isn't it?" he asked. "I've been coming down here a lot. Something about it. It feels important."

I shook my head in agreement. "Brings you back to yourself, in a way," I said. "At least, that's what it does for me."

"I don't think so," he said. "Not for me. I think it brings me away from myself, actually."

We were quiet for a few moments as we looked out to the now blackening sky.

"Maybe that is the kind of the same thing," I said.

"Maybe," he said. "But you and I, Selena, we are very different." He released his grip on the smooth metal. Something in his voice was unsettling. My moment shifted around it, but before I had a chance to ask him what he meant, he spoke again.

"Come with me," he said. "We'll be late."

And he started to walk.

"Late?" I asked, scurrying to catch up. "For what?"

"Our ride," he said, pointing toward the water. Two boats, alight, bobbed up and down on the darkness.

We walked toward the dock, and Arun took my wrist as we boarded one.

"The ferry," he said. "Best mode of transportation to Brooklyn."

I was soothed by his touch and by the undulations of the water beneath me. We made our way up to the front of the deck, and watched the lights glimmering across the horizon. Manhattan was just as beautiful from a distance.

I put my hands on the railing as the ferry picked up speed, my hair twirling in salty rings around my face. Arun placed his hand close, and layered his finger over one of mine. We were silent. There were only the distant sounds of city, the purring of the engine, and the lapping of small waves against steel. There was still so much hanging over us. It felt wasteful in that moment, however, to put my energy anywhere beyond the lights reflecting in our eyes and his skin resting lightly across mine.

We docked across the water and made our way to a restaurant not far from where we were let off, surrounded by trees and with a view of the water. It felt like a different world there, such a short trip from the land we stood on before. It was dark and quiet inside, small overheard lanterns guiding our way.

We enjoyed a French meal by candlelight, pushing our necessary conversation into the background until Arun abruptly broke ground.

"Are you seeing anyone else right now?" he asked, as I brought a julienned carrot to my mouth.

Though his blunt questioning didn't surprise me anymore, I brought the carrot back down to my plate.

"I wasn't sure we'd ever go there," I said.

"All in good time," he said.

I unfolded and then folded the napkin in my lap. "Well, you are, right?" he asked again, this time his voice more delicate.

"Yes," I said. "I am."

I paused, playing with the edge of my napkin, and then asked in return, "Are you?"

"Seeing anyone?" he asked. "It depends how you define it."

"Define it however you'd like," I said, my throat tightening.

"I'm dating, here and there," he responded.

It stung. Of course, it stung. Surprisingly, however, there were no waves of intense jealousy stabbing me at my core. I swallowed slowly, and let it sink in. This was the reality. The only thing that shifted was my awareness of it. So really, at its essence, nothing had changed at all. For months, my mind raced with possibilities. Questions. Concerns. Suddenly, the details mattered less. I didn't know why, but they did. I wondered, of course, through the sting, who these women were and how close he had gotten to them. But not with the same arresting preoccupation. Maybe his presence removed some of my ego. Or maybe, the answers were beyond the details.

Before I had a chance to respond, he was back to me, leaving his response hanging in the air between us.

"Who is he?"

"Someone I had dated a little while back," I said.

"Justin?" he asked, remembering our toast over Japanese food.

"Yes."

"Is it serious?" he asked.

"It could be," I said.

"Could be, or is?" he probed.

I shrugged in a small way.

"It's heading there," I said, "but I'm here, aren't I?"

We fell silent.

"What about you?" I asked. "Anything serious?"

"No." He took a bite of his filet and wrestled it between his teeth.

"I'm just going with the flow. I have a lot on my plate," he said. "I'm a single guy living in New York, Selena."

He put a lot of emphasis on that statement. Like it was his trademark. Like he needed me to understand it without question. Like it was never going to change. That, beyond all else, is what drilled into me. My composure was beginning to crumble.

"Amongst other things," I responded, eyes on my vegetables. "Is that why you disappeared?"

"Disappeared? I haven't disappeared. I just have a lot going on."

"You know what I mean," I said.

"You know," he said, with some bite, "it's ok to be alone for a while. You don't always need someone around."

"I agree," I responded with sharpness.

"So why do you need to get serious with this guy? It obviously didn't work the first time."

"I don't *need* it," I said. "We just enjoy being around each other."

He let out a quick, harsh laugh.

"What?" I asked, my eyes a little wider.

"You..." he said, "it's obvious." He wiped his mouth on his napkin and took a sip of sparkling water. "You want someone to save you."

"What are you talking about?" I said, eyes narrowing. "Save me from what?"

"Look," he said. "You're a beautiful girl. You're smart. You're awesome to be around. But you're a little lost..."

I waited for him to go on.

"You don't love your job. You don't know what you want to do next..."

"And?" I asked, anxiety mingling with the beginnings of anger.

"What's the point?" he said.

"The point of what?" I asked.

"Of doing it alone," he said.

I looked at him challengingly, hoping I was wrong about the direction his words were headed in.

"You'll find some guy," he said, insolently, "who will make your life easier. It's how it works."

I turned suddenly furious.

"Make my life easier?" I said, with fire in my eyes. "Make my life easier *how*?"

"You'll find a guy to support you, emotionally, financially, and otherwise, and you won't have to worry anymore."

All efforts at maintaining my calm extinguished in an instant. To think that he saw me that way, it stabbed at me. I felt my insides twisting and engulfed in fire.

"It's just how it works," he said, coated in a concrete that none of my fire could penetrate.

"No," I said through gritted teeth. "That is not how it *works*." My voice now swimming in angry waters.

"No?" he responded calmly.

"No," I repeated. "This life is mine to live. I will figure out what I want to do and I will do it well and I will do it on my own. And if I meet someone who wants to walk my path with me, then great. But not because I plan on taking a damn thing from anybody!" A person at the table next to us looked over at me, and I lowered my voice to an angry whisper. "Do you truly look at me that way? Where the hell is this coming from?"

My eyes were filling with tears. They were just at the point of spilling over.

"Don't cry," was his response.

His cold and empty response.

I created a point on the edge of the napkin, and blotted each eye with it, letting the salty water disperse through its fibers, and make its way from me to somewhere else. I was shaking. We were silent for minutes, letting time tick slowly around us. I didn't want to look at him. His hurtful words continued to stab at my insides, and through the burning, he looked different. Harder. Pain's lens, coated with anger's hue.

What had I done to make him see me that way? That dependent and selfish? What lens was he watching *me* through?

"This is crazy," I said. "I don't get it."

"Let's just forget it," he said. "I got carried away."

"Forget it?" I said, and then laughed under my breath, while he remained silent. He took the napkin from him lap, and placed it on his plate.

"So, is that it?" I asked, trying to decipher the overarching message behind his cringe-worthy words. "You, for some reason, don't trust my intentions?"

"No, that's not it," he said, breathing out heavily. "I got carried away. We just... we want different things, me and you."

"How do you know?" I asked, defeated. "How to you know what the hell I want?"

"You're right," he said. "What do I know?"

And then he fell silent. We both did. And then we got up and boarded the last ferry back to Manhattan.

We were quiet the entire way, pain wrapping around my skin and seeping into my very soul. Layers of it. Layers and layers of pain and realization. Of what it all meant. Of where it was all headed. I couldn't find a single word for it. Not one word until we were back on land.

I walked ahead of him, quickly, finding my footing, and made my way off the boat, back to where we started but eons away.

"I should go," I said.

"Why?" he asked, and I couldn't tell if he was being evil or ignorant.

"You don't have to go," he said. "You don't. I don't like you traveling so late. And your bag is at my place."

I swallowed hard.

"We can talk more at my apartment," he said.

A let out another small, sarcastic laugh.

"Or, we won't. Whatever you want," he said, leading us away from the water. "Come on."

It was late. And leaving things that way? Hanging in the air with stinging discomfort? It would only make things worse. Worse than before. Worse than not seeing him at all. Worse than it had ever been. I pictured myself in weeks to come, replaying it all in my head, smothered in silence with no satisfaction. Instead, I followed him up the five stories to his apartment with heavy legs and an even heavier heart.

He did not exude his usual warmth then, but he wasn't cold and unmoving as he was at dinner, either. He was more like a blank slate. A shell of who I thought I knew.

I went into the bathroom to remove the tear-stained makeup from my face. I took my time. I had never avoided his presence before, but in that moment, I couldn't even imagine looking him in the eye.

Arun was already in bed when I returned, and I got in too. I turned away from him.

"Selena?" he whispered. "Tell me what you're thinking."

I wanted to speak. Let words and thoughts and emotions fall out of me so I didn't have to hold them all night. But nothing would come. I shook my head *no* as a tear fell down my cheek toward the pillow. I watched the room through the same fizzing darkness as the first time I was in Arun's bed, only this time, it was stifling.

After some time, I heard his breathing become steadier and heavier. I turned around to look at him, and watched his shoulders rise and fall for a few moments and I knew he had fallen asleep. I laid there recounting the night's events, over and over again, feeling no relief from my tight muscles. The night transformed from a beautiful relief to a painful deluge at such an abrupt speed that my head was spinning. How could he sleep so peacefully while I laid awake, mulling over every intricacy of the pain I felt—the pain he had caused? Was he that blindly unaware of the magnitude of effect he had on me, tonight, and always? It was more likely that he just didn't care.

It wasn't even the fact that he was dating other people, and uninterested in anything beyond the casual. It wasn't even the fact that I was sure of that now, and that no amount of denial or hope could any longer tell me otherwise. It was his lack of sensitivity following the painful blows to my chest. It was unfathomable. Feeling hurt by him felt different than any other hurt. It was more pungent, more stinging. His words felt like a validation of all of my irrational insecurities. They were harsh. Mean. They stirred up shame and doubt, fears of not being good enough or not strong enough to take care of myself. Discomforts relating to an unstable financial future and in the ability to ask for help. Issues with reliance on other people or things to make me feel safe. My inner child reared at me, telling me through its small voice of intimidation that I couldn't stand alone. That I would always be dependent and afraid.

I got out of bed at 3am, and walked into the living room. I couldn't lay there anymore, allowing my poisonous thoughts to choke me of sleep. There was subtle light coming through the window from the city streets. I stared for a moment from the other side of the room, then filled up a glass with cold water and pulled a stool from the kitchen table to where the window was. I curled my legs up tightly toward my chest.

The undeniable reality seeped its way into my consciousness with vigor. We were each swimming in our own realities and there was no middle to meet in. Or, at least, we couldn't find a middle without some sort of balance. A balance we didn't have. A balance he didn't even want.

I sat there, allowing the painful knowingness to settle into my chest. I thought about the details, and the rest I let simmer below my surface. Our dissipation was obvious, but the true intricacies of our situation weren't. I understood those only abstractly. It was a clouded and stunted comprehension. We were beyond simply that night's words and harshness. Beyond our other relationships, experiences and desires. Those reasons were simple. It was something bigger. Something beyond that. Just because I couldn't comprehend the abstractions didn't make them less real.

Either way, I knew what was coming next. It was the definiteness of it that choked me more than anything. No more hope, no more denial. Reality isn't always comfortable. Sometimes, it's downright treacherous.

I sat there until the first hint of sunrise mocked my heavy eyes and forced me to go back to bed, at least for a few hours. And when I woke, it was to a glaring sun, chirping birds, and a chest so tight I coughed when the loveliness hit me.

I rolled over and there was Arun, turned toward me, watching me wake.

"Good morning," he said.

"Good morning," I replied quietly, without looking him in the eye.

We were silent for a few moments, the space between us holding all of the heaviness, and keeping us far away from each other.

"I'm sorry." He said it softly. Kindly. But for the first time, his voice sounded small. He looked down toward the sheets and away from my eyes, and sighed. "I'm sorry, and I didn't mean those things. It was..." and then he shook his head. "I don't know. But I didn't mean them."

I shifted my focus toward him and rested there for a while, taking him in. I wasn't angry anymore; I had burned that away overnight. It was exceptional sadness that sat in its ashes. I knew his harshness had to come from somewhere. Some experience he had, some frustration that was lingering below his surface. Things boil over when we cover them up and we are too filled with them, like a pot of rice with the flame too high, sticky wet water running over the sides. I didn't believe it was really all about me. Unless, of course, it was all about shaking me up. The pain was all I could really be sure of.

I took my hand and ran it through his hair. He responded quickly, nudging his head into my arms, burrowing there while I stroked him. We laid that way for a while, without words, our touch softening whatever remnants of pain still lay triggered within us. He was my cause and my cure. The closer I got, the more it hurt, and the better it felt.

He took his left hand and ran it down the curve of my hip. He lingered for a while, and then squeezed me there, simultaneously burying his other hand under the side I was laying on. In one swift motion, he pulled me on top of him. He wrapped his arms around me tightly, and I placed my cheek against his, my arms curled up against his chest like a child.

I felt myself starting to warm, my desire for him starting to seep out, making its way around my emotions like lava around rock. The confusion I felt for my longing made it burn even more. I wanted, more than anything, to give him all of myself. It pulsed inside of me. And I could feel it pulsing inside of him.

He took his hands down to my lower back, raising my shirt so that his hands could lay on my skin. He ran them down further, and I felt the heat on my skin where they touched. He motioned to remove the little clothing I had below, and as he did, I tightened against him.

I wanted to give him all of myself. But all of myself wasn't there for me to give.

"I can't," I whispered.

I felt his chest rise and fall. He took his hands to my face, and lifted it.

"I want to..." I said, "but..."

"You can't?" he said, looking me straight in the eye, weaving his melodic voice past my ears and deep into me. As I was lulled into his hypnosis, he abruptly, harshly, turned me off of him.

He grabbed my hips from behind, and threw himself into me, still clothed. He was hot with emotion. I could feel him through our layers.

Desire exploded around me. I was drenched in longing.

"No," I whimpered, moaning lustfully.

Our desire, laced with our poignant emotions, had a visceral effect on me. But as he thrust into me again, I clenched my fists. I thought of last night. I thought of what was coming next. I thought of Justin.

"No," I said, this time more resolutely, and I clumsily flipped myself over to face him, leaving him kneeling above me with fire in his eyes and everywhere else.

We stared at each other this way for moments, our breathing heavy and in rhythm with one another's. He inhaled when I exhaled, comforting me with mutual pulse. We softened there.

"I have to go," I said, so quietly I could barely hear it myself.

He slumped slightly into himself, and ran his fingers once through his hair. He looked so beautiful, towering over me with the gentleness I thought we had lost, his shirtless skin smooth and soft. He leaned forward, shoulders defeated.

"I know," he whispered.

He looked toward me for a moment more and then reached over to the bedside table and into its drawer. He grasped whatever was inside in his palm, and then opened it in front of me. Four pieces of what looked like slick black metal stood stacked in his hand.

He fought their charge and pulled them apart in the center, holding two pieces for himself, and handing two pieces over to me.

I turned the pieces of smooth metal around in my fingers, our distant reflections laying blurred across its sheen.

"Magnetic hematite," he said. "From a lover of magnets, for a lover of stones."

My eyes misted over and I held the stones tightly. I put my other hand to his cheek and held it there. I squinted my eyes slightly, so that I could see his face through the mask of cement that he spent a lifetime chiseling out in perfect form. I was sure I saw beyond his eyes, then.

I was sure I saw his soul.

PART TWO

The Moon

The moon stays bright when it doesn't avoid the night...
—RUMI

13

Knock, And He'll open the door.
Vanish, and He'll make you shine like the sun.
Fall, and He'll raise you to the heavens.
Become nothing, and He'll turn you into everything.

—RUMI

We all long for connection. That all-encompassing delving, of seeing through the veil, behind skin and bone, right through to the soul. These types of connections are the purest form of human interaction. But these connections are rare. They cannot be crafted, molded, or confined. They transcend our ego's understanding of relationships, but if we are open enough to allow such breathtaking dynamics to flow, we can be transformed by their unique power.

Our soul may know these things before we do, so we have to learn to listen to its soft voice. It whispers to us all along.

A year had passed since our last meeting, and aside from happy birthday wishes and the most basic of corresponding responses, we hardly spoke at all. The first few months were pretty horrendous, much like the first time I grieved the loss of him, but with the increased intensity that comes with finality. Questions went unanswered. Fears remained unhinged.

I loved him. I still did. That didn't change. I feared that he wasn't the person I thought he was. That his intent on that last night was a malicious one. Worse, I feared that he never truly saw me in the way that I thought he did. That his expressions were coming from a distance between us that I was wholly ignorant of. These were fears, though. They weren't the reality that I felt in my core. And fears are so often laced with mistruths. Though I could never make him want me the way I wanted him, I refused to believe that there wasn't some truth in what we had, because it was the most intensely real thing that had ever touched me.

As time passed, I started to shed the initial agony, but I never stopped thinking about him. Not at all. Not ever. Arun had awoken something in me. He had done something to me that could not be undone.

Not everything we experience in this life will be comfortable. I get that. Sometimes, we have to suck it up and float in something that doesn't feel *good*, but for whatever reason, is *necessary*. But I also don't think it ends there. Where does our control over the process come in? Do we have any control at all? I've come to believe that it can all be a part of our path, and simultaneously, be up for reform. Another paradox, you know? That we have a destiny, but the choices are still ours to make. That even the mundane has purpose, and even when we are in the trenches, there is gratitude to be found.

It had always felt dishonorable to move beyond the incontrovertible understanding that *it could always be worse*. So, I at times confused gratitude with a life that was static. I worried that moving beyond something that I had grown out of meant that I didn't appreciate it. But, when I met Arun and all gratitude and passion and life exploded before me, something shifted. I saw life, my life, differently. I understood how short life is. How fleeting. So much potential is laid before us. So much promise and passion. What had made me believe that gratitude and growth had to be mutually exclusive? What good were any of us doing for the rest of the world, for the expansion of our society and our consciousness, by staying stuck in any place that didn't help us or the people around us to grow? There is no shame in striving.

Even through the pain, I was growing. Maybe, through the pain, I was growing even more. Arun had planted within me the seeds of transformation. A new enthusiasm for life, an inspiration to be more and to be better, and an unceasing and unquenchable desire to live life in the ways I had always been too afraid to live it.

And although I wasn't able to fully be that person yet, I wanted to be. That was the change. That was the start. Higher ground was becoming more and more of a requirement.

I continued to desire a greater understanding concerning our unique dynamic, but it was a cryptic undertaking at best. Anytime I tried to force clarity, the purity that was at the very core of our interaction seemed to disintegrate. I was not yet ready to fully grasp its graceful enormity, though somehow, I was aware of my own ignorance. A knowing that something is bigger than ourselves, while not fully understanding that something, is a form of faith, and my experiences with this electric soul were too paramount to discount as inconsequential.

I wondered if the truth would ever be shown to me concerning what made us so different; what it was about our relationship that was such an inspiring force. In the meantime, I had to simply be grateful for my experiences with such an intense soul connection, however fleeting. It was perhaps the first step in a more graceful direction. However nebulous my understanding, gratitude was the light helping me see through the layers of fog. Helping me keep my footing as I stepped forward into my cloudy unknown.

Our interactions, Arun and I, created a delving into my soul that was unparalleled, and one that was unique to any other experience. It was that feeling of being met somewhere. An in-between. Somewhere pure, that I had never been. The feeling was new to me. Addictive, like a drug, it ran through my veins, and I was gradually withdrawing from its high, learning to accept that I would never feel harmony with another with that kind of transformative strength again.

The thing was, just because I had a uniquely powerful experience did not mean that I could not have other forms of beautiful experiences in the future. It was important to remind myself of that. There are different types and levels of connection, and there would be others to embrace.

If one day we are blessed to witness the most phenomenal sunset, the colors meshing, layering, and glowing in such a way that our heart flutters like never before, the beauty of all sunsets we had seen before and all that we would see in the future would still remain. Though our unique sight had caused our lens to expand, every other beautiful sight would still maintain its own essence of beauty to be celebrated. Different, perhaps, but still sensational, as all sunsets are.

I was grateful to have seen the most dazzling one of all, but I refused to let it blind me.

And with that, I started to move forward, one step at a time. It always hurt. Always. It was a deep and throbbing longing, way down within the deepest corridors of my heart, and when I allowed it to flood me, it permeated every nuance of myself. But that longing meant I had something worth missing. If memories are part of the joy that creates the tapestries of our lives, then I was blessed to have so many beautiful ones weaving their way into my consciousness. When I looked back on our fleeting moments together, through the pain I found something powerful. I found that even through the hurt, I had a lot of love in my heart. Perhaps, through the hurt, I found even more.

I knew that in that love, there laid a secret. We may not always be privy to all the answers, but we intuitively know when we hit on something important. I began to focus on this. On love. As often as I could remember, to live from that place. In that place, the sadness still existed, but it couldn't make me hard. There were secrets I kept tucked away—secrets like hope, which never seemed to fully dissolve. A part of my heart, a corridor that was designated only for Arun. A part that wouldn't let him sink too far into the past. But even with those things hidden below my surface, I carried with me enough love to start shaking myself from that dark hold. To move forward beyond him, beyond the space of our relationship that for some reason had become toxic, and had become a place where that love could not thrive.

And gradually, like a flower learning to let the light in, I opened to Justin.

It took time, but with his patience, and my diligence, we moved forward with kindness, softness and laughter. With him, there was no demanding, and there was no fear. He made it easy to feel safe, and to trust that I could place my pain to the side, at least for a little while, and feel a different but very sweet joy in the presence of another.

As time unfolded, from this place of greater purity, I fell into a graceful love. It was impossible not to. Justin was everything that love is. The relationship became a very particular type of beautiful. The type filled with the softness of each other's breath on our eyelashes, and whispers on lips that met slowly and warmly. Through its grace, my healing continued.

I was truly healing. I was. I know now, however, that there was more to that truth. That something was brewing, deep within. That a seed had been planted that I was unconsciously watering, every day, unaware that through its nourishing, a blossoming would occur. An opening that my Self as I knew it could not house. I had no idea how much work lay before me. If I saw the abyss before I dove in head first, I would have absolutely frozen in fear, never to discover what awaited me within.

We have many beginnings. My next one started on an overcast Friday in November.

I sat at on a swivel chair at my desk in an office that had no windows. I had been at that job for a while, a position that offered a lot in the realm of fast-paced experience and a little in the way of creativity. I may not have found passion in the work, but I happened to be pretty good at it, and that created just enough comfort to keep me stationary for a while. Staying there did not correlate with my newfound drive, however; the one that proved impossible to ignore.

On that particular day, I was a little late for my break, as I was buried under piles of work all morning. It was almost comical, the way the responsibility continued to materialize in front of me, conquering my desk in a mess of pages and sticky notes. But, I needed to step out. I was feeling a bit strange. For the last week or so, I had been sporadically experiencing a subtle lightheadedness that I attributed to the stress of work, the incessant staring at the computer screen, and most importantly, the unceasing tug at my insides that I was not where I belonged.

The work will be here when I get back, I thought, though I wished it wouldn't be. I grabbed my things and made my way out of the office. It was too cold to sit outside, where we usually liked to congregate, but a few coworkers were eating and chatting in the dilapidated break room. I took a seat by them, pulled a granola bar out of my bag, and exhaled the stress of the morning.

"We're talking about this magic show we saw last night," said Mac, the print director. "It was gross. It wasn't magic, it was gross. He poked the needle straight through himself. Right through his arm. You just saw it hanging there, and coming through at the other end. And to show us it was real, I guess, he held it over an empty glass and squeezed. Seriously, blood came pouring out, man. I'm telling you, it was gross."

He continued his detailed and gory description, but I stopped listening. I lowered my granola bar down and my jaw tightened, making chewing laborious. Whatever was already in my mouth became lodged in an instantly dry throat. I squeezed my fists and swallowed hard.

"Did you see it?" he asked me.

"No, I didn't see it," I said, with an obvious wince.

He laughed. "Can't handle a little blood? Don't feel bad. Me either."

Usually, no, I couldn't handle a little blood. But not like that. Just the thought of it and I felt a surge of hot anxiety rush through my body. I was breaking a sweat. I started wringing my hands together.

"Can't handle it..." I mumbled.

I was envisioning the bloody scene on loop. I took my phone into my hand to find something to distract myself, and when I looked down at the screen, its contents blurred. In trying to find a simple technological explanation for something otherwise unnerving, I blamed the screen instead of my eyes. Nevertheless, I squinted them, searching for focus through their narrow apertures. In doing so, the screen lurched away from me and then back again. My eyes, like camera lenses, out and then in, and then out again until the blur was gone. I had never experienced anything quite like that before and I was instantly rattled, realizing with great possibility that I may pass out.

The guys talking around me were nothing more than muted background noise to my ringing ears.

"You know, I'll be right back," I said, dropping my granola bar on the table and sliding my phone into my pocket. "I need some air. I'm not feeling very well."

I got up before they could respond, and walked toward the door in a haze, wringing my hands together, breathing quick, shallow breaths. *Please don't faint at work*, I thought, and the fear of falling made the anxiety even worse. My head was swimming. My feet didn't feel as if they were hitting the ground in the way that I was used to. I had to force them to land more squarely so that I could sense the hard evenness beneath them. I had always been a bit squeamish, but not like that. It was turning into a full-blown panic attack, bloody visions running through my head in an incessant loop, torturing me in their reels that would not quit. I wanted to rip them out of me and the more I wished them away, the more they persisted.

I used to play a game when I was a child. The rules were simple: *don't think about a strawberry*. I'd sit in a quiet room and test myself with disciplined thoughts. As many times as I tried, I could think of nothing else but that waxy-red, sweet sustenance.

I made my way outside and took a long, deep breath. I didn't have my coat on, but I didn't notice the cold. I was overwhelmed by heat, still swimming through a blurred reality. The ground looked as if it was undulating beneath me, and the clouds looked like a cotton mosaic, dancing through the sky in a way that I was sure no one else was seeing them dance.

I stood there for minutes that felt like hours, and let the cold enter into my lungs, where it dispersed its chill throughout my cells. Slowly, I started to notice the prickle of cold on my skin, and I knew I was coming back to myself. The world through my eyes started to regain its composure, shapes falling back into sharpness. The ground stopped sloping, returning to plateau. I stood there for a while longer, allowing any hints of calm to expand inside of me. The anxiety was still coming in sharp waves, but its intensity was lessening, and the waves were spaced further and further apart.

Once I felt ready enough, I inhaled one more cold, deep breath, and went back inside. The warmth felt pleasing, which I took as a good sign. I made my way back upstairs, carefully avoiding any interaction with my coworkers, and back to my computer. I hoped the piles of work would be a welcomed distraction, but as soon as I entered my cocoon of a cubicle, the anxiety started up again. What the hell was I doing to myself? Obsessive thoughts pounded away at my equilibrium, sapping me of any of the calm I had found outside. I was having trouble swallowing, forcing each gulp down a throat that seemed to be made of sandpaper. I could feel my eyes turn dark, filling with something distant. Nausea started to rise in my stomach, which was twisting in knots. None of it made sense. It was as though I was being flooded by years' worth of anxiety in moments; old illogicality that I thought I had rid myself of. The lightheadedness was returning quickly, and I held on tightly to my chair.

My phone rang.

"Hey Len. Can you come over here for a sec? Quick question," said the Carolyn, the Art Director, through the phone from her desk in the adjacent room.

"I'll be right over," I choked, even after clearing my throat.

I dreaded the interaction, but again, hoped the forced distraction would serve me well. I lifted myself up and made my way over cautiously, as if any missed step could leave me tumbling head first into a ditch that my blurred vision wasn't able to ascertain. The room oscillated around me.

"This file you sent me," she said, "the print vendor is having some trouble with the resolution and..." Her words started jumbling in my anxious brain. I looked her in the eye, again willing myself to focus, and her face blurred, lurching to and fro like my phone screen had done earlier.

"Are you ok?" she asked.

"I'm ok. Yeah," I mumbled.

I backed away as if she were made of something venomous.

"Hey," she said. "You're really pale. Are you sure you're ok?"

"I feel dizzy," I said.

"Come," and she led me back to my desk, where she sat me down and fanned me with a manila folder. "Maybe you should go lie down."

"Yeah. I think you're right," I said, my body at that point trembling so violently that my voice shook with it. "Maybe I should go home."

"You shouldn't drive in this condition, Len. Isn't there someone you can call?"

I thought for a moment. "My uncle," I said. "He lives nearby."

I spent a lot of time at my Uncle's since I was a child, and since he lived so close to my office, I'd take my lunch break there sometimes. Uncle Remy, recently retired, was home to receive my call, and was up and out to pick me up before we even hung up the phone. Carolyn told me to stay put, as she would let my boss know I had to leave, and was kind enough to walk me out when my ride arrived. He was there in a matter of minutes, and shortly thereafter, I was sprawled out on his couch, with a large glass of water, a warm blanket, and a huge flat screen television on the wall in front of me.

"Let me know if you need anything else," he said graciously, as I laid my head down.

"This is perfect," I said. "Thanks so much."

Once I was alone and safely positioned within the confines of the couch cushions, I felt massive relief. Feeling unwell had always been the most prominent source of anxiety for me, and feeling trapped in my windowless cubicle, surrounded by the negativity of my office only made things worse. I was so glad to be there that, for a little while, with my head against the pillow, the discomforts quelled.

I closed my eyes, hoping I would drift off into a restful sleep, but even through my weariness, I laid awake, parsing through the details of the day. The events, my feelings, my reactions—they all felt extraordinarily out of my control. They didn't feel as if they were mine, but I couldn't deny my experience of them. I wondered if the experience of something alone is enough to consider it our own. This felt more like being infiltrated by something outside of myself. It was dark, and heavy, and smoky, and I saw it twisting its way around my organs, squeezing hard and taking up room where peace had once been.

We have hundreds, thousands, of thoughts every day. Our bodies experience countless sensations. We fluctuate in emotion and we feel and we analyze and our minds are rarely still. It doesn't seem right that all of this would be ours. I felt suddenly more vulnerable, more aware of external influence than ever before. I felt like a sponge that wasn't saturated with myself, the empty space leaving room for my surroundings to soak in. Perhaps the negativity of my work environment was starting to make its way to my insides. I felt that I needed to remove myself from the toxic situation, but at the same time, also learn to better protect myself from this kind of external energetic invasion, no matter my circumstance. Surely, I thought, now that I was removed from the confines of the office, in a safer place, I would feel better. I would worry about Monday when it arrived. I had an entire weekend to rid myself of whatever this was.

As I made my way back to my car a few hours later, however, sure that I'd be well enough to drive myself home, I again felt that fear rush through me. Not to alarm my Uncle, I breathed through it, and thanked him for his hospitality. He dropped me off by the driver's side, and watched me climb in. I smiled through clenched teeth, gave him a little wave, and waited for him to drive off before I closed my eyes and pressed my head hard against the back of my seat, hands clenched tightly on the steering wheel. It was a thirty-minute drive. One that I made five days out of the week. One that I usually enjoyed, taking advantage of the alone time to think, to listen to music, to unwind while gliding down the pavement. This time, as I pulled out of my parking spot, it felt more like driving forward into a vast and dangerous unknown. The road stretched before me, lengthening ten-fold with every inch I rolled forward. Anxiety was building, taking residence in my racing heart, and my head was again swimming, making it difficult to focus.

The obsessive thoughts returned. Bloody ruminations ate into me, creating a stale taste in my mouth. I elaborated gory scenes in my head, torturing myself with their details. The reactions were visceral. Every time I stopped at a red light, I clenched the steering wheel harder, sweating palms merging with its leather. My vision was unfocused, and I worried that my lightheadedness was becoming too intense for me to continue. But, I wanted out of that car. I needed to get the drive over with before things got worse, or as I feared it, I lost consciousness.

My thoughts were making me ill with fear and disgust. Swallowing became such a chore that I dreaded each time I had enough moisture to move away from my tongue. My head felt large, floating atop my shoulders like a helium balloon. I felt the pressure mounting. Focus was shifting in and out, and the world before me took on a muted quality, as if my car was moving underwater. I took my hand and opened my fingers, pushing my palm hard against the top of my head. It was the only form of relief I could find, and I kept it there whenever I could take it off of the wheel.

When I finally pulled up in front of my home, there was relief, for a few moments, at least. My safe space was what I thought I needed to feel well again. But the high of this wish coming true left me as soon as it arrived, and my next wish took precedence: stop thinking. I wished I could shut my brain off, or at least change the station. I wished I could stop smelling the metallic, rusted scent of fresh blood and picturing it rushing through my veins. I wished my own heartbeat didn't make me cringe.

I made my way into the house, slowly, stumbling slightly, gripping furniture and holding walls as I passed them. Madeline wasn't home. I found the couch, and curled myself up in its corner. I sat there with eyes wide, frozen in hunched terror, torturing myself with thoughts that couldn't have possibly been mine.

Could they?

I wondered if anyone could go crazy that quickly.

14

Be empty of worrying.
Think of who created thought!
Why do you stay in prison,
when the door is so wide open?

—RUMI

The next morning was blanketed in memories of the night. Frightening thoughts reared their heads like rabid dogs on short, chained leashes. I could hear their gripping snarls through sharp clenched teeth, but they could not quite reach me. The memories remained, but the depth of emotion that I felt the night before did not, merely lingering the way dampness does after rain.

I threw my legs over my bed and let my feet hit the floor with vigor, moving quickly and with purpose so as not to hear the snarls. I made it to the window with hastened step and opened the curtain. The chill seeped sharply through the glass, the crispness of fall quickly turning to cold. The sun that fell across my face was warming, however, its light hitting my closed lids. I soaked in its offerings.

The sun did not shine for me, for my body through that window of that room, rolling out of that bed with hair in knots. It would shine whether I was there or not. Whether I felt its rays across my skin, my nerve endings sending messages to my brain telling me that it felt pleasure in the form of warmth and Vitamin D. But still, it warmed me in its seemingly caring way while memories bobbed, up and down, up and down, on the surface of my conscious waters.

What had happened yesterday? It felt like another lifetime of experiences, eons away, yet still in my here and now. It was a part of a play, a movie, a script that was my life. It was a misprint, or a blip or some kind of mistake in the simulation of my essence. I was afraid that in trying to understand it, I risked it becoming real.

So, I shoved it down. Not too far, but just far enough. A strange and dark phenomenon confined to its place in time, for it had no right to permeate a sunny Saturday that smelled like late fall. Instead, I went to yoga and walked on the beach. I went grocery shopping and took a long, hot shower. I cleaned my room and rearranged my closet. Any excuse to occupy myself, cycling through distraction in a way that was nowhere near ordinary but that felt safer than the alternative.

That night, Justin had to work late, and wary of the slow pace of loneliness, I made plans to meet Madeline at my mother's house for dinner.

"How long until it's ready?" I asked, inhaling the steamy smell of roasting garlic.

"A half hour or so," Mom said, and I felt the remnants of nervousness prickle the skin of my stomach.

"I'll run out and get us a bottle of wine," I said, already up and collecting my coat and gloves. "Do you want anything in particular?"

"Surprise me," she smiled.

The store was just up the block, but the air was biting. Colder than it had been. The whipping wind made my ears hurt. I moved quickly, of course, and let the air numb the spaces where any piercing thoughts threatened to surface. My shoulders were tensed and up near my ears, my gloved hands curled up in the sleeves of my coat. I waited impatiently for the light to turn at the corner, and then ran stiffly across the street, the lights of the storefront soon bathing my face in neon. The door was heavy. I opened it with some exertion, and then slid myself swiftly and fluidly into the heated exterior, avoiding a few extra moments of cold.

The salesman greeted me with a friendly hello.

"Let me know if you need any help," he said.

"I will. Thank you."

I looked up at the sea of choices ahead of me, bottles scaling the walls and the shelves and the counters. I could read every single label, if I wanted to. I could be there for hours, focusing solely on bottles and body and red and white. Such a protracted treat of eloquent distraction.

I made my way over to the Cabernets. The most approachable were there at eye level, and just a little further up were the rarer vintages. I let my eyes scan the shelves toward them, stacked elegantly, rows and rows merging through mutual glass casing and individualized by unique labels. I spotted a particularly wonderful design, simple, but impactful: a single white wildflower amongst a dark background of sharp shapes. Blossom, it was named. A Chardonnay. I thought of Arun and the crisp taste of the night that we met. I thought of its freshness on my tongue, of sitting just close enough to him on the couch so that he could catch hints of it on my breath, holding the glass with one hand, and his words with the other. I could almost smell him through my reverie.

Its poignancy was jarring, and I inhaled sharply in response.

The bottles on the wall lurched to and fro, similar to the day before. I shook my head from side to side with subtlety, and blinked my eyes like a small, frightened bird. It didn't help, so I closed them tight, searching for balance in the dark. When they slowly rolled open again, I fixed my gaze to the ground, and blindly grabbed the first bottle within arm's reach.

I made my way to the counter, wary of any harsh movements. I imagined my insides constructed like a house of cards; one of which a light breeze could demolish. Send fluttering down into an unorganized heap of hearts and spades. I waited on line with the bottle clamped under my arm, wringing both free hands, this time not because of the cold.

Low blood pressure? Hormonal imbalance? Brain Cancer? I ran through the possibilities of rationalization in my mind. Hunger? Hunger. That must be it. My anxiety was masking it, but my body needed sustenance.

I had eaten very little that day. Hypoglycemia ran in my family. Sugar drop, we called it. Blood sugar drop. *Blood.* The word seeped into my crevices, hot and thick. I made a tight fist.

It was my turn to pay. The wine was more expensive than I'd planned on, but I didn't care. I needed to get out of there. I feared, again, that I would not be able to maintain a standing position. The cashier looked like he was immersed in a fog, his words further away than they should have been and his features slightly out of focus. I was in a cloud. Or underwater. There was a sheen in front of my eyes that no amount of blinking would undo. He took my credit card and took his time as he turned around to swipe it and print both his receipt and my own. I stood there, anxiously impatient.

The top of my head was tingling. The very top, right in the center. I pulled my hood up.

The cold outside didn't bring me back. Instead, its biting wind threatened my house of cards. I tightened the hood around my head and made my way home, fear beginning to burn, coursing through the passageways under my skin. I imagined it mingling in my veins, rushing through them violently and smelling like rust, and I walked a little faster. The black sky swam around me. I stopped for a moment to gather myself. The air rushed around my ears, taking strands of hair and whipping them across my cheeks.

I breathed the cold in deep, and looked toward the spinning sky. The moon was still, luminous, and full, it's soft blue light washing over me like warm water. It was the only thing I could see clearly, this center of the vast sky that seemed to blur and spin around it. I let the light cascade over my skin, calming the burning fumes of fear with its touch of liquid luminosity. The earth began to still in its peace, recalibrating as it had when I stood outside of my office and the undulating clouds balanced out and became horizon.

The air was beginning to numb my edges, but I stood outside for a while longer under the entrancing moon, swimming in a different reality. I didn't know what that reality was, aside from the fact that it was at one with the iridescent glow. Despite the fear, something held me there. It felt like meditating but with my eyes wide open, upright and alive.

I looked at my skin on the back of my hand and I saw the glow reflected there, sure and palpable. Then and now, this and that, before and after—I was shifting shapes too quickly to keep up with.

"I was getting worried," my sister said, as I came through the door in a trance. "What took you so long?"

"Indecisive," I mumbled, as I unpacked the bottle and placed it on the table.

She walked over, and gave me a tight hug.

"I've missed you," she said, brightly.

We hadn't seen much of each other that week with our busy and conflicting schedules. I was happy she was there to greet me, but I didn't want to tell her about my episode. To say I didn't want to worry her would have been noble, but it would have simply been an excuse.

"Catch me up," I said, changing a subject that I was the only one privy to. "How was work?"

The marinara sauce was bubbling in its large iron pot and I walked over to stir it as Madeline poured over her day, the steam dancing in wisps on my cheeks. The garlic and tomato filled my lungs with warmth and home, enlivening my senses and making me extraordinarily aware of my surroundings: the wood floor under my feet, the clanking of plates as my mother set the table, the yellow glow of the artificial light of the kitchen against the night outside. In my awareness, however, I felt far away, as if I was watching it all through a lens from the place I had stood under the moon. I watched it all and I watched myself, a newfound and baffling perspective.

Something was shifting. There was something in it that reminded me of that moonlight. It felt oddly sacred, even through the fear. I couldn't bring myself to speak it, to bring its essence to life in words. It was too abstract. It made me feel tired.

The three of us sat down to eat and it was just like every other time, habitual in its essence, masking my obscurity. This time, however, my dissociation was more pronounced. I let it simmer behind my quiet smiles, and when I returned home that night and the house was still and dark, I sat near the window and looked toward the sky. I hoped that night, the shelves of wine dancing in front of my eyes in a manner beyond metaphor—I hoped that night held the last of it.

That's something I've learned about hope. Sometimes it adheres to the wrong things.

15

It is said that God's light comes from six directions.
"From where?" asks the crowd, turning left and right.
If only you could look neither way for a moment.

—RUMI

"Come on," said Jason one day, convincingly. "One cup of coffee."

Even prior to the last month of unrest, I hadn't seen Jason in a while, and I was starting to feel guilty for my distance. From him. From everyone. I agreed, fitting my winter hat to my head that had become like a security blanket to protect me from the undulations.

We chatted through basic subjects, and I sat in a robust fabric chair, appearing relaxed, but pushing forcefully against my anxiety as the clock ticked toward the time that I could be alone again. That's what I had started to do when I was around anyone: hold strong until I could bow out gracefully, as if, when I was alone, things were actually any better.

"What happened with Arun?" he asked, when my peppermint tea, steeped in a to-go cup with images of coffee beans around the exterior, was almost finished.

"I haven't spoken to him," I said, with seeming curtness, but in reality, an anxious throat.

I had enough to worry about. I was generally avoiding social situations for the last couple of weeks, but maybe my avoidance of Jason ran deeper. I didn't need any more stressors in my life. Arun included.

"Crazy what all of that turned into," he said. "Isn't it? I mean, life is funny sometimes."

"Funny is a good word for it," I said, my eyes focused on a brown spot on the white ceiling.

"So, what happened?" he asked. "It just didn't work out? Business *or* romance?" He laughed.

I gave a small laugh too in courteous response and looked down at my phone, pretending to see something important. I didn't want to tell him what had happened with Arun. I didn't want to tell him about any of it. About my swimming head or about the peculiar place I was in. From the outside looking in, it didn't seem much had changed at all. It just felt different. Everything did.

I was on edge. Jarred. Uneasy and dysphoric. A subtle darkness wafted in like a slow-moving storm cloud. When it got too close, I'd expand my lungs to exhale it away, but the problem came in its momentum. It was always headed in my direction. It was slow, but strong, and as soon as it was able to recalibrate from its altered course, it headed right back towards me. I was afraid to let down my defenses, even for a moment. It was an exercise of will, and though I was not winning, at least I was staying afloat. The slightest showing of weakness and I knew I was done for. If I let my guard down for even a moment, I could be blown into hysteria.

Why was it there? Why was this intruder trying to invade my space, constantly aiming to obstruct my clear sky? And, most importantly, how would I get rid of it?

My practiced stronghold grew wary as weeks passed. The emotional unrest. The physical instability and constant lack of grounding. The lightheadedness, almost all of the time. Sometimes it was worse than others, as in that night in the wine store, but the discomfort was always present. The world just looked a little different. Not as crisp, not as steady. I went to three different doctors and had all kinds of tests, ruling out allergies, equilibrium problems, hormonal imbalances, and migraines. Every test came back with no red flags, and each doctor told me I was "in perfectly good health."

Could one be in perfectly good health if they never felt healthy?

The peculiar place I was in was rather peculiar indeed. Was this something tangible, a malady that was decisively altering my state? Or, was it possible that this was something much more frightening—something that was all in my head? If nothing was quantitatively wrong, could these maladies be something I was creating?

I worried about this. About my mental health. I became more and more obsessive about my fear of blood and illness, and believed that it was possible that my irrational fear was causing a consistent state of physical imbalance. As concerned as I had always been about my physical state, however, I had never experienced anything so pronounced in reaction.

It was a chicken or egg scenario: what came first, the fear of discomfort or the discomfort itself? Either way, it was quickly becoming a vicious cycle.

As the weeks passed, it only got worse. My mind started to play games with me. I felt worse when I thought of blood, or vomit, or broken bones, so I frustratingly and obsessively imagined cringe-worthy scenarios on loop. Often, I would picture my heart pumping surges of blood through my veins, imagine the sloshing sound it made as it sped through my insides, smelling like sweetness and rust. I couldn't escape my beating heart; a constant reminder. I was a prisoner of body and mind. Instead of avoiding the thoughts that caused my hazardous reactions, my brain thought it would be interesting to try the opposite. My own thoughts became a slow and unceasing type of torture. I was afraid to drive because I had too much time to think with the quiet of the road. I was afraid to lay my head down to sleep because with closed eyes I had nothing to take myself away from the visions. I was gradually being taken over by that black cloud. It edged its way toward me with applaudable persistence.

Work was miserable, sleeping felt impossible, and joy was being gradually sapped. I was swimming upstream. It never tired, but I did. How long could I fight it?

"Are you ok?" Jason asked, as he watched me mull over the unexplainable.

"I am," I said, "but I think I have to go. I have something I need to take care of." It was half true. "Can we continue this some other time?"

"Sure we can," he said, with concern on his face. Not many people saw that side of him. The sensitive one. I got up to leave, hugging my empty cup, looking small and tired. "Are you sure you're alright?" he asked.

"Fine," I lied. "Just a lot going on, you know?"

I gave him a quick hug and scurried out to my car through the grey dampness. It looked like snow but it felt more like rain, the wet air sitting in my bones and taking residence there. I had a short drive ahead of me, only five minutes or so, but the peculiarity was rearing its head with increased strength. I waded through the fear and made it back, though I was shaky and uneven by the time I got home, and the top of my head was tingling vigorously.

I grabbed some frozen fruit from the freezer, hoping it would do me some good, as again, I was lightheaded, and hadn't eaten much that day. I forced an icy slice of banana into my mouth, the cold meeting sharply against my warm tongue. Something was not right. I pushed against the food and my throat, and when I tried to swallow, it was as if my muscles stopped working. I mulled the piece of fruit around in my mouth for a while longer, determined to push it down. Spitting it out would be a form of surrender, admitting with a gross display of chewed up food splattered against the inside the garbage pail that something was wrong.

I felt angry, steadfast in my refusal to allow another strange phenomenon to take over my physicality, but there was a ball of something lodged in my throat that was as large as it was uncomfortable. With effort, I brought the piece of fruit around the obstruction and down past my passageway, but nearly choked when I did, coughing and gasping through the soggy taste. I felt something then in the pit of my stomach. It was a rock-bottom feeling; a metaphorical reaction made real. I felt darkness down there, a thud, and then a cloud of dust. It happened instantly, and it grew almost as fast. It rushed through me as hot and as heavy as molten lava, reaching into every bit of me. I felt the pricking of sweat on my forehead, the dreaded and instant nausea that comes with panic, the clammy hands and impossibly dry mouth.

I pushed the bag of fruit to the side as if it were poisonous, and got up to shake myself out, pacing up and down my floor, wringing my hands and sucking in air. I was in deep panic now, the ball in my throat expanding exponentially until I felt I would be sick, deepening my panic so acutely that my ears started to pop and my eyes blurred. My body trembled, every sense warped and muddied. I begged some unseen force for reprieve.

Everything passes, I thought. *Nothing can last forever.* I continued to pace the floors, passing time between that torture and the future in which I would feel relief.

But it would not pass. Whenever I started breathing again, fear threatened and then rushed through my veins with greater force and poignancy. Whatever this was, it was bigger than me. The dread washed over me, made of tar and burning rubber. Nothing would quell the terror. Never in my life had I been so afraid. Fear that had no need for reason. It found a place to take hold and it destroyed all resistance. I felt it, running through me as if it had structure. As if fear itself was something tangible, taking form and molding itself around my organs, wrapping around my insides and squeezing the life out of me. It made me cringe with nausea and my heart pound with heat.

Days were short then. Darkness fell upon the earth so early that the night permeated well into daytime hours, and by 5:00, the sky was already as smooth as hematite, cold and black. In all my years of struggle with anxiety and depression, never had I experienced anything like that. Never had I experienced anything so protracted and acute.

The walls hummed with their nothingness. So much silence everywhere. So much silence everywhere, but none inside of me.

The cloud came in with the silence, and I was defenseless. It came in and it smothered me and I let it. It choked me. It took any space it could find between my cells, and it filled it. It took my peace and suffocated it, and took my joy and sapped it dry. It took all of the light and it asphyxiated it, until all that was there was blackness. It was a cancer, killing everything it touched. It rolled slowly over me because it could. Because it was so strong, it could take its time, mocking me as it gradually took life as I knew it.

And I could not fight it anymore.

I fell to the ground, and I stayed there.

It was minutes. It was hours.

It was despair.

It was terror.

I must have been in deep, because it was as dark as the sky.

16

If you find the mirror of the heart dull,
the rust has not been cleared from its face.
—RUMI

"Take a deep breath," she said. "Start with a deep breath."

Athena was on the other line. I called her out of desperation, somewhere before midnight. I called her crying so hard that my words hardly sounded like words at all, just a jumble of sounds thrown into a heaving storm.

"I don't know what is happening to me." I wailed. "I need help." Tears were accumulating on my sweatshirt. I sounded small and terrified, my plea close to begging.

"Listen to me," she said, calm and firm. "Listen to me. Take a deep breath."

I knew she meant it, so I inhaled and let my lungs expand.

"Ok," she said, "Tell me what is going on."

I wasn't sure how to describe it, so I threw my words together loosely, one fragment at a time. I told her about the episodes. The dizziness, the thoughts, and the blood. The incessant tingling on the top of my head, the ball in my throat, and the panic coursing through me. I told her about the despair. That I couldn't stop it. That it would take over, running through my veins as if it was a tangible thing, burning away at my walls and filling me with smoke. I told her that I was weak, that I was hardly eating and that I could not sleep. That I didn't know what was happening and that even at its worst, my emotional turmoil had never been close to as treacherous.

I told her that I must be going crazy, and that I would do anything, absolutely anything, to make it go away.

"It feels different," I said, my voice obviously quivering. "I am having trouble putting it to words. It's like an entity, a cloud that enveloped me in its blackness and that is making its way through my body, tangibly and with force."

She listened. For a while, she didn't say a word. And then she stopped me.

"Lena," she said gently.

Her voice was gentle, ethereal, and filled with awe.

"Maybe this isn't as dark as you think it is."

I was quiet for a moment, letting the words seep past my defenses.

"What do you mean?" I pleaded. "I've never felt so miserable."

"I know," she said with compassion. "I know. I do not at all deny the pain you are feeling. I am not minimizing that."

She was quiet for a moment, too. She must have heard my short, shallow breaths.

"Have you been spending a lot of time doing your energy work lately? Have you spent a lot of time in meditation? Tell me where you've been at with all of it."

"Yes, I've been doing a lot of energy work," I said. "More than I ever have. Every day, but nothing seems to help." I took another breath then found some more words through clenched throat and garbled thought. "I've been working with my chakras the last couple of months in class."

"What kind of work?"

"Clearing and healing." I swallowed hard. "I've been focusing intensively on one at a time, working from the root up."

"And this month?"

"The last. The crown." I swallowed again. My mouth was so dry that my throat muscles moved, but with empty purpose.

"And when did this tingling start? On the top of your head?"

"Three weeks ago," I said. "I feel it so intensely sometimes that it alters my vision. Things seems to lurch to and fro, and there is a sheen over my eyes. God, it's so hard to explain," I said.

"How interesting," she said, with subtle awe.

"You think it's related?" I asked. "To my energy work?"

I was always the youngest one in my meditation classes, and the most inexperienced, for lack of a better word. My wise and practiced classmates often spoke about physical reactions to their energetic processes, but I never truly understood it. Without the understanding, I viewed their reactions abstractly. That perhaps they were feeling a hint or suggestion of something, describing their emotions symbolically through their physicality. I didn't think they were fabricating anything, but I always looked at it as less concrete, like when someone describes nervousness as butterflies.

"As bad as it feels, this may not be the dark force you think it is," she said again.

"What then?" I asked, nervously.

I stood by my bed like a small bird, timid and fragile, clasping the phone in my weak grip and pressing it to my ear. She went on.

"When a light shines on our dark places, we see things that have been hidden."

I blinked.

"Light?" My words were short and stumbling.

"A growth process," she said. "A part of your spiritual evolution. A shaking out of what you don't need anymore, and a filling up with something higher."

The tears started to accumulate again. My bottom lip quivered as I fought them off. I was confused, grabbing at thoughts that were filled with intuition but fizzling before they had substance. My mind was muddled, too scattered to put pieces together.

"Can you explain it to me?" I asked. "Can you help me?"

"I've experienced similar things to what you are experiencing now," she said, "in my own way, of course. But this is your process, Lena, and it's not for me to decide what it is you are experiencing. What does it feel like to you?"

I thought quietly. I thought about the last few weeks, the bizarre experiences, the out-of-this-world sensations.

"It's a process, Lena. One your soul decides upon, and the rest of you agrees to, whether you realize it or not. I am here for you however I can be, but it's important you look at this, deeply and without preconceived notions, to see what you find. You have all of the answers. You are the only one who does."

To someone unaware of the particular type of genius that surrounded everything Athena did, or someone outside of the realm of spiritual curiosity, this perspective may have appeared fantastical. I knew better. I didn't take anything she said lightly. I just needed to understand.

"But you think it's possible? You think this could be a spiritual experience?" I asked, looking for something concrete. Anything I could grab on to and change.

"Think about it, Selena," she said. "Think about the energy work you have done, and take it a step further. Everything in this Universe is made of energy. We are no exception. Even our thoughts hold their own unique frequencies and vibrations. When we start manipulating our vibration, when we start altering our energetic state, things change. We change."

I nodded, flooded by something that felt true, but that I could not fully grasp.

"When we start to do this kind of work, *really* do the work, releasing the dense energies and the things that no longer serve us, and bring ourselves in line with a higher frequency, the process can get a little uncomfortable."

"Am I doing something wrong?" I asked fearfully.

"Of course not," she said with consolation. "There is no wrong here. Your soul knows what it's doing. It's important to trust yourself."

"Trust myself?" I asked, sapped of faith.

"It's all yours to discover," she said.

"But when will it stop?" In that moment, it was all I cared about, Aunt Athena's wisdom lost to the ethers. "How can I make it stop? If I'm getting used to a new vibration, isn't a couple of weeks long enough?" Every word I spoke sounded like a plea from a younger, naive self. A self that was cowering in fear's corner, dependent and confused.

"Trust yourself, Lena. Fear is very dense. It is there with purpose, and it is part of the process of release," she said, "but it can also be the thing that holds you back."

"But what do I do?" I asked, nearly begging for answers.

"You trust yourself. You breathe through it and release the fear whenever you can," she said. "And you grow."

It was almost as if I didn't hear her.

"You've experienced this?" I asked. "For how long? When did you start to feel better?" My obsessive line of questioning beat in my head like the second hand.

"Everyone is different. Everyone's ascension process is different."

"Ascension?" I asked.

"Lena, just breathe. You don't need answers right now. You just need to *be*. Do things you enjoy. Get out in nature as much as possible. Spend time alone. Spend time with people you love. Create. Live. Love. Everything is going to be ok, and then, it is going to be spectacular. You are on a hero's journey. A journey toward the heart. You are headed toward a place where all of the density doesn't want to exist in the way it always has. When you get there, it can't."

A hero's journey. I felt a small glimmer of something behind the skin and bone of my chest. It wasn't dark like everything else.

"Our world is changing," she said. "Many brave souls are pioneers now, advancing the collective consciousness through their courageous soul-work. Digging deep, you know? Healing and rising."

"I don't feel very brave." I said, meekly.

"You will," she said, definitively. "Don't forget how well I know you. You are stronger than you think you are, and there is a reason you are here."

"It sounds like a massive undertaking. What if I don't want to?" I said meekly. "What if I don't want to do this?" I felt so afraid. So tired. A single tear got too heavy to hold on, and ran down my cheek, navigating the curves of my face until it went tumbling down to the ground below.

"Who is the *I* you are speaking of? Your ego and your higher self are not always in agreement."

"Mine usually aren't." I thought about Arun. I thought about the bliss and the fear.

"Will this help me?" I asked. "This process? Will it help me move forward in my life differently than I have in the past?"

"If you want it to, it will. It's that simple. Be open and allow it. Your soul is here for a purpose, but you still have the power of choice," she assured me. "How you grow is up to you. The path you take to get there depends on you."

"But how can I be *choosing* something that is taking over?" I asked, frustrated by the enigmatic nature of the conversation. I was too afraid for mystery.

"Why not?" she said. "Why do these things have to be mutually exclusive? It's deciding to take the leap. It's like jumping."

"Jumping?"

"Leaving the ground on your own accord and then leaving the rest up to the way the air circulates around you. Leaving the rest up to gravity, and the speed at which you are flying through space."

I could almost feel the breeze on my cheeks, and by the time I hung up the phone, I felt the dampness slowly return to the inside of my mouth. So many thoughts undulated within me. There were the thoughts of fear and dread that still draped themselves over my consciousness, but then there was also something else.

Perhaps I wasn't going crazy, slowly from the inside out. Was it possible that instead, I was in fact experiencing something miraculous? I paced the floors contemplating the last month, the bizarre circumstances that permeated my days, the strangeness that threatened to take my sanity. My lens was clouded. My heart knew there was something there to see, but the rest of me would not give in without understanding. A compulsion that was becoming all too familiar.

I went over to my computer, and opened a new tab. I typed in one word: *Ascension*.

I read. I read and I read. I took pieces that were mine and pieces that weren't, and merged it all to create a reality that was still as murky as a cloud wet with rain.

At 3:30 a.m., I fell asleep at my desk, and at 5:30 a.m., I walked myself to bed. I slept then, but not soundly. Sleep, it seemed, was as rare as comprehension those days.

17

You were born with wings.
Why prefer to crawl through life?

—RUMI

    I woke, still bleary-eyed from a long night of research and a chest filled with fear. My eyes had run over every word with a gripping sense of urgency. I could not stop. I wanted to know everything. I needed to. I rubbed the sleep from my eyes and curled my legs to my chest, my black rimmed glasses leaning on the bridge of my nose, my feet cold but uncovered. My eyes scanned stories on the computer screen, digging through heaps of information, following so intently that I wonder if I had time to blink.

    What some called a Spiritual Ascension Process, others called a Spiritual Awakening. It seemed they were one in the same, but with some differences, as some people experienced an awakening that was spontaneous, whereas ascension seemed to be more of a gradual process; an aching growth, a burning and expansive trajectory. Either way, it felt like the most important thing in the world to label what was happening to me. Even if it was just fear talking, there didn't seem to be any other way but to intellectualize my experiences, obsessively researching other people's stories like an addict reaching for the very thing that caused torment. I believed discovery would soothe me, but like a drug, it left me fearfully craving more, perseverating over findings until my next question arose, or the next fearful experience came up for interpretation.

I heard the front door open and then close. Boots against the wood floor. A knock.

"Morning Len, you good?" Madeline asked, out of view and muffled.

"Hey Mady," I said, distracted. "Good, yes, come in."

I looked away from the computer for a minute, and brought my legs down. She opened the door with concern on her face.

"Breakfast?"

My cheeks were gaunt.

"I'm not hungry," I said. It was a lie from my body, but a truth from my fear. "Just got home?"

I knew she had been at her boyfriend's place, but it was easier conversation.

"Yes, but I'll be around for a while. Can I at least make you some tea?" she asked, with obvious concern.

"I'm going to take a walk," I stated, with unintended bluntness.

"Are you sure?" she said, eyes narrowing. "It's freezing out."

She was right. Bitter cold.

"I'll bundle up." This time, I gave her an elaborately forced smile.

She made her way toward the living room and I put on a pair of leggings with a pair of sweatpants over them, my warmest boots, and a hat that covered my ears. I heard Aunt Athena's voice. *Get out in nature as much as you can.* And I made my way down to the beach.

The sun was shining blindingly bright in a way that hurt my eyes, but somehow, it was pleasing, for the only part of me succumbing to the numbing wind was my bare face that was soothed by its warm light. The anxiety draped across my insides since the night before and was gaining in strength. It made me feel sick to my stomach, the acid and fear inching up toward my throat. I let the air enter my lungs through my mouth, cooling the hot acid fear with its fresh cold.

My new knowledge was piling up and augmenting my terror. Had this only just begun? If all of these bizarre things were happening to me now, what else would happen? What else *could* happen? Could this get worse? I had read horror stories. Stories of people becoming ill, their bodies unable to adjust to an influx of high vibrational light and instead crumbling under the weight of crippling pain and debilitating fear. Internet tales of people warning the world of the dangers of delving into the menacing expanse of spiritual growth, a place of no return where our bodies and minds could be forever lost amongst powers beyond our strength and will. Would that happen to me? Would I crumble under this pressure? If the only way to move to the other end was *through*, would I be strong enough to navigate it? And if I was somehow strong enough, what would get me to the other side?

When I was 7 years old, I took swimming lessons. I remember standing on the side of the pool, looking down into the water, shivering from the wet cold. My hands were clamped in a tight fist below my chin, my arms pressed against my torso for warmth. My toes curled around the concrete edge, and I felt the tenseness rising in the stomach. How could I find the courage to shift my reality from standing firmly on that ground to submerging myself in that ominous depth? In that water, there was nowhere to catch my footing. If I did it wrong, I would go down. And, the higher I flew, the deeper I would go. In my childish way, I understood that. I didn't want to explore those depths. I didn't want to fly.

As I grew older, I never strayed far from the shore. I let the water encircle me, but my feet were always planted on the ground, sinking slowly into the sand like roots. I felt the earth beneath my feet but only the earth I was used to. Only the earth I knew. I was afraid. Afraid of not being good enough. Afraid of not being strong enough. Afraid that if I took one step too far away, I would get lost. Afraid if I dove too far down, I would stop breathing, and if I reached too far up, I would crumble, the uncharted altitude too grand for my fragility.

The afflicted, the ones who took the time to pour out their stories on internet blogs, touted their solutions like talismans with frustrating irony. That the answer to moving forward was to be found in abandoning everything. Releasing attachments and all of our earthly ties. That the route toward wholeness came in diving in headfirst, letting go, accepting what came. Most importantly, it was doing all of these things without fear.

Moving forward in strength, amidst it all. But if moving forward through it was the very thing causing the fear, how would that be possible?

I cursed aloud.

The terror and dread washed over me again like a cold ocean wave, but thicker, like it was made of mud. I was weary with its weight but I started to walk, turning left and navigating the periphery of the shore. There was no one around but the birds overhead, soaring again through the early cold. The sun was laying itself down against the ocean, glimmering in the bright morning. It rippled in its blinding beauty, moving with the flow of the water with no effort and always in perfect time. I wanted to be like that light. I wanted to be like that water. I wanted to stop the incessant thoughts that pounded in my head, the rushing darkness that pulsed through my veins.

I continued to walk, staring unwaveringly out toward the horizon. My heart knew perfection. It saw it in every glimmer on water and sand, trusted that it could run through my crevices when I inhaled deep. How, then? How could I feel so much misery when I saw so much beauty? It was right there in front of me, flowing around me, singing inside of me, but I was not it. It was right there, and just out of reach.

My warm boots felt strange against the sand, bobbing against its erratic surface. I felt sick, but I kept moving, determined to reach the undetermined goal that lay ahead. The beauty took its salty rays and seeped beyond my layers, reaching down into my heart. It overwhelmed my eyes and made my cheeks wet. I started to cry, heavy and loud. The wind took the sound and made it its own.

"God, you are so beautiful," I whimpered aloud. "You are so beautiful and I want to be like you."

I walked faster then. I spoke to myself and I spoke to the air and I spoke to anyone who could hear me. I knew someone was listening. I could feel them in the light on my face.

"I can't do this," I said, through streaming tears. "I can't." Despair ran through me, hot and deep, and I let it. I let it take its long fingers and reach toward my core.

"I am sad," I said, "but I am strong. I am crumbling, but I am beautiful too. Somewhere, I am beautiful like you. I need to find it. I need to find where it is."

The words kept coming from a place that I didn't know, and I walked. I made it far enough, and then walked a bit further, all the while tears streaming down my face, the wind pulling and dancing around me. I affected its trajectory but it didn't care. It just kept on blowing, taking some of my salty tears and all of my words with it.

I saw the sky differently there, in the quiet of that place in winter where people did not come. Its colors were softer and so were the hums of the ocean, trance-like and otherworldly. I was alone with the flow of the Universe, longing to be a part of it. It crashed against me, over and over, trying to mesh with me. Nearly begging as I did.

"If I can't be like you," I whispered through a tear-choked throat, "thank you, at least, for letting me feel you."

I stopped and turned squarely toward the ocean, and breathed it in. Nature, in that moment, was my meditation. It felt warmer there. Safer. The despair still draped itself over me, but the fear was losing its grip. I felt it slipping, sliding across my consciousness like oily rain. It was a place I'd find in meditation sometimes; a place of being-ness without fearful thought, where the moment was only the present and I was comfortably frozen in it. I had never experienced it with my eyes open.

The ebb and flow of the crashing waves made its way effortlessly up and down the shoreline like a moving meditation. *It's going to be ok*, it told my ego. *It's going to be ok*, it told my physical and emotional self. It spoke to me. I could hear it. I did not drop my gaze. I stared out into the healing waves, the light dancing before my eyes in spectacular rhythm.

And then the water began to lurch to and fro, much like my phone had, much like the deep red bottles of wine. But this time, it was more powerful. More vast. My entire field of vision moved toward me and away with unmistakable vigor. I watched the waves crash close to me, as if they were going to douse me with their drenched fingers, and then instantly, they were just as far away. The light swirled on them now, defying all rules and reason, glistening on crests and valleys that were supposed to be in shadow. Everything was bright. There was nothing out of reach.

I could not feel my body. I believed that if I looked down, I would see my feet drifting up from the ground, hovering a half foot from the earth. I was sure of it, and simultaneously, completely sure it was imagined. So, I didn't move. Not yet. I knew if I let the fear in, it would take it all, choke it out of me and force the magic to cease. I didn't know what was happening, but I knew it was something I had to hold on to, at least for a little while. For moments, moments that felt like much longer, I let it take me. I let this beautiful thing happen and I had no control over what I was seeing, how I was relating to the space around me. There were no rules as far as perception. It broke all barriers of space and time. It was somewhere else, and so was I, but it was also right where I was.

A voice. It whispered in the breeze. It was so elusive I could barely make it out with my senses, but it was trying to tell me something important. Instead of hearing it, I felt it. It whispered to my heart, so I had to know it there.

You will be a beautiful light.

A flash shone brightly before my eyes then, radiating off of the shining water and blinding me for just an instant. I blinked and started to lose my grip. The undulations of the ocean became almost too much, overwhelming me in their oscillations and reminding me again what it felt like to be afraid. When I couldn't hold on any longer, I knew what to do. I shifted my gaze to my feet.

There they were, planted on the sand. The wind was throwing grains of it up over the top of them and accumulating along their edges like they had never left the ground. When I looked up again, the ocean was exactly where it was supposed to be, though still out of crisp focus. I stared at it for a while longer, and nothing else happened aside from the usual types of glimmering motion. The light danced atop it, again following the rules that light loves to follow.

Everything was still slightly unsteady and covered in that sheen. I thought perhaps I would pass out, but then I thought perhaps I wouldn't.

I turned around to walk home, the sand blurred and dancing beneath me. My Divinity had come out to play, and in that moment, at least for that moment, I had a feeling it would keep me safe.

18

There are a thousand ways to kneel and kiss the ground;
there are a thousand ways to go home again.

—RUMI

"Please come. Just for a little while. We'll leave whenever you want," Justin said over the phone, his voice small in an attempt to hide its melancholy.

I quieted.

It was almost Christmas. Considerations shuffled in fast succession, and Aunt Athena's words again floated through my consciousness. "It's the holidays, Lena. You've got to get past yourself for a little while. I'm not saying always, but sometimes. Be with the people you love. Your family, your friends, Justin...they're all worried about you." The gift of peace of mind, she called it. Showing them that I was maintaining some semblance of self beyond my vacant looking eyes and pale face.

My experience on the beach a couple of weeks prior created a huge shift in me, cracking again at my foundation. It didn't take away the pain or the fear, that didn't only linger, but persisted with gusto. What it did do was prove to me that my soul did in fact have a plan. That I was undergoing a transformation that was beyond any usual description, and that, if I paid enough attention, I could begin to open up to the possibility of the miraculous. In short, it not only made me believe in miracles, but gave me the experience of one.

All of this made it difficult to communicate with anyone at the time, and even for someone so practiced in the art of mask-wearing, it felt impossible to pretend everything was as it always had been. No one understood how much energy I had to put toward simply existing, never mind creating the illusion of anything more. I cringed with the knowing that I was hurting the people around me through their incessant concern, unable to combat the innate selfishness of my state.

Justin attended this Christmas party every year. He painted a picture for me of a home adorned in white bows and silver sparkling ornaments that hung upon an elaborate 10-foot-high Christmas tree. Of people chatting joyfully, dressed in their winter best, martinis lined with peppermint rims in hand, music playing outside under a tent with heat lamps and white glimmering lights, and elegant hor d'oeuvres served on the periphery of the dance floor.

He was intent on bringing me on his arm. It was almost irrationally important to him, but I understood what it represented. Even with his extraordinary patience, there comes a limit to one's disappointments. He was trying his best to be understanding, but how could I explain something to him that I had hardly scratched the surface of myself? I was afraid to attend the party. Truth be told, I was afraid of everything those days. I felt panic from the moment I woke up until the moment I went to bed, and even then, there was no rest, for fear never stopped bubbling inside me like a thick witch's brew, foul and ill-intentioned. My normal shifted so quickly to this all-encompassing state that I could hardly remember life without it.

"Ok," I said over the phone, my voice shaking. "Ok."

I could feel his smile on the other end, imparting courage.

In the darkness and chill of my new winter, I cared little about appearance, but on that night, I put in some effort. I had to. I found a tight black cocktail dress hanging in the back of my closet and pulled it up over my thin body. It zipped up without any resistance, draping loosely over my flesh that hugged my bones tighter now, taught around my skeleton. I added a cardigan sweater to hide the angles of my shoulders, and once my hair and makeup were in place, and I was draped in stockings, a pair of stiletto heels, and dainty silver jewelry, I felt almost pretty. I had forgotten what that looked like on me.

Justin picked me up in his black suit and black Mercedes smelling of cologne and kindness. "You look beautiful," he said. He didn't sound surprised, but he sounded relieved.

"We clean up well," I smiled, hiding the slight tremble in my hands by placing them into my jacket pockets while my heels clinked against the concrete. The anxiety was dry and thick, like cement was before it set.

We arrived a little late, so the party was already in full swing; crowded, loud, and filled with flashing lights. I was instantly overwhelmed, breathing through acute and sudden panic, and thankful I was surrounded by so much movement that few would notice. I felt it in my throat again. I imagined vomiting in the middle of the dance floor; a worst fear come to life. I wondered how many times I had been afraid of a worst-case scenario that never happened. I wondered how many hours of my life I had wasted on that kind of thing.

We removed our coats and made our way through the crowd. People kissed me on the cheek and greeted me with friendly embraces. They smiled and drank and moved lightly from space to space. I wandered through the room like an actor in a play. None of it seemed the type of real that anything used to seem.

"A drink?" asked Justin.

I hadn't been drinking. My head swam enough on its own. He got me a glass of club soda, and I clutched it between my shaking fingers.

Just breathe, I repeated in my head.

We made our way outside, where the dancing and the lights and the carousing was happening. Soon, with Justin's arm around my waist, and the unavoidable conversation with friends we had not seen in some time, I started to settle in, the pinnacle of panic slowly abating. There was something soothing about the warmth of the air under that thin-veiled tent. The lights illuminated it in a soft way, its orange glow laying fuzzy along the interior and contrasting peacefully against the night sky. It reminded me of a sky lantern, floating over the earth, encasing its magic but giving the world a glimpse of it through its translucent skin.

And it hit me that quickly. I remembered.

It would happen that way sometimes. I would remember something that I didn't know I knew in the first place. I remembered a time and place I didn't know I had ever been. It was as sure and clear as anything, and simultaneously as enigmatic. There were no details to the memory; just a foggy déjà vu. But I remembered something in those lights. The loud and jarring sounds of the music started to mesh together until it sounded like I was underwater, floating through the soft current with all of these people and breathing just fine.

It looked this way once before. I remembered, before I knew I was remembering. Remembering a time beyond myself and my body. The night I met Arun, and we stood in that bar, the lights and the colors and the sounds meshed and moved like that. I stood there seeing something that I was sure no one else was seeing. Did that make me crazy? If it did, maybe that was ok. Now that I had seen it, it could never be unseen. It was otherworldly there, with a peaceful magic that I couldn't quite understand except that life was more beautiful when I arrived. I was alone there, but more connected than ever.

Light, dark. Dichotomy. Always present, always alive, always happening at the same time.

"Selena?"

Justin touched my shoulder, but he didn't shake me. I turned toward him without disturbing the air. I thought perhaps I was glowing. My eyes filled with soft mist. I was slow and gentle, and I spoke that way too.

"My love," I sang, "isn't it beautiful?"

"Isn't what beautiful?"

"All of it," I said.

"Yes," he said, and I knew we were seeing different types of beautiful, but that was perfectly all right.

He must have seen a light in me then that he had not seen in some time. I could tell in the way we laughed with people and we let ourselves. I ate hor d'oeuvres and appreciated flavors in a way I had not in some time. I kissed him softly on the lips without fear clenching my throat closed. It was peaceful there, in that place, where I remembered magic and he remembered me.

He held me from behind, wrapping his arms tightly around my shoulders. His suit jacket rode up from his wrists and I held him there.

"Tomorrow morning," he said brightly, kissing me on the side of my face, "let's go Christmas shopping."

It made me smile to hear him that way; hopeful and filled with love. He was riding his relief. He was hoping I had returned to him, never to leave again to someplace that he couldn't find me. And I let him. I even almost let myself, agreeing softly with a graceful smile.

I wanted to hold that moment. I wanted to live it. Let it cloak me like the sweater that hid all of my sharp corners.

But underneath it, there was still the skin and bone.

When I went home that night, I turned the lights off, and my darkness came too. It came back with a vengeance. I couldn't hide from myself; at least, not for too long. I wondered if the higher I went, the harder I would fall. I wondered if I would ever be able to hold that space again, where light was easy and I wasn't afraid to breathe. I didn't sleep for one minute that night. Not one. I tossed in a blanket of fear. It draped itself over every inch of me, drowning me in sorrow and frustration. I got a taste of joy. It was sweeter than I remembered. Why did it have to leave so quickly?

Why did it have to leave at all?

When Justin showed up the next morning, he knew he had lost me. I wore sunglasses in the car to hide my tears, but he could see them when they reached my cheeks.

The thing about the light shining on the dark places? For a while, it makes the dark looks like it's stronger.

It isn't. But it really looks that way.

~

The next few months went on the same way as the night of the Christmas party, filled with the most magical vitality and deepness dipped in the darkest of places.

There was beauty everywhere. Grandeur in breeze and flower, in sunset or spinning moon, in children and animals and lovers holding hands. Everything made me cry. I released tears with joy and gratitude, while wading through deep depression and incessant, seemingly unending anxiety. The irony itself was excruciating. My body ached with beauty. My mind pulsed with the edges of understanding, while its demons fogged me, battling clarity. I felt like a plastic container, housing something that was too hot. My edges started to melt and mold around what filled me, and it oozed out, spilling over the top, scorching me, but connecting me to the ethers with its succulent steam.

I knew there was something I was missing. If I could only find the courage, I thought, to fully embrace the path I was on, I would discover the truth behind it all. If only I could dive into the unknown with full abandon, leap from my illusion of safety, I could rid myself of that pain once and for all.

My process went through stages, clearing dense and painful energies out of my space one at a time and with intense velocity. My soul did not want to take it slow. I was on a full-speed-ahead growth trajectory. Spinning in a tornado that used its winds for cleansing. It pulled everything out of me that did not belong, and left behind empty space in its wake that was longing to be filled with light. Anything that had ever pained me in my life, anything that I had ever pushed to the side, any irrational fear or faulty story I had told myself, came to the surface for healing. I couldn't keep anything hidden while immersed in such a bright light. It shined in every dusty corner. A contracted throat and a need for truth. Clouded vision and a need for perspective and clarity. Aching and convulsing muscles and a need to move forward through fear. Inability to eat and a discomfort with the fragility of life; the power food had over my very sustainability. The lightheadedness that spoke of my teetering between two realities; what I came to understand as two dimensions.

I think one of the most interesting facets was my inability to be amongst crowds. My veil was so thin between self and everything else that other's energy pulsed into me like piercing sound waves. I had no protection against it. I was like a sponge, soaking in everything around me, and when that everything was not mine, or did not belong, I'd feel it pulling at my fibers like ripping steel wool. I'd feel the pulling in my head the most, the threads of my brain edging away from each other with rough tension.

And it went on this way, teetering between light and dark and navigating all the in-between, until that fateful night in late March. It was a time I intuitively knew would come. It was a time I had been afraid of.

It was the night I hit rock bottom. The final push.

I had been trying so hard to maneuver through the fear. To let the light take me. To wade through the exhaustion with a motivated heart. Maybe I was trying too hard. Maybe I was forcing wholeness too much. Maybe in all of my acceptance, I wasn't truly accepting any of it, because acceptance meant accepting even when I could not be brave. Maybe I was just tired. Whatever it was, after all of the instances of peak followed by valley that happened along the way, I finally cracked.

It started like so many of the other episodes, gratitude evaporating into the damp late winter sky like melting snow. *People go through so much hardship*, I thought, *and I can't even handle this blessing?* Guilt and pain rushed over me like boiling water, burning away my ragged outlines. Depression wafted in and anxiety and panic pulsed into every edge and every inside. I spent the whole night awake, pacing the floors, tossing in my bed, fighting with all of myself the terrifying physical urge to vomit it all out. I was starving for a reprieve that so many months later, I wasn't sure would ever come.

I thought about Amelia, her elegant coat no longer against my face. I paced the floors, imagining her footsteps following close at my heels, tripping me under their billowing softness. I thought about Arun, his strong smile, his confident gate luring me toward a gleaming mirage. I thought about my place in this world, a ghost amongst statues, willing my faith toward a glistening and disputed ethereal truth.

At 3:00 in the morning, I went outside. I fell to the ground, my knees in the grass, my head hanging low over my body, and my worn muscles no longer strong enough to hold it up. I sat there like that, hunched over, knees iced over where they met the ground. Tears hit below me with aggressive force, slicing audibly into blades of grass. A realization flooded me. It was the heaviest thing I had ever felt.

I didn't want to live. Not like that. Not anymore. And somehow, that wasn't the scariest part. The scariest part was knowing that I would never choose to go. I would never leave this life, leave my family behind, or leave this gift I was given. This gift to breathe this air and see this sky. That is what scared me the most. No matter what, there I was. No matter how much I hurt, no matter how much I cried, I wasn't going anywhere.

I grabbed at the ground, gripping blades of grass between my fingers. I ripped them out and held my fists up high, their roots scattering their lush soil into the air and then down around me. I picked up my gaze and looked to the sky. Tears were streaming down my face. The stars twinkled in them.

"Please, help me," I begged. "Please, make it stop."

I knelt there, sobbing, pale and thin, speaking to the stars and speaking to the sky. I spoke to the Spirits I felt around me. I saw their glow against the night, encircling me, their hearts expanding wide and arms reaching towards me. Offering something. Offering themselves. I didn't see them in my mind or with my eyes, like someone who is hallucinating might. I saw them from somewhere else. My chest pounded.

"Please, help me. Please," I repeated.

I didn't care how I looked, or who heard me. I yelled it passionately through my thin paleness. I repeated it over and over, until it became a whisper, and then over again until I was too tired to go on. I watched my words float toward the sky, where they were held in tender arms and molded until they were shining too. I watched these hearts around me, expanding until they were so bright and so close that I thought I or the sky would explode in their beauty.

I felt them hold the pain. I knew, with every shattered piece of myself, that I was not alone.

All of this time, I was never alone. All of this time, when I needed help, all I had to do was ask.

I felt them take the pain and I felt it seep out of me, bit by bit, leaving space for things that were softer. Kinder. I felt them smile in their generosity, and in my trusting of their light. Fear and disbelief extinguished inside of me as if it were made of nothing but that mist all along. As if I was the only one who made those things real. In that moment, there was clarity, inside of me and around me, augmenting the peace that wafted around me and connecting me to all of it and them.

I let gratitude and love shine from me. I made sure that it did. I let it shine as brightly as I possibly could.

When my voice could speak no longer, and my eyes were all but closed with exhaustion and dried up tears, I rose up. With arms peacefully by my side and face toward the heavens, I watched a light cross the sky. A flame thrown from one hemisphere to the other.

I went inside, and I fell into a deep sleep, stars shooting across my dreams. When I woke up, the sun was shining, and for the first time in a long time, it didn't hurt my eyes.

19

Dance, when you're broken open.
Dance, if you've torn the bandage off.
Dance in the middle of the fighting.
Dance in your blood.
Dance when you're perfectly free.
—RUMI

In retrospect, I can pinpoint so many pivotal moments on my path toward awakening, but I suppose that is the path itself. Every moment leading to the next, unfolding in its graceful way, cascading from experience to thought to emotion and back again. Every moment creating a tapestry that is life and is Spirit all wrapped into one.

Like submerging sun-kissed skin under a cold ocean wave, there is no way to prepare for a light like that. It takes us, and we adjust accordingly.

I remember the *time*. It's an overarching aspect that I remember. I remember how much I focused on its intangible presence. Passing, slowing, moving through space and bringing my story with it. It moved, regardless of my joys, and unimpressed by my sorrows. It unraveled in sleep or in waking, in breath or in fear. It would not still, and it would not rush. And it was the only thing I thought could save me.

I remember, too, when I started to hate it. Time. I didn't want to float in it that way. When fear drenches everything in its black tar, existence slows. Life became wading through muck, the incessant and taunting tick and tock, no longer gliding down the hours but jerking along with the second hand, each jolting movement shaking us from ourselves.

As time would have it, just as quickly, it all changed. But I had to let the time keep moving. I had to let it take me. I had to let it hold me, carry me to a place where I was wide awake. A place where I could see more clearly—that was the difference. To my eyes, that have never been opened so wide before, the light was blinding. It rushed in and my pupils cowered. My lids would clamp shut but I'd pry them open, allowing it to burn, again and again. And, my heart, it was flooded by something beautiful, but there was no room for it until fear stopped taking up so much space.

Life is light, and it is dark. It is dichotomy. Paradox. Balance. Harmony in disparity. We can't have one without the other. Somehow, in our darkest moments, we are open to the most light. Somehow, the deeper it seems we are falling into the abyss of the dark earth, the closer we are coming to the sky. To the other side of the tunnel that shines the brightest. There is no direction in this paradox. It is infinite. Cyclical. Eternal. It feels like we are falling down, when in reality, we are soaring. Soaring gracefully up toward the heavens.

My world had always been the ground, and then it wasn't. The sky took precedence. My soul longed so much to be free of its enclosures that it grew, and it grew, and it grew until it ripped at my seams. It cracked my heart so wide open that it shattered. Sharp shards of red glass heart, clinking against my rib cage, disintegrating slowly. The light was unrelenting. Like ocean waves eroding the shores, it took its long fingers and massaged the pieces until they crumbled. They turned first to coarse sand, and then to dust. The light burned through their elements and turned them to mist. The light danced in the mist and used the shadows to create a new heart.

And then the light made it beat again.

The light must be the Divine. A miracle, defined. Life, and all that we are.

I don't know if this is always a truth about light, but maybe we can make it one. Maybe, we just have to open to it. Allow it to flood us when our hearts are the darkest. Open wide and raw. To its miraculous healing power. To its silver lining. To the Divine. Maybe, it's the answer. It's the thing that can lead the way through this twisting, unpredictable, mysteriously miraculous thing we call life.

Maybe we have to let ourselves fall, because in the falling, we rise.

A year. A year of seconds ticking by and hour hands moving as slowly as glaciers. A year of light dancing in shadows and rebuilding a heart so that it could never again be shattered. In this moment, that time is nothing but an instant. A blip in a journey that is so vast. A point in a grid of expansive enormity. A breath of eternity.

There were many pivotal moments on my path to awakening. Each one taught me something. Each one showed me that I could be brave. That I could trust being thrust into the unknown and let it take me, even if only for a short while. Even when it was uncomfortable, or painful, it did something to me that was filled with goodness. Each experience opened me, took all of my abstract beliefs, all of my intuitive feelings, and all of my daydreaming thoughts about this other reality, this reality that is only peace and light, and for moments, it took it all and made it solid.

Whatever is out there in this vast Universe, whatever is conscious of our inner workings beyond our rational understanding, knew something that I didn't. Even if I didn't need proof, the things I experienced, the powerful things that helped me not only believe in the light, but to feel it with every aspect of myself, opened me in an inarguable way. It instilled in me a belief beyond hope and laced it with clarity.

I had to hold this belief and trust its transformation into knowing. Once seeds are planted that are watered by our souls, it is only a matter of time. Like a lotus, we have no control over our blossoming. The shifts gradually begin cracking at our cemented semblance of self and create fissures for the light to get in. We dig our hands deep into our dirt, excavating the darkness from the lush soils of our souls, and we keep our belief near us through the pain. We grasp at it as we face risk and cling to it as we face fear. It steadies us if we tremble.

In my turned-up earth, I finally started to smell my vitality again. It smelled very much like spring. Something lingered in its breeze that reminded me of truth, because when I inhaled, I noticed the stirring. The truth is like sun or season and every warm breeze, singing in every phase of moon. We can feel its subtle whispers in our chest, pulling us and lighting us up.

I surfaced slowly and all at once. I had been reborn. Rebuilt in an instant that my clenched eyes once saw as a forever. I let myself shatter, and I survived. I let myself crumble, and I grew. I handed myself over to the light, without even realizing I was able, and I let it fill me. I handed myself over to love, without even understanding what I was doing, and I let it become me. Soul couldn't crumble. Soul couldn't drown. Soul wasn't afraid to soar. Soul whispers to all of us, but there are voices we must quiet so that we can hear it. It sings songs of truth in our ears. It lulls us into peace when we are walking against the winds. It gives us the strength to let the current take us.

I will always have a lot of growing to do. The journey of discovery that painted my moment also colored my past with its great hand, and will bring my future to life in its light. But it finally looked different. I was more ready to hold it. I was a butterfly, pieces of cocoon still stuck to my wings. But still, I had emerged. I could feel each particle of enlightened essence as each one of my cells. See every moment as the miracle that it was. I wondered if I could fly then. Maybe, when it came to things with wings, I was more like a baby bird. I had acquired the power; I just didn't know how to use it yet.

Soaring takes some practice. And there was no reason to rush it.

My practice came in meditation and in awareness. Intensive meditation and awareness. My understanding of the world around me, and how I reacted to it, began to change. With the grip of anxiety lessening, I was able to start working with my transformed self in a new way; looking toward how to move forward more gracefully, learning how to let fear flow through and then out. I was able to start looking toward healing instead of letting ills sit inside and rip me up.

My Self wasn't what I had always believed it was. It was so much more. Through my experiences, I learned that I had much more control over my own reactions than I had ever imagined. I couldn't believe how much I had accepted and succumbed to for so long. So much pain and so much sadness that I believed would just be a sporadic but integral part of who I was. What was the point of being so afraid all the time? Sure, fear had its benefits. It was there to protect us, keep us safe from harm. But sometimes, it took on a life of its own, coming out of its depths when it was not welcome.

Each moment, no matter how uncomfortable or intimidating it may seem, there is an important fact to hold in awareness: we are alive. In our aliveness, there is an innate safety. A promise. That no matter what the circumstance, in that very instant, we have not been overcome. I'm not talking about looking toward moments in the future, or looking back to all of the moments that have passed. I'm talking about this very moment. And this one. And this. Blink. Swallow. Beat. You're ok. You're ok.

There are unquestionably awful things that can happen in this life that are worthy of fear and pain. Unfortunately, there are, without doubt. All I'm saying is, when working with our own intense gut fear reactions, the type that holds us irrationally, the type that holds us when it isn't welcome, presence is something we can work with. Whatever came before, we cannot change. Whatever is to come next, will come. But in this very moment, and in this one, if we are truly present, is there anything to be afraid of? Fear of the unknown can't exist in a moment of knowingness. Fear of unknown can't exist if the unknown is only later, and we are now.

Whatever is happening, that is what is happening. And if we can be aware of it, whatever it is, it hasn't beaten us. And if we can be aware of it, maybe we can even change it. Whatever it is, we are at least still moving through it. Maybe, just maybe, we are even finding a bit of gratitude there.

It is amazing how extraordinarily difficult it is, with thought and ego and physical feeling constantly vying for attention, to stay present. In order to be there, we have to remind ourselves constantly. Luckily, even the practice of reminding ourselves to practice is grounding, pushing us into awareness.

The energy of fear is extraordinarily powerful. We are able to feel fear to a profound degree. We are able to feel it rushing through our veins and at one with our very heartbeat, and because we are able to feel its power, we may think it is stronger than we are. It isn't, of course. We have the ability to manipulate fear, eradicate it with a shift in perspective or with something as simple as a focused thought. As soon as we label it, pull it apart, see it for what it truly is, it starts to wither.

I started to focus on the energy of fear a lot, and not in just separating from it, but also in accepting it when it came. Part of the miracle of being human is the ability to feel. I didn't want to numb myself, but I needed to find some balance, and I needed to stop making every uncomfortable sensation into a catastrophe. If in my moment I felt fear, I started to practice this acceptance. *You are feeling fear now. Learn from it. Let it flow through you. This will pass. These moments are their own. And the next ones will be their own too, and they will be different than the ones before.*

I worked more intently in meditation on moving my fear energy. I could look at it, shift it out of my space when it truly didn't belong there, and even use its strength when I needed it. And it wasn't only fear I could do this with. I could look at and play with anything. My meditation teacher loved to use the word *play*. I always liked how simple that made things. We assign such intense meaning to these things that control us, that we forget the grander perspective. That we are here in this life to experience all of it. That we are whole just as we are, and still part of something so much bigger. That this whole life, our whole story, is ours to create. We grow older, but that doesn't mean we always grow outwards. Sometimes, we have to remind ourselves to keep growing. To shake off the shackles that come with conditioning.

I learned to speak to my inner child when I was afraid. To tell her that everything was going to be ok. Sometimes I wonder if I ever embraced my inner child, even when I was her. I was always scared, then. Children shouldn't carry those things. The heavy things that adults carry. Children are often closer to essence than adults are. More pure, unadulterated, the world not yet weighing down their pristine souls. Their carefree innocence allows them to explore without the imagined barriers. Right?

I thought I knew that little girl. I thought I knew of her every intricacy. Her every thought and fear and beautiful sparkling dream when she looked up at the sky. I thought I knew her and what I knew was her fragility. I knew she was small. The poor thing. I never let her be brave. She knew how. Of course she did. Every child does, because they are the closest thing to our untarnished souls. The closest thing to our hearts. I didn't let her. I kept her encased, safe, dependent. I kept her there because fear told me to.

It wasn't my inner child that was carrying those things later in life—the heavy ones. It wasn't her at all. Those things were the ones she wanted to help me rid myself of. Those things were the ones she was brave against. Fragile? No way. She was unbreakable. I was the lucky one to have held her there. She was as light as clean air but never weightless, because she was too busy holding me and the sky, while keeping us grounded in the lush earth.

She came into the world with a soul older than me, with enough wisdom to know that I'd catch up eventually. All those years later, I wasn't a little girl anymore, but I finally felt young and vibrant enough to be an adult. To understand that fear was not who I was. It was a part of me, but it was not me. I was introduced to the shining little one that was always inside, pushing me, enlivening me, silently making me brave. All these years. Even when I resisted. Even when fear told me I couldn't.

So much had changed since it all began, and I had grown so much, but there was still so much to process, and a lot of work to be done. I was working hard in my meditation practice, and making great strides, but I intuitively felt there was another step I should be taking. I searched the internet for a therapist. It felt well past time to reach out for support. Someone outside of myself. I came across a woman with bronze hair and shining eyes. She was a psychoanalyst, but cultivated a spiritually-based practice, which seemed like just the right combination for my abstract needs.

The thought of delving into all of it with someone outside of myself was daunting, but intuition was speaking more loudly than my thoughts, and for that reason, I followed the call. Elora's office was an hour away. On the day of our first visit, I was running late, and there was a lot of traffic on the highway, cars honking as I inched forward. The first hints of anxiety bubbled up over my collar, but it was nothing I couldn't handle. I plucked out some tools from my mind's repertoire to ease the tension as I considered turning back. I knew that I would be rather late, and it didn't seem like an appropriate way to start the new relationship. As I turned the curve to make my way onto the second of three highways, however, the change in direction altered the ways the rays of sun fell across my face. I squinted a moment through the glare, and saw something fly in front of my windshield.

Two somethings. A pair of Cardinals, circling each other in the sunlight.

I watched them in the air, their vibrancy shining against the soft blue sky, and in miraculous contrast to the congested concrete of the highway. I knew there was no turning back then. Of course there wasn't. And, when I arrived, after apologizing for being late, I spoke about the Cardinals that brought me there.

Elora was beautiful. Calming merely in her presence. "Turn around," she said with soft smile, pointing to her desk at the far side of the room.

There sat a photograph of a cardinal, and another hung on the wall close by.

The Universe has such a beautiful way of getting us to where we are supposed to be.

20

When my soul soared to the blessed sphere
I was free of the tyranny of "why" and "how?"
At last the thousand veils lifted and I could behold
the hidden secret.

—RUMI

"Close your eyes," Elora said, with voice as smooth as silk.

This was our fourth visit. For the first few weeks, we talked. A lot. There was so much catching up to do, and I felt safe to express my truths in her presence. For Elora, it seemed nothing was too far out of this reality or too deep within grounded earth.

I closed my eyes, nervous, but trusting. I didn't know what to expect, so I went into it the best way one could: without expectations.

First, she brought me to a calmer space. A deep breath, an exhale. A deep breath, an exhale. I felt the chair beneath me, and sunk more deeply into it, noticing the comfort of the billowing fabric. My hands laid softly on my lap and my breathing became steadier, following her rhythm.

We moved forward then into some kind of hypnotic exercise. I imagined myself on the very top of a hill, and as we counted down from ten to one, I visualized myself walking down and around a twisting path. Lower and deeper. My footsteps appeared on the fine dust of the earth and I smelled the trees lining the way. With each count, I sunk further.

When I got to the bottom, the path opened to grassy earth and a tall staircase. I climbed it, counting the stone steps, up and up. At the very top, there was a door. It was massive, towering over me, each of its polished wooden planks larger than my whole body. Enormous brass knobs stood just at arm's reach, and I turned them, hearing a deep clank as I moved them in their sockets.

Inside lay a majestic structure with no roof. Clouds of soft color created an infinite ceiling. They shifted quickly above me in an undulating kaleidoscope of rhythmic motion, as smooth and soft as pastels weaved over the curve of a soap bubble. A huge hallway lined with pillar-like structures reached up towards the heavens, and on each side of the massive room were two smaller hallways, each cloudy and dark. Elora asked me to choose: *left or right?*

I thought for a moment, and then I decided to feel instead.

"Left," I said quietly aloud, slightly startled by my own voice.

I turned to the left and started to walk, and when I came to the dark entrance, a shining orb of light dropped elegantly into the space in front of me. It was bright white, its core glowing brilliantly and its illumination draping effortlessly over the walls and my face. *Go ahead*, a voice said. *Don't be afraid.*

I walked forward into it and I felt a dip, as if I had just ridden over a hill and my stomach couldn't catch up with the declivity. Everything went dark. Part of me, the fear part, wanted me to open my eyes. But I kept them shut and lifted a foot in my mind's eye, taking one more cautious step forward. When I did, the clouds lifted and the black turned into a deep, midnight blue. Clarity enhanced as I moved forward, though the deep blue hue maintained, coating everything in its formless depth. A beach. I smelled it first, and then it came into focus through the thick air. There was dark sand beneath my feet, and the ocean roared, hearty and alive.

It was dusk. Deep dusk. It was as damp as rain, but none fell from the sky. It just floated there as part of the blue air. There was a chill, bordering cold, but not quite. The midnight blue was turning quickly to black again, but it hadn't. Not yet. I saw a woman. Her hair was long and black, its coils whipping in the strong wind. She stood at the shore, the waves that rolled along it grabbing at her ankles and soaking the bottom of her dress. Her clothing was that of a woman from long ago; one who wore layers under ornate, thick wool.

She walked forward. I watched her, drudging through the shallow shores, her dress heavy, weighing her down with wet cold. She pushed on. I could not understand. I wanted to reach out to her, but I was suddenly stuck in place, unable to move, forward or away. My words got caught up in the wind and they were whisked up into it. No matter how loud I yelled, she could not hear my screams.

She walked on into the ocean's depths. I heard a sound of crackling sharpness. I was watching through her eyes. And then I wasn't. And then I was again. I was dipping in and out, first seeing from my far away, and then there, feeling the numbing cold. She walked on. She walked on and the water lapped around her chest and I saw the splashes heading toward my eyelids. It was so cold. The dark was rapidly descending.

A wave came. I saw it rolling in from a distance, and then it was right there in front of her, her body's drapes too heavy to lift with it. She stood there, weighted and afraid, water pouring over her hair and covering her in its blackness. And then she lost her footing. The strength of the retreating wave was stronger than her frozen garbs, and it took her in its reaching fingers. It pulled her feet from the sandy ground and it took her. I watched it take her with salt in my eyes and something pounding in my head and heart. I didn't just see it then. I felt it.

I felt the fear.

My head. My head that was atop the body that was sitting on the warm couch started to spin. My eyes were closed, but it felt as if the entire room were spinning full circles around me. Full three-hundred and sixty degree circles. I broke into a sweat, every bit of skin drenched in the intensity of the moment. I took my hands and I gripped the couch tightly, determined to stay there. Determined not to open my eyes. I spun and I spun and I brought my focus back to the woman. The one who needed me to see.

She was drowning. Her dress looked elegant then, weightless under the waves. She reached up, searching for the moonlight, but it shattered on the waves where it couldn't be grasped. She struggled, and she gasped, and she choked. She died there, under the water. I started to sob, uncontrollably and with fervor. I sobbed anxious sobs, seeing her pale white face lifeless as porcelain under the waves.

"Stay with it for a moment," Elora whispered. "Breathe."

I inhaled. I was almost surprised I could. My screen went black. I let the tears pour out of me until they tired.

"Take another deep breath," Elora said. "And then, when you are ready, you can open your eyes, and tell me what you saw."

And I told her. All of it.

"Tell me what it felt like," she said, with much more calm than I had.

"She thought she had to die," I said. "That's what it felt like. Like she didn't belong where she was."

I thought for a moment. Tears rolled down my face.

"Like she thought she had to die, but then when she actually put herself in that water, she changed her mind, and it was too late. It felt like fear. Like the ultimate regret."

Elora continued to listen, urging me with her gentle eyes to go on.

"It felt like terror," I said. "And I had this feeling...this feeling that she knew too much. That she was somehow ahead of her time."

Elora nodded her head in understanding. An understanding I didn't even have.

"And what about now?" she asked.

A tear rolled down my face and then I choked on the rest of them.

"For her, or for me?" I asked.

"For the both of you," Elora said.

"She's gone," I said. "She's been gone for a long time. But..."

I stopped. I didn't know how to explain it.

"She was me," I finally said. "But she wasn't."

Elora shook her head in recognition.

"She can be both," she said.

She let me sit with it for a moment.

"Another paradox to wrap myself around," I said.

"What about that is paradoxical to you?" she asked.

"Something about being—and not being—at the same time," I said, clumsily. "This woman was me, and obviously not me, because I am here, and she is gone."

She shook her head, prompting me to go further.

"Maybe," I said, "she wasn't just a vision."

I thought for a moment more.

"It didn't feel like just a vision, you know? The whole thing didn't feel like just a dream. It felt like…" I narrowed my eyes in deep contemplation. "It was more like a memory."

Quiet.

"A past life," I finally said.

"And what does that mean to you?" Elora asked.

"I'm not totally sure," I said. "It reminds me of these instances I've experienced during my awakening process. This act of remembering without knowing exactly what it is I was remembering. A clear knowingness of something beyond myself."

"Can you give me an example?" she said,

"It was this ethereal thing," I said. "It would happen when the light was falling just the right way, and when I was calm and open enough to receive it. Usually, it was beautiful. This time, seeing this woman, it hurt."

Elora looked at me compassionately.

"Who was this woman?" she asked me, definitively.

"She was me, but then," I said. "In a different time, but as if we share the same soul."

I sat in silence then for a long time, letting tears run down my face in quiet succession.

"She was so scared," I said. "Especially once she realized her mistake."

"Can you tell me more about that regret piece?" she asked.

"I think she brought that with her," I said sadly. "The energy of that. It's heavy."

"You saw that it was heavy for her?" she asked.

"Yes. And I felt it too," I said, shifting in my seat. "I think I still do."

"What does it feel like now? Can you relate to her in that way?"

"I don't know," I said. "I think I can feel her regret in the form of fear. That heaviness, you know? I guess that's how I can relate to it."

"So, you don't feel the regret itself, but the accompanying fear is your experience of it?" she asked.

"Yes," I said. "We were both afraid."

"But what is different now?" she asked.

I sat quietly again, watching the carpet and hearing the clock.

"What is different," I said, "is that this time, I didn't drown. I don't have anything to regret because I kept pushing through. But for whatever reason, the fear lingered. Lingered maybe without substance, or maybe it lived in me based on a reality that was no longer mine."

"So, what were you really afraid of, all that time, while you were experiencing the pinnacle of your awakening process?" she asked.

"Pain," I said, definitively.

Elora was silent.

"And, discomfort…and the unknown," I added.

Elora still did not speak.

"Well, and failure, I guess," I said.

"What would happen if you failed?" she asked.

"I don't know," I said. "I'm not sure, but I was afraid of it anyway."

"What was she afraid of?" Elora asked.

"Death," I said, matter-of-factly. "She was afraid of a lot of things, but ultimately, at the very end, she was afraid of death. And that's the fear she carried with her."

She was silent again.

"Maybe," I said, "all along, I feared living in pain, but it was that old fear that I carried. A fear of failing. Her fear of death."

Elora looked at me softly, and with compassion.

"Is that possible?" I asked.

"You tell me," she said.

I shook my head. "So..." I looked beyond her with lines of contemplation wrinkled across my forehead. "What now?"

"Let's say we change the story," she said. "Let's go back in."

And so, we did change the story, in all its glorious paradox, not erasing its existence but altering my current experience of it. I watched her soul, my soul, rise above the water, the moon dim in comparison. It hovered there, the wind howling through its light, removing fear as if it were made of smoke. Blowing away regret like a layer of ash while the ocean lapped against her body.

Another being appeared. She was made of light also, shining just as bright, if not brighter, emitting a brilliant golden hue. She took the woman's soul, my soul, in her arms. Together they flew up toward the sky. Toward a peace that I could not see, but that I was sure was there.

21

It may be that the satisfaction I need
depends on my going away,
so that when I've gone and come back,
I'll find it at home.
—RUMI

The experience in Elora's office reminded me of where I came from. It was something I already knew, but had forgotten. It reminded me again of fear's realness and simultaneous illusion, pushed down into layers of life and experience, and buried beneath the dust and the rubble and the magic and the mystery.

Learning to manage fear was one thing, but there were other layers to comprehend. Where does fear *come from*? Where did *my* fear come from? Was its foundation solely based in my innate personality structure and molded around experiences in this lifetime? Or is it possible that it came from someplace beyond that?

We can't prove the existence of past lives. The concept itself is, to some, a laughable farce. But is it really such a crazy, absurd, nonsensical notion? Or is it possible that there a deeper truth there; an undeniable existence that lives in the very core of our experiences? Even if we can agree that energy cannot be created or destroyed, and therefore, our energy must travel through time and space for eternity, does that mean that this energy can in fact live on through generations of experience? And if so, that we are able to access these experiences beyond conscious memory?

I wanted to believe in the possibility of seeing beyond this moment in our physical lives. That we are connected to a vast past, present, and future within this space in time that may not be as definitive as we think it is. Could this become my truth from an inner knowing, or did I need more than that to constitute it as real? All of the things that were saving me, all of the things that were making me whole again, were beyond physical proof. They were feelings, visions, understandings, intuitive stretches of the heart that were leading me toward wholeness. Energetically, intuitively, and metaphorically, what I saw and experienced felt like truth. Logically, it was hard to wrap myself around.

I suppose where it came from meant little in comparison to its impact. I felt like I knew myself better. In my compassion for this woman, I imparted compassion within myself. I was given some sense of reason. A new manner of contemplation when it came to my introspective and phenomenological studies of fear. A new layer, augmenting my understanding.

Is this fear an integral and necessary part of my present moment, or does it come from someplace *else*? The shift, the releasing of the fear of that story, the allowance to change its surrounding energy, cushioned me. It was as if I was carrying this intense fear reaction for generations. Carrying it into my present where it no longer had use or basis. It made sense for her to feel that way then, but holding it in my here-and-now didn't do any good.

When our external world begs for proof, truth stands in its science like cement: unmoving, rigid, and unforgiving. When we stand in knowingness, it feels different. When we stand in Spirit, we can swim through our own depths, a reality that is as enigmatic as mist and mercury, but just as palpable. I realized that when I crashed into the encased rigidity of the thinking mind, my flow turned to something that stuttered. That's not to say that my introspection was not important. Actually, it was an integral piece. But when it really came to the core of things, it was in meditative trust and intuitive knowing that I felt most graceful. When I came closest to understanding the mystery.

There is so much we still don't understand. We learn more every day about ourselves and the Universe and the particles that make us up. Even if this most terrifying reality was true, that the beauty that I began to base my life upon was not truth in the usual way and that all of the magic did not exist beyond the confines of my mind, isn't our mind connected to the rest of it anyway? An integral part of the whole of this body we reside in, this earth we lay our feet upon, this Universe that is our breath and what our breath becomes?

How narcissistic, I thought, to believe that there exists no greater truths because we as human beings have not yet quantifiably proven them to be. How bold to believe that there is no forever here, while simultaneously understanding that we are made of the stuff of the stars?

What will give us this proof? And do proof and faith have to be separate entities? If experience is proof, then I have lived a life of this magic, and have proven its miracles again and again. If experience is not proof, what keeps us believing? I think this is where faith comes in. Faith doesn't have to be blind belief or naively subscribing to irrationality or impossibility. It can be as simple as understanding that we don't understand. Knowing that some beauty may be too vast to fully grasp with our minds, and only with our hearts can we be flooded with its light. Knowing, with all of ourselves, that blurred periphery does not mean that nothing exists outside our field of vision. Perhaps, when the truth finally floods us, our faith is the thing that prepares us for the light of truth that would have otherwise been blinding.

There are those of us who look at the ground as we walk, and there are those of us who look toward the sky. We sky-gazers have a certain look of otherness. When we look as if we are far away, it is because we are. When we take a deep breath, or many, and leap with reckless abandon from the comfortable and the safe, diving headfirst into the unknown, we explain ourselves simply: *The sky made us do it.* It had us believing in something more. It filled our hearts with something that tasted like magic. We saw a love that was not ordinary, and when we jumped, we let the air take us, and we soared.

Truth, then, may be as simple as trusting ourselves. It is living in the magic, while merging with the lushness of the earth. It is knowing there is a vast and expansive *more*, while simultaneously living fully in our present, and living it with as much fervor as we feel in our expansive heart's view. It is not anyone else's, and it is everyone else's. It is a thread that weaves us all together, and it is that which makes each of us unique enough to grow. We teach each other, we learn from each other, we support each other as we dig our toes into the sands of our realities, feeling each individual grain between our toes.

I had to live my truth. What other choice did I have? The difference was, I desired to not only live it, but to become it. To bridge my earth and sky, my science and my magic, letting what was everyone else's and mine mingle in the ethers between our breath until they created something that was even more beautiful. I never started believing in the impossible. I only started trusting my belief in something greater; a grounded spirituality in which I was one with the earth while my heart was in the sky. My awakening process was moving to the next step, merging my worlds and realities in deeper layers of truth. And, what a beautiful process it was.

For something that so many people in the world are experiencing, the awakening process still remains largely unspoken and wholly misunderstood, often carrying with it a stigma of destruction and nonsensicalities. Even as someone who spent years in spiritual circles, this experience was still something I had never considered as possibility, especially in its all-encompassing nature. When it arrived, I felt muddled and alone. Scared, crazy, and misunderstood.

The process has been kept a secret behind layers of illusion. A vow of silence for all that grow under its miraculous weight. But why?

The information that I did find during those times I was searching for answers, pouring questions over internet pages like they were my elixir vitae, was frighteningly ungrounded. The process was painted in such a negative light. Lightning bolts of information warning against the dreadful pain of transformation. Threats of mental breakdowns, physical crumbling, excruciating emotional turmoil. If you didn't do it right, if you weren't strong enough, if you didn't understand, if you didn't eat right, if you didn't meditate enough, if you didn't sleep enough or carry around the right crystals or breathe in the right way, you would fall. You would live in a pained state forever, a spiritual purgatory, painted in your failures to transcend and your unworthiness to grow toward wholeness.

Other people's words and experiences had permeated my space and created even more fear. Though a healthy level of pain can be a surefire route toward transformation, none of it had to be that threatening and ominous. I know that now, but I was absolutely guilty of the same fear-based thinking that infiltrated the spiritual community. Why were so many of us so afraid of a process that should be beautiful? Why was such an intimidating, negative and terrifying picture painted from the miraculous?

I believe that firstly, we are afraid of what we don't understand. We, as a species, like to have the ultimate grip on our reality. When something arrives that is out of our realm of comprehension, we must remedy the resulting anxiety with answers. We feel uncomfortable without clarity. It feels dangerous. Vulnerable. We feel unsafe when we don't have control. We forget that vulnerability can be a great strength, and that sometimes, in the relinquishing of control, we can find the answers.

Secondly, we have a relationship to discomfort that is rooted in our physical bodies with aversion. Discomfort is, well, uncomfortable. Sometimes, even painful. So, we label it as negative and snap into a mode of fight or flight when it arises. Sure, there are certain forms of discomfort that are dangerous. Forms that needs to be remedied as quickly as we can remedy them. Warning signs for deeper physical issues, something our body is trying to reject or to heal that it needs our help with. But sometimes, discomfort is just another part of the dance. Another state, like peace or joy, that will come over us, sit within us, and then move on. Without discomfort in any form, would we ever grow at all? Without fear, for example, how would we protect ourselves or learn about core issues?

Perhaps we must see them in fear's light so that we can move past them, ridding ourselves of their hold for good.

Thirdly, I think fear is contagious. Someone else is afraid of this, so it must be bad, and now it's happening to me. We forget that everyone is different. That every process is a unique unfolding of circumstance and perspective and the will of our own individual Spirit. We are surrounded by so much fear energy that it can seep into our space from the outside in. And, in the most vicious of cycles, this fear begets more fear. We cower in it. We let it become a part of us. And the more it takes over our space, the harder it is for us to see the truth of our experience.

It is the fear that is the most painful part. It is the fear that can make anything look dark. The fear brings out our insecurities. "I'm not good enough." "I'm not strong enough." "I'm not worthy." We feel small in comparison to the rest of the Universe. We may even feel weak in comparison to other human beings. But the fact that there exists great universal forces does not mean we are at their mercy. We forget how powerful we really are. How connected. Once we start to realize that we have the power to create our internal experiences, things start to change.

This dance is a beautiful journey of interconnectedness. We create and are therefore created, and we are created and therefore create. We love and we are therefore loved, and we are loved and we therefore love. It is like that with anything. The most eloquent cycle of giving and receiving. Of being and striving. Of being gifted and instilled with life and all it is made up of, while still creating that life as we walk it.

Much of my physical and emotional turmoil was created by me. It was up to me how graceful my process was. It was up to me to shift painful energies when they needed shifting and up to me to accept when I couldn't. Maybe I needed the pain. Actually, I'm sure I did. It put me knee deep in a growth trajectory I may not have been able to experience otherwise. But that was just me. As Aunt Athena said, it was all mine to discover. I didn't understand then. I didn't understand how much power I had over my own process. And, in times that my power couldn't overcome my pain, I would still be held safe.

A spiritual awakening is a magical journey of miraculous unfolding, not to be confused with a torturous abyss. When people tell you must suffer, you may feel compassion for them for they are stuck in an in-between, but you needn't hold their truth. We can be grateful for any lessons fear teaches us, but we are here to breathe light.

If you are changing, growing, expanding, if you are learning how to align with something higher, something more pure and light, know this: it might not always be easy, but it doesn't have to be so hard. Whatever your process is, trust it. Trust yourself. You have everything you need to be whoever you want to become. And your soul will not lead you astray.

PART THREE

The Earth

*When lovers of life get ready to dance,
the earth shakes and the sky trembles.*
—RUMI

22

Anyone who knows me, should learn to know me again;
For I am like the Moon,
you will see me with new face every day.

—RUMI

"I just want my girlfriend back," Justin shrugged as we walked along the shoreline, leaving footprints behind us and looking out toward the foggy horizon.

My awakening process was, in many ways, life itself. But still, in most others, it was a hiatus from life as I knew it. During the pinnacle of the growth process, there wasn't much room for anything else. But what about now?

In my unintended selfishness, I left Justin out to dry. He gave me compassion and he gave me patience, and I had no choice but to take it, along with a heaping serving of guilt. Even when I was right next to him, he saw in my eyes that I was in a far-off place. He didn't know how to reach me there, and I didn't know how to invite him in.

As I started to settle back into life on the other side, and the monotonous upheaval had abated, finding balance became a necessity. I didn't want to stop doing the work, but I had to learn how to bring my learnings into the world around me. Connect the ethereal with my every day.

I hoped all along that my awakening process would eventually instill in not only me, but in the people around me, something beneficial.

I hoped that, somehow, I could share the light that filled me. I brought this hope with me all along; a promise tucked away for those I loved. That once I was feeling well again, I would give as much as I could give back to them, even if just in small ways. A smile. A touch. A vibration. An energetic boost or sharing of some sliver of wisdom. But when I came back, nothing was the same. Whatever gap existed between Justin and me before, however slight, had become a gaping canyon. We couldn't understand each other. We found joy in different things. Our conversations were muted by everything that stood in between us, and we could not hear each other through that intangible space. I lived in one place, and he lived in another, even when we were breathing the same breath.

We loved each other. That did not change. And my gratitude ran so deep, that I was determined to try to make it work. I had to. But not at risk of losing myself. It was a balancing act that was as crucial as it was arduous.

Perhaps love shouldn't be so hard. But also, perhaps it is the only thing worth trying so hard for. I wasn't sure which was more true, so until I figured it out, I couldn't change a thing.

The lack of clarity was tiring, but I moved forward with its weight. We both did. We, as a couple, deserved at least that much. And maybe I could have held that weight for the both of us while I was finding footing in this new life. Held us up as if that was the only thing to hold. But it wasn't. There was something else, and it crept in stealthily and hung on me even heavier.

I found *him* creeping into my thoughts again.

Arun came back first in dreams. I watched our memories while I slept, picking out the most emotionally charged to either aid in my slumber or jolt me from rest, depending on the nature of the story. And soon, I wouldn't just see him at night, blurred and mystical, but also in waking, when I would daydream about him with sharper contours and brighter colors. I wondered about his life and where he was and what path he took to get there. I wondered if he ever looked up at the sky when I did. I wondered if he ever wondered about me too. I wondered all of those things, and I felt sorry that I did, for it was the last thing Justin deserved.

I never stopped caring about Arun, and I was sure I never would, whether he was in my life or not. Where before, I could keep it behind lock and key, soon it began to flood me again.

Though its pinnacle was behind me, my awakening process was still causing shifts, albeit more gracefully. I was so wide open that what I had resonated with before was changing. I was in tune with something higher, and Arun had always been that for me. He had always been that other place. I understood that part better, or at least, I understood aspects of it. That perhaps his innate vibration matched closer to my new one. Of course I was magnetized toward him before, while my soul was craving his particular light. Later, while my soul was basking in its own glow, it must have craved its mirror.

Weeks past and the dreaming and the daydreaming and the wondering became something more commanding. Arun began to permeate my thoughts, wholly and completely. I missed him with a consistent and powerful ache. I wanted to tell him my story, and all of its intricacies. I wanted to share myself with him, and I longed for his understanding and recognition.

He was everywhere. Like Amelia, I felt him on the breeze and in the rays of sun.

The difference between the missing now and the missing then, when our relationship (for lack of a better word) had crumbled, was in its grace. I missed him, and I let it flow through me. I felt it ripping at my heart, and when I felt it (just as when I felt unsteady in the blinding light months before) I welcomed it. I knew that in it was something higher. Something nourishing, even in its discomfort. Arun was feeding my soul, even from so far away. The more I missed him, the more I grew. Love expanded inside of me, toward him, and out toward everything else. I learned of love more decidedly then. That it was not just me to him, or anyone to any one thing. It is the very air we breathe. It is the very life we live, if we live it from the heart.

So, how could I stop loving him? I couldn't. It was inspiring me in astonishing ways. I saw love in everything, and the more it touched me, the more it touched the people around me, too. Maybe this was the answer. Love's contagion. Either way, there was so much love, it even started to spill over to Justin, which, speaking of irony, was one of the most ironic bits of all. We were both so undeniably touched by love's light, it almost didn't matter where it came from. There was more laughter then. It was a gift to bask in.

The greatest difficulty was being alone in the grandeur of these realizations. I wanted him to know. I wanted Arun to know that he was one of the things that was bringing me back to life.

And, it went on that way for months.

One morning, I was sitting at work with headphones in my ears, and a song came on that made me think of him. I can't remember which it was, because most songs made me think of him, but on that day, and for some reason, it held me with greater strength than most other times. And as I listened, picturing the way he would smile if he liked the melody too, I remembered something I had read that morning. A short line of text on my daily calendar pages, nestled between the date that hung large at the top, and an image of rolling hills at the bottom.

Today, have no regrets.

I swallowed around a lump in my throat, thinking about all the words I could not say.

Would it hurt to say hello? I thought. *Would it really be that bad?*

Desire pounded in me, filling me to the point of distraction. Desire can quickly become longing if we let it, and then it takes on a life of its own.

I would just say hello. Ask him how he was. Speak casually while I filled myself with him. Or, I wouldn't. I would transcend the desire like I had so many times before, not in the way I wanted to, but in the way I thought I should. Perhaps, this was the right thing. Or perhaps, I wasn't even sure what right meant anymore. Maybe, it simply came down to what was the most regrettable.

Focus on your work, I thought, *until 2 o'clock, at which time you will take a break, leave the office, breathe in the fresh air, and come to a grounded decision.*

As extraordinarily busy as the day was, it was even harder to focus. My heart and brain were clashing and making such a ruckus. I finished up the last of an arduous project, and by 2:30, I grabbed my things and headed outside. My phone sat in my bag. I hadn't look at it in over an hour.

It was late summer, and my black Rav4 sat baking all day under the afternoon sun. I rolled the windows down and set off toward the water, where I could eat my salad with my back against a tree bark. The small lake was only a few minutes away from the office, so I arrived quickly and got myself settled, letting the sun fall over me while budding excitement caressed my chest.

I could resist it. Of course I could. I didn't want to. But I could. Indecision tugged at me as I pulled my phone out of my bag to draft a long overdue message without wholly deciding if I'd send it. At 2:00 on the dot, however, I had received a message that, once seen, changed my plans without question.

Was I seeing things? Could it be? I looked away, and then back down again, making sure my eyes weren't playing their tricks. But there it was, in plain sight, staring at me from its space on the screen. I looked up again, this time to get my bearings and to thank someone I could not see. The clouds moved in the shifting sky. It hadn't moved that way in some time but it was different in that, this time, my reality was his too, and right where I could touch it.

Lena, he said.

That was it. My name. Just my name.

Arun.

I sucked in a bit of breath, but there wasn't much room for it in my chest. I was filled by too many other things.

I stumbled upon something interesting today, he said.

I steadied each shaking finger as I found the letters. *What's that?*

Your name, he said, *and what it means.*

My forehead crinkled. The shaking radiated from my hands to the rest of me, like electricity through thin tangled wires.

Stumbled upon? I asked.

Don't think I'm not up on my Greek mythology, Selena, he stated, with less sarcasm than most.

I laughed. The sun pounded down on me as profoundly as my heart pounded in my chest.

Or should I say, Goddess of the Moon?

It's a lot to live up to, I said, sweat accumulating on my neck and cheeks rosy with tangible emotion.

You're doing just fine. I could see the crooked smile it was laced with. *And there's more.*

More? I asked.

Of course, he said. *Isn't there always?*

There is. I waited. I caved.

Tell me.

Do you know what my name means?

I didn't know. I wished I did.

Tell me, I repeated.

He sent me a picture of the afternoon sun. The same one I was sitting under.

You're kidding... I said, though fully believing. I smiled as I thought of fire and soft night. The cycle of light and dark. The inspiration and the inspired.

Do you want to hear something else? I asked.

Always, he responded.

I was just thinking about saying hello. On my lunch break.

You mean it?

I mean it, I said.

But you didn't? he asked.

Well, I said, *you beat me to it.*

Ah, he said. *The simulation.*

Simulation? I asked.

The Simulation Hypothesis. That all of reality is a computer simulation. If coincidence doesn't exist, this must have been a glitch.

I laughed. The sun and the moon and our elaborate views.

Maybe more like synchronicity, I said. *Something like divine timing.*

Like something, he said, *for sure.*

Something.

How are you? I asked.

I'm well, he said. *Working a lot. What's new by you?*

Oh, you know, I said. *Life moving ahead in all its messy synchronistic glory.*

He smiled then. He showed me on the screen.

How's Justin? he asked, and even my eyelids halted.

I didn't respond for a minute or two, my silence filled with emotion and undertone. It felt strange to see his name from Arun. They were worlds that should not collide. *He's well*, is all I said. What else could I say?

Good, he said. *Sometimes I cheers to him, like old times.*

I laughed out loud, a small short laugh, then swallowed it.

Shush, I said. *And you?* I didn't need to elaborate. He knew what I meant.

Single guy, just going with the flow, he said, making sure I remembered. *Let's catch up sometime. Over a drink.*

I stopped again, because those last words made my chest swell. I wondered if he meant them. He probably did, just not like I would have meant them. Not with the same weight.

There must have been a perfect and balanced response, but it was just out of my reach. Doing the right thing meant responding in a way that would not hurt Justin. Right? Was that what was right here? The thought of seeing Arun's face, however, being next to him again and smelling his midnight-wide-awake was almost too much to take.

We have a lot of catching up to do, was all I said.

And I watched the cursor blink until it was time to leave.

23

When I walk on the path, when I enter the house of Love,
I see you.
You are the King in every town.
I see you in the sun, the moon, the stars,
I see Your alter in every plant, in every leaf.

—RUMI

"Our time was short," I said, "but powerful," summarizing a story that carried the essence of magic but of which seemed words could do no justice. I looked down at the carpeted ground.

"I loved him then."

"And now?" she asked.

It was the first time I had told Elora the story of Arun and I. The first time I mentioned him to her at all.

"It's my secret," I confided. "In many ways, I still do." I swallowed around it.

She leaned her head down in half a nod and turned it slightly on its side. "What happened?"

"He didn't feel the same way," I said, my voice small.

"He ended things?"

I thought for a moment. "Not directly," I said. I tucked a strand of hair behind my ear. "Not in the way you'd imagine."

"What made it different?"

"He just wasn't there," I said, mulling over the thoughts as I spoke them. "I ran to save myself."

Elora took a slow breath, eyes fixed on me. She waited, giving me time to make sure that my words were complete before she spoke her own.

"He was your opening." She said it almost matter-of-factly, but it was coated with a thin layer of fascination. And then she fell silent again.

She did that sometimes. Prompted my stillness. Left me to decide whether I wanted to look into her eyes or at the ground while I processed our last discourse. The silence was under my control. It was my choice as to when to break it. This time, I let it elongate. I heard the clock ticking, but nothing else. I watched it all on fast-forward, clips making themselves visible in flashes and then falling into the background. Our meeting, our coming together, and our falling apart. My falling apart, followed by complete decompensation, and then comprehensive restructuring. Returning, rebuilding, expanding. And then I saw him. Drifting back into my life with gentleness at first, and then with increased insistence. A chill prickled on the back of my neck and made its way down my spine. My gaze was down, but I didn't look at the ground. I didn't look anywhere really, except for within.

When I did finally look up, I was wide-eyed.

"Unbelievable." I uttered it under my breath.

"What are you experiencing?" She asked.

I repeated her words. "My opening." I tasted them on my tongue, and she looked at me while I swallowed them. "Of course," I said. "I've never looked at it like that before."

"Like what?"

I thought for a moment.

"I was always aware of the unique effect he had on me. But I hadn't realized how connected it all was."

She sat, silent, watching me process it on my own.

"Of course," I repeated, as the clock continued to click time forward. "When I look at it now, with time's distance, it fits perfectly together." My forehead wrinkled and then relaxed. "He came at just the right time. He showed me what I needed to learn. And then I had to be on my own to learn it."

I took a deep breath, appreciating the disparity between wholeness and emptiness as realizations poured over me like cascading whispers.

"And Amelia," I said. "Amelia too."

"What about Amelia?"

"I always knew how life-altering her passing was for me, and how much she had gifted me, but there's something else there. Something even bigger." I stopped for a moment, and my somber face softened. Elora watched the emotion paint itself over the room, allowing me to put the pieces that made up my heart together. Her long skirt draped itself over her crossed legs, her hands holding one another and a gentle smile on her face.

"It's like, she prepared me for it. For him."

"How so?" Elora asked.

"Maybe, if it wasn't for her passing stripping me raw, I would not have been ready to let Arun in."

Tears started to emerge from my eyes, almost heavy enough to fall, but not quite. They sat gently along my lids, savoring the moment of soft emotion. My heart expanded in my chest, reaching out to the both of them somewhere in the invisible.

"A gift," Elora said though soft smile. "The first step in the inevitable immersion of which a dense reality could never accept. Cracking through your walls. Leaving your bare heart open."

A bare heart that was to be drenched and beating in moonlight. I paused.

"I needed them to teach me. I needed their help." The afternoon light stretched in from the window and reached far across the room, falling warmly across my sandaled feet. "They gifted me my awakening." The words were so full of truth that I spoke them from somewhere deeper than my throat but they were light as air. It's funny how quickly we can shift from ignorance to wisdom, wading for years through murky confusion and then surfacing in crystal-clearness.

"Awakening through love's energy is a rare gift," said Elora, as clarity settled softly in my chest. I waited, hoping she would say more, but she remained silent.

"A rare gift," I repeated. "How do you mean?"

"Everyone's spiritual process is unique," she said. "There are some that experience spontaneous and intense awakenings, perhaps soul-directed and without preconception, or even strived for through intensive meditation experiences or ceremonial work. A painful experience, a near-death experience, or some other intense and perspective-altering life circumstance are often the things that shake people out of themselves, and open them to something higher. Other processes are more gradual. Softer. Life's energy building up over time and then eventually spilling over into everything. It seems your process has a little of each, gradual but full-speed ahead, brought on through your decisive spiritual focus, but also, somewhere beyond your consciousness. But your openings are based in love. It is pure love that is your driving force. Even when it doesn't seem so, it holds you in its foundation. A miraculous path."

The light of love washing over me all that time, so beyond what I was used to that I understood it as pain. My shoulders fell soothingly from my neck and I let out a slow, satisfied breath. Somehow, Arun just became even more important. He was not a chapter in a book that was my life, to be placed in the past with the flipping of pages. He was a thread that held the whole thing together. He was weaved into every word. He was between the lines and he was outside of them.

I had so many questions that I didn't know where to begin. My new realizations didn't have much structure yet. They were somewhere beyond my ego in a place without reason.

"I feel so full that I am empty," I said. "Does that make any sense?"

"Can you explain how you mean it?"

I thought for a moment.

"I'm so flooded by realizations that you'd think I'd be lighter. You'd think I'd be clearer."

"What do you feel?" she asked.

"I'm...satisfyingly overwhelmed," I confirmed. "It's like the light. It's so vast and bright that I can't wrap myself around it."

"I understand," she said, eyes unblinking and holding me.

"What should I do?" I asked.

"What have you done in the past, when something was too vast to grasp?"

I thought again.

"Let it unfold," I said. "I let myself unfold."

She nodded. "For now, just be with it. Use it as a way to practice."

"Practice what, exactly?" I asked.

"Practice loving for love's sake."

"Sounds simple," I said. "But it's not."

She smiled warmly, and I drove home in filled up silence. It was dark, and oncoming headlights filled my windshield blindingly, but only for moments at a time.

When I got home, I stepped straight into the shower. I contracted against the scorching water until my skin adjusted, and time slipped by with my thoughts until the bathroom was filled to bursting with misty hot steam.

I shut the water off and shook myself in the figurative sense. In the literal one, I dried myself off.

I thought about our conversation. About Arun and Amelia and their life-shifting presence. There was another truth there; a certain serenity that came with the beginnings of understanding. A relief from ignorance. The beginnings of grasping the vastness of something bigger than comprehension but paradoxically begging to be understood. No wonder I had not let him go. No wonder he sat there in my heart all of that time, beating with me and filling me with the very light my soul had been searching for.

But with these understandings came new confusions. Questions, solitary musings, and a healthy serving of guilt. Did I have something to feel guilty for? Sure, I wasn't exactly exercising transparency concerning my interaction with Arun the other day, since I hadn't mentioned it to

Justin, but it didn't feel worth upsetting him over. Arun was a very sore spot for him, and as honest as I always was with Justin, I wasn't sure I should breach that conversation. It would only worry him, create more fear and frustration at a time that we needed to embrace our togetherness more than ever.

On the other hand, to say it wasn't worth upsetting him over may have been an excuse; an exercise in denial, downplaying its importance with textbook unfaithfulness: *it didn't mean anything, I swear!* But what had I really done wrong? Arun was an important part of my life, and Justin knew and understood that, at least to a degree. Of course, he didn't comprehend how intricate that importance truly was, but then again, I had only just begun truly delving into the depths of it myself. If I hadn't even fully comprehended it yet, how could anyone else understand it? To tell Justin that Arun was an integral part of my spiritual process, that it was imperative for me to process it and for Arun to be in my life, no matter my circumstances, would in all likelihood seem a laughable justification in maintaining my attachment.

As for my conversation with Elora, how could that have been wrong? Guilt-inducing, perhaps, but wrong? I had to be honest with her, and with myself about all of those things if I was to ever truly understand them. Wasn't that at the core of the entire process? Learning and growing and not hiding from any of it? Concealing those emotions from my therapist, or from myself for that matter, would not do any good.

I suppose it was the hugeness of it; the massive realizations and the deep feelings that were all based around another man that brought on the uneasiness when I thought of Justin. The guilt came in its secrecy, but at least for that time, the process had to be mine. If Arun was in fact a driving force in my spiritual maturation, then I had to give it time to breathe. I couldn't shove the important things down anymore. I had learned my lesson.

It would have to be taken one step at time. Learning about Arun's impact on my spiritual journey and focusing on bettering my loving relationship with Justin did not have to be mutually exclusive. I was so enthralled by the levels of connectedness that were abstractly unfolding in my consciousness when it came to Arun, that I was confusing it with my physical reality. We were not in each other's lives beyond a few text messages a year. There was no way I could let irrationality get in the way of what was important. It was simple, really. I was the only one complicating it. And for what? Arun did not have to be in my life physically for me to be able to process those things. That wasn't what it was about. It was about me understanding the gifts of my past that continued to mold my present. It was about delving into the next stage of my unfolding. It wasn't about romance. It was about opening, and expansion, and energy. It was about love, but only for love's sake. With Arun wasn't the only place I could feel it. I could take it with me anywhere. Take it with me, and share it with the man who was there, pouring it over me, always. The man who wanted nothing more than to be love for me every day, without doubt or pretense. And we were worth fighting for.

"Is something wrong?" I asked that night, as the television flicked cold blue across our faces. My legs were crunched under me and toward Justin as he looked straight ahead.

"No," he said.

"Are you sure?" I asked, moving closer.

"Yes," he said, and I dropped it out of fear of starting a conversation we would not be able to stop.

24

I am so close, I may look distant.
So completely mixed with you, I may look separate.
So out in the open, I appear hidden.
So silent, because I am constantly talking with you.

—RUMI

Justin was turned away from me when I woke the next morning. I reached over and put my arm around his shoulder, over to his chest and squeezed myself against him. He stirred but did not turn.

"Good morning," he whispered through his grogginess.

"Good morning," I breathed, kissing him on the back of the neck.

I considered running my hand down his torso, and gripping him where I had not touched him in a while. He rarely initiated intimacy anymore. I blamed myself for that, too. For a while, he thought I was too fragile. I think he had trouble putting that behind him. Once you hold something fragile in your arms, afraid to break it, it's hard to love it any other way.

I rubbed his chest, hoping he would want more. Hoping he would turn to me and place his lips on my neck.

"We're going to be late," he said.

I took my hands back and he got up to shower. We had to get to work, but we weren't running out of time. Or maybe we were. I didn't know anymore.

I got out of bed too and grabbed my clothes from the section of closet designated for me, and unlatched the ironing board from its hook. I then went over to Justin's dresser. His shirts were neatly folded in one drawer, and his pants in another. I removed one of each.

He came out of the bathroom with his towel wrapped around his waist, his smooth dark skin still damp and slightly glistening. He was very attractive, always, but times like those, it was almost breathtaking. I wondered if he ever looked at me that way anymore.

"Thank you," he smiled, when he noticed the iron heating on the board. He came over then and wrapped his arms around me from behind. "I'm sorry I've been a little withdrawn," he said.

"It's ok," I said, softly. "Is there anything you want to talk about?"

"I don't know," he said, loosening his hold and slumping his face gently upon my shoulder, his cheek touching mine with freshly shaven smoothness. "I just feel so unsure sometimes."

"Unsure of what?" I asked, gazing into the space in front of me with sad eyes that he could not see.

"Of you. Of us. I just get this overwhelming feeling sometimes. That you are still not all here."

I was surprised he was opening up. The shower must have washed away some of his armor.

"I know," I said. "I've put us through a lot."

"It was something else last night, though. I can't explain it. I just felt it," he said.

This wasn't new for Justin. His intuition was strong, but he didn't like to turn toward it. I think it scared him, and I think because it scared him, he thought it only showed him dark things.

"We both have a lot on our minds," I said, honestly, "but I'm right here." I took his hand in my own.

"I know," he said, and he hugged me a little tighter. "I'm just afraid. I don't want you to go anywhere."

I turned around and squeezed him back.

"I love you," I whispered.

My eyes teared up with it. "I love you so much." I was almost surprised at how deeply I meant it.

He was silent for a moment and then he let go of his grasp.

"Can I ask you one question?"

"Of course," I said.

"Have you spoken to him lately?"

"To who?" I asked, as if I hadn't known. It was more reflex than it was deceit.

"Arun," he said quietly, without looking me in the eyes.

"Not really," I said.

"Not really? Does that mean you have or you haven't?" he asked.

"Only once," I said.

"When?"

"A week or so ago?" I said, in question to enhance the nonchalance, as if I did not know the precise time of day.

He took a short, hard breath and sat down on the couch.

"I knew it," he said to the ceiling with a slight shake of his head, words drifting off somewhere beyond me. "What did you talk about?"

I sat down next to him.

"Nothing in particular," I said. "Just catching up a little."

"Ok," he said, simply.

"Ok," I said. "Does this upset you?"

"No," he said, and then quickly recalibrating his words, "I mean, yeah, a little." He looked down at his hand and picked on a piece of skin around his cuticle. "I mean..." he repeated, "I would never tell you who to talk to or not talk to."

I looked at him, all beauty and kindness alight. "All history aside," I explained, "he's my friend." I wondered if it was true.

"I know," he said, "I know. Listen, it's cool. It's not a big deal. But if you ever decide to see him..."

"What?" I asked, as calmly as I could, though I felt my face getting warm.

"I couldn't handle that. That wouldn't be ok."

I swallowed hard, hiding as best I could the sudden and sinking heaviness I felt in my gut.

"Ever?" I asked, with an almost imperceptible shake to my voice.

"Is that a problem for you?" he asked, with an edge to his.

"No," I lied. I thought of some of those last words, their glimmer of hope bringing an indescribable and undeniable light to me. *We should catch up sometime.*

"Forever is just a really long time when it comes to promises." As soon as I said it, I regretted it, realizing how stinging it was.

"You can do whatever you want," he said with a flip of the hand. "I'm just telling you what I will and will not stick around for."

I looked down and cleared my throat. He'd never spoken about his feelings toward Arun and I so outwardly before. I was happy he was expressing it—for showing me a truth that he had kept buried under his selflessness. It was undeniable that my daily thoughts alone could rip him apart. I wanted to never hurt him again. Of course, that is what I wanted. But how would I stop?

How would I stop?

Forever ran through me hot and sharp and I let it burn. I felt it scalding the same place in my chest that burned the last time I saw Arun. The last time I looked into his eyes. And then I looked at Justin, and I saw the weight on his shoulders. The one he held because of me.

This would have to be it. This would have to be the thing that I would do for Justin. I would feel the pain of this forever and love him through it and he would never know of its gravity. I had done it before. I had learned how to hold pain. Now, I would bare it for the both of us.

"You are beautiful." I kissed him gently on the cheek and then hesitated for a moment, inhaling deeply but silently. "I understand. I'm here. Exactly where I want to be. And I am not going anywhere."

All I had to do was make it true.

I watched the subtle colors of relief come over him. My cheeks flushed as well, perhaps because of the strength that comes with determined martyrdom, and perhaps because the pain edged its way up. It would be a thing to cleanse us; a sacrifice of some of my peace to create more of ours. In his lack of awareness of it, I felt even stronger. A silent gift of love.

He kissed me then, long and hard. He lifted off the couch and prompted me to follow, letting his towel drop and bringing me closer.

"I want you," he sighed, with softness and surrender.

"We'll be late," I whispered.

"Who cares?"

He pulled my shirt over my head, and ran his hands down to my chest, taking each breast between his fingers and playing at my skin until it was warmed and ready. He lifted me up and brought me back to the bed, removing what little else lay between us, and dipped his fingers slowly inside of me. I took him in my hands then too, and he pressed his mouth against mine and exhaled warmly on my face.

He got on top of me and gently, slowly, and with loving rhythm, became a part of me.

"How do you feel?" he asked.

"I feel good," I said, breathy and awed.

"Lena?" he asked, eyes to mine.

He moved my hair off of my face and placed it behind my ear.

"I love you too."

And he made love to me, his wall not crumbling but softening, merging around his enamored desire. It was peace, and whatever let us have that moment, we allowed it. We wrapped around it together.

When the pleasure built almost to bursting, I kept my eyes open. I was afraid if I closed them, I would see Arun. I was afraid he would be a part of it. I kept my eyes open so that I could only see Justin. In that moment, I wanted him to be my bliss so that I could also be his. I kept them wide open and watched him groan, and then I watched him fall over me limply.

Only when he kissed me on the forehead and got up off the bed did I let myself blink.

25

Is your face a beautiful blossom or a sweet torture?
I have no complaints but my heart is tempted to let you hear
of its sorrows.

—RUMI

A poignant form of irony is tainted happiness.

If happiness is a well of crystal water, a drop of ink would be the seemingly innocent pollutant, growing and merging until its legs spread so wide, it meshed into the great space and all its intricacies with such vastness that it couldn't be seen by the naked eye. But we know it's there. That the very chemistry is changed. And that knowing is the worst part. We try to keep it down, ignore it, move forward under its weight with feigned lightness. But it pulls at us. Lays in us. Merges with our sculptured life as if we ever had any control to begin with.

Anything that reminded me of him inspired this presence of heavy knowing. And most things reminded me of him.

"I didn't know you liked Guinness," Justin said one night, when he ordered me a glass of wine and I changed the order. "I'll have one with you."

"I never heard this song," he said on another. "Where'd you hear it?" I'd shrug and make it a little louder.

"I didn't know you wanted it that way," he said with pleasant surprise when we were skin to skin and I asked him to push harder into me.

I don't know why I did that. Sometimes, I just couldn't help myself. And when the light was falling just right across the clouds, I saw him in them, and snapped pictures for him that I never sent.

Thing was, I had learned to live without Arun before. I had learned how and I had gotten pretty good at it. Sure, I was feeling flooded then, cascading realizations of our unique grandeur forcibly surging through my consciousness. But if I had done it before, I could do it again. Love him from a distance. Love without him in return, but still, with the everything else that came with it.

Living without Justin, however, was another story. That was something I had no idea how to do. Even with all of the ups and downs, we had become like family, having spent nearly three years by each other's supportive sides. Things were solidifying again. Becoming more graceful. I didn't ever have to fear him walking away or hurting me with harsh words. I didn't ever have to feel lonely and unsafe with him near me. I didn't have to ever feel unloved. It was always given to me, unconditionally, and there was always a space to place my own in return. I was happy. We were happy, together.

Letting Arun get in the way of that would be illogical and ungrounded. If he was present in my life to help me grow, to help make me into a better and stronger and more loving version of myself, then I had to use that for good. Walking away from Justin did not make any logical sense. For what? Roaming thoughts of an unrequited love?

For weeks, months, Justin and I loved each other vigorously, while all along I felt the pain and I let myself, allowing it to keep chiseling at the deceit in my chest. It was important and deserved; a panacea to the duplicity. It was the only thing that made me feel deserving of Justin. He was too pure, and me, tarnished by thoughts that would rip him to shreds. I let the pain burn away at me, setting the evil I felt into flames. I watched it char and then become ash and return to the air. In the space left behind, I planted seeds for our relationship to flourish again.

If Justin knew anything about this, he hid it just as well as I did, pretending he didn't notice the occasional heat prickle up my cheeks. He never said a word about it, and neither did I. We smiled together, held hands, draped over each other gently in sleep. We were the white picket fence and the shining romance; the perfect actors on love's stage.

And we moved forward. June rolled around with its bright nights, the sun setting so late that the sky held surprising splashes of color.

"So," Justin said, the beginnings of the moon's lavender-blue sky reaching through the window and softening his cheeks, "a big birthday is coming up."

"Not too big," I smiled.

"Thirty? Big enough," he said. "How do you want to celebrate?"

Big enough. I guess it was. When I was navigating through all that heavy *time*, entering into a new decade held steady in my mind as a light at the end of a long and dark tunnel. It was a place that I could mark in the midst of elusive time. *By then, things will be ok*, I thought. *By then, I will have grown so much that I can start enjoying life again.* And there I was, breathing again, feeling vital enough to focus on the reaching tributaries of life that are beyond base survival, and still, an integral part of it, like love and everything it touches.

"I just want to be around the people I care about," I said. "A small dinner, or something?"

"Leave it up to me," he said with his warm smile, and I was cradled in gratitude.

When the day rolled around, Aunt Athena woke me bright and early with a phone call, wishing me a happy birthday in her sing-song voice, and I got out of bed with a smile.

"Another year," she said. "Can you believe how far you've come?"

It was almost too grand for believing. I was a different person a year ago. Too choked with fear to notice all the joy.

"Hardly," I said, tears peeking out of their enclosures similar to the way they once had, but this time, mirroring the early sun.

"I am so proud of you," she said. "A miraculous shift. You are a warrior, my dear. Hard work pays off, doesn't it?"

I smiled broadly through the further accumulation of tears.

"Thank you for always being there for me," I said. "I don't know what I would do without you."

"All you, Lena," she said. "But you already know that. Now, your gift!"

"You didn't have t-" I started to say, but she stopped me.

"Don't be ridiculous. Now listen," she said, and she spoke quickly. "It's a little obscure, but I really think it comes in perfect timing. I stumbled across this incredible woman's work. Degrees of separation brought her into my life, so it seems we were meant to cross paths, and I feel that now she is now meant to cross yours. She does these readings, and I'm gifting you one. I only had to provide her with some of your information. Birthday and such. I hope that is all right."

"Of course it's all right," I responded brightly. "What kind of reading is it?"

"She looks at your soul map. Your unique soul journey. Your unique energy. Where you have been and how you got there and what lessons you are learning along the way. Why you are here."

"Interesting," I said, completely intrigued, and only somewhat skeptical, since nothing really surprised me anymore.

"You'll see how you feel about it when you read it. She channels the information. She has been phenomenally spot on for me. Her teachings have helped me understand things I never would have thought to look for. And, well, no matter what, it's a lot of fun!"

"I can't wait to read," I exclaimed.

I hopped on the computer when I hung up the phone and downloaded the attached file. It was from an intuitive named Chondra, and crafted specifically for me. It included a detailed history of my soul, identifying in its ethereal yet straightforward way where I was on my spiritual journey, and spoke of the endless lifetimes I had passed through as a lover of wisdom.

Pages and pages of words that described me in eloquent ways, outlining my personality, my strengths and weakness, my desires and those other types of souls I connected with most flourishingly.

It spoke about my awakening journey in this lifetime, a lifetime in which my soul was meant to make leaps and bounds toward a greater understanding of the universe and my own heart, should I allow it. It spoke about other lifetimes, in which I wasn't ready. In which it hurt too much. I swallowed hard around it. It described my journey in a poetic way, and so appropriately, that there had to be something there beyond coincidence. It was incredible how closely it all resonated with me. How it made my heart open; a feeling I had gotten rather used to when I was near something true.

Either way, even if it was simply a story of amusement and wonder, it was beautiful. I was still in love with the idea that my 'Self' could have in fact been here longer than thirty short years.

I sent Aunt Athena a thank-you email for the gift that came from the perfect person at the perfect time, and then went over to the couch where the sun was sending its early morning diagonal rays across the cushions. I would need to read it again, all the way through, to allow it to appropriately sink in. To take in the sections that I had glazed over. But at that time, unlike in the past when I had to quickly devour every bit of information I could, I just wanted to sit for a while. Sit in gratitude for the chapters in my life that had led me, page by page, to that very moment, inhaling life and breathing in every intricacy of it with appreciative awareness. There was peace there, in the early beginnings of a morning and a new phase of my life, and it stayed with me as I walked through the day. I had not been that present in a long time. There was a feeling nestled deeply in my grateful chest. A bubbling excitement that mingled effortlessly with the predominant peace. Good things were coming. I didn't know how, or why, but I knew that they were.

I thought back on a promise I once made—when the clouds were dark and choked me of life upon inhale and my thoughts smelled like burning coal—that never would I forget to appreciate the contrast. And, for that reason, it felt extra lovely to be alive in that day. To be able to enjoy life with all of the beautiful people that were a part of it, breathing in air that smelled like ambrosia for what seemed like the very first time.

Warm water feels warmer when your hands have been cold.

A little after 5 o'clock, I left work and walked to my car. I got inside and kept the windows rolled up, soaking in the warmth from both light and air. I turned the keys in the ignition, glad the work day was behind me. Glad that I could go spend quiet time meditating on my next chapter, before the following night's festivities that Justin had arranged.

And then I heard my phone sound.

It was so warm in that car, but still, I felt a chill run up my spine. My phone had been sounding all day with well wishes and birthday songs. This time, however, it sounded different. It was heavy with something, the sound elongating and vibrating against the windshield. I removed it from my bag and when I looked at the screen, the chill was instantly replaced. The name glared at me, lighter than the screen, lighter than the sun that massaged my skin, but with just as much heat.

Happy birthday, dear Lena.

Well, I'd like to tell you I rose above my innate reaction in the most grounded way. That I was able to access the harmoniousness of the peaceful state I had created and remember my mission. That would be valiant, and noble. But it was not the way it went.

Instead, I opened all four windows and brushed the hair away from my face, heat rising from my core. I put my phone down and fought the single tear that threatened to fall, hanging there between the world I had tried to create and the one that was threatening to crash down upon me. As soon as it got too heavy, the tear came tumbling down, and with it, a deluge. I leaned my forehead against the steering wheel and sobbed.

The silence, feigned peace, and deprivation of truth's emotions built up in my denial and then came pouring out of me. Two months' worth of longing shook my shoulders under its weight. It took this simple contact to crumble every bit of wall that I had constructed. I was completely at his mercy. The dam I had built was completely powerless under even his most subtle tide. I had done a lot of growing, but I had not grown out of this. In the time I spent denying it, I almost believed I could rise above it. If I could not, what were my options? Continue to deny it? Learn to dance with it? I didn't know.

This love was everything, and it was not only excruciatingly unrequited, but somehow wrong. Somehow, its very existence inspired guilt and destruction. But it would not be shoved down, because it also inspired everything else. Everything beautiful. It came out in my tears when it had nowhere else to go.

Maybe, there are some things that are just not meant to be triumphed over. Maybe, this had nothing to do with power, and everything to do with grace.

Maybe letting go doesn't mean surrendering.

There were too many thoughts to process just yet, and my eyes were too fogged by tears.

Arun, I typed. *Thank you.*

I watched the three dots pop up on the screen, the ones that show that someone is typing too.

So far, so good? He asked.

So far so good.

You're very old now, he remarked sarcastically.

Yes, I said. *Very old.*

And wiser, I hope, he said.

Through my biased lens, those words were heavy with meaning. Even if they weighed nothing to him, they were heavy to me.

I'd like to think so, I said.

How are things?

Things are well, I said.

How's work? The family?

All well, I said. *Thankfully.*

He paused for a few minutes.

How's your boyfriend?

I paused too. I couldn't lift his words at all then. I didn't want to talk about Justin. I didn't want to say that everything was fine even though it wasn't and even though I should.

I didn't want to tell the truth, to him or to myself. And I couldn't lie to either of us either.

I put my phone down, and turned the keys in the ignition. I pulled out of the parking lot and into traffic, contemplating the words to say, but none of them seemed just right. They were too crafted. Only transparency was right in that place. Only transparency was ever right with Arun, but for some reason, obscurity lingered in every conversation.

I refused to look at my phone again while I was driving. I was distracted enough by my running thoughts, and I had to focus on the congested road. Words, so many words. His, mine. They ricocheted in my brain, uncomfortably, and made my shoulders tight. I put on music, and I shut it off. I opened the window, and I closed it. I heard my phone sound again.

I waited. I waited. I couldn't wait. I pulled over.

That good, huh?

Sorry, I said. True.

I was driving, I said. True.

My hands shook.

I have trouble talking about him with you, I said.

True.

Why? he asked.

Why. Why did I? Because I didn't want to tell him we were happy? Because by expressing that happiness, Arun would never know how much I thought about him too? Every single day? How much I cared about him? How much he was a part of my unfolding? Saying I was happy left out most of the story.

Or was it because I didn't want to tell him I was unhappy? Because really, that wasn't true. Because that would be a slap in the face to Justin, and a gross underestimation of the importance of both of them in my life. How could I be unhappy, all discomfort and pain aside, when I had so much beauty surrounding me, in so many ways? A kind and loving partner, another who gifted me open eyes and an open heart, and enough love for all of it?

The story was too complicated for a simple answer. Maybe that was why. Maybe I needed to say more. Maybe that was the problem. Unfinished business. Too much to say, and never a chance to say it. And obviously, a text message was not enough.

He ran through my blood and was a part of my bones. These words did not suffice.

It's a long story, I said.

Can you tell me sometime?

I'd like to, I said.

When? he asked.

I was shaking now, from head to toe. Justin's words doused me in their finality. "I'm just telling you what I will and will not stick around for..."

My heart pounded, resounding in my chest and reverberating through the rest of me.

I don't think I can, I said.

Of course you can, he said.

I was frozen, fearing my own threatening insolence.

This weekend, he said. *Are you free?*

That weekend. My birthday. My celebration the following night. I suddenly cursed it, and instantly felt the fiery guilt illuminating my stomach.

This weekend is no good, I said.

Busy?

Birthday stuff, I responded.

Next Tuesday. Let's meet up after work.

Something mingled with the guilt. It cooled my insides.

In person? I asked, taken off guard.

Of course, in person, he said. *What we are doing right now, is not talking.*

Then what is it? I asked, stalling.

What it is, he said, *is not good enough.*

I was so distracted that I could hardly notice my heart pounding fast and hard against my rib cage. I was an addict being handed the only thing I wanted and the only thing I didn't yet know how to find the willpower to refuse. I couldn't go. I couldn't. But I couldn't find it in myself to say no, either. I tried. I typed words and deleted them and watched the cursor blink.

I see you typing, he said. And the words "I can't" lingered there, undelivered, my thumb hanging over the send button.

Until my phone rang, that is.

26

*Your task is not to seek for love,
but merely to seek and find all the barriers within yourself that you have
built against it.*

—RUMI

"Hey?" I said.

"Moon," he responded. "I wanted to hear your voice."

I blanched, choking on delight. I had not heard his in so long. Its melody weaved around me and into whatever space lay empty in my chest.

"Are you still driving?" he asked.

"Not at the moment," I said, while my car idled on the side of the road.

"Ok, good," he said. "I want to make sure you're safe."

I wasn't sure if I was, so I just said "thanks."

"Where are you?" I asked. "It doesn't sound like Manhattan."

There was a breeze muffling his end of the phone, and I heard bird sounds.

"Part of the beauty of this city," he said, "is its versatility. I'm walking along the East River."

"Sounds lovely," I said, looking out at the stretches of concrete before me.

"So," he followed, "Tuesday?"

In the comfort of his voice, I had almost forgotten what was coming. The anticipation of self-inflicted injury caused a locking up of my muscles and hot skin prickling with cool sweat. I knew where I was finding the strength, but is anyone able to take such a leap without hesitation? The instinct for avoidance of anything heart-shattering is too strong for most of us. I fumbled in quiet vacillation.

"Tuesday..." I said. "Tuesday is not going to work out, either."

He didn't answer for some time. The silence was heavy. I felt sick in it.

"No?" He asked.

"No," I said.

"Is this your decision," he said, "or someone else's?"

"Mine," I said, voice small and nervous and leaving out most of the story.

"You're ok with this?" he asked.

"Ok with what?" I asked, unsure of how he meant it.

And he was quiet again, which was a bigger blow to the chest than most other responses could have been.

"I understand," he finally said. "I'm sorry."

"Me too," I said, and then I tried to speak the next words, but I couldn't find any. Sounds got caught and I stammered until all I had was that and I guess he didn't have any more either. There was silence for some time, not awkward but empty, until he said "ok" and I said "ok" and we hung up the phone.

I stared into blank air for a long time, deflated. A new fear prickled at my edges. I thought I had known all of them, but it prodded me with a fresh and rapidly increasing intensity.

He had no idea how hard it all was. No idea of the truth. I didn't explain to him what happened, or what my heart was filled with. The pain and confusion sat within me, but none of it reached him. And I was so close to having the chance to remind him. To show him what it meant to be in each other's presence. Without that, all goes to dust. It was taken from a dream as real and luscious as a crisp piece of fruit, and made rotten and black. I had nothing then to bind us but that invisible thread, running between empty words and separate breaths.

I had to remember. I had to remember why. I thought of Justin. I thought of the soft smiles and all of the love.

Focus, I thought. Focus.

It was cold there, standing in that storm like a statue, letting the snow and icy wind pelt me in the marble face, but I had done it.

I was surrounded by endless love in my life but in that moment, I felt alone. I will be honest with you, because even though I wasn't proud of it, I had to be honest with myself. Sometimes, we just can't help it. Sometimes, in moments, the darkness just has to live. No matter how much we have seen. No matter how much we have grown. In that moment, I felt totally and utterly alone. There was no bubbling in my chest then. There was only silence.

There were no more words that day. I left the music off in the car on the way home, and didn't answer any phone calls. Not from Justin, not from my mother. My mouth was too dry to speak.

When I opened the door to my apartment, I kicked off my shoes, and made my way to the couch. I was hungry, but I didn't feel like eating. The sun hadn't yet set, but it hid behind thick clouds, blanketing my apartment in grey. I didn't turn on the lights. I didn't want to. I lit a candle that flickered softly, and we both merged with the muted surroundings until night fell.

And then I closed my eyes. I took my hands and placed them atop my legs, facing up toward the sky. I connected myself with the ground and with the stars and with the air around me. Quiet. And I let it come.

My second past life regression was experienced alone.

27

In the darkness of the night,
you pitched the tent of the moon,
and sprinkled water on the face of wisdom as it slept.

—RUMI

My vision went from blackness, as black as the air around me, to the twinkle of something in the distance. It grew from the center, fuzzy, misty, and clouded. It was comprised of muted tones, beige and the faintest greens and yellows. It expanded, cottony, blurred and impressionistic, until it took up my whole closed-eyed vision, stretching from edge to edge and beyond, and gradually solidifying.

I saw a girl, a young woman sitting in a field, her long blonde hair wavy and whipping around gently in the breeze. She wore a long cotton dress, patterned with delicate flowers, and covered in the center by an off-white apron with a thin lace trim. Surrounding her was overgrown grass and tall wheat, swaying gently in the breeze to a rhythm that sounded soft, in melodious movement with her hair and the clouds.

In the distance, there was water. It was misty there, and I could only make out the shadow of it. It existed beyond what I could properly envision from my vantage point behind the girl, but I knew that it was vast and deep.

She turned around, and I saw her face. It was more detailed than it would have been in a dream. I saw the curves of her nose and the blue of her eyes. She could not have been older than sixteen, but she looked wise. Older than her years. She was so gentle. She made me feel pure.

She turned and looked out into the distance, and when she did, her eyes came alive. She stretched out her arms, and someone appeared. A boy. A man. He seemed to be around the same age, or perhaps slightly older. He wore brown trousers with loose straps that extended up around his strong shoulders. He walked up to her and took one of her hands in his, placing a wildflower into the other.

The room started to spin around me, much like the last time, but faster. Faster and stronger. I clenched my eyes shut. I grabbed onto the couch cushion and I held on tightly and my vision spun with it.

Love oozed from them. There was no other way to describe it. It fell all over me. It was the purest and most beautiful love I had ever seen. They spoke to each other without words, peering into each other's eyes and each other's souls. They removed each other's pain and filled each other with hope. They softened each other and they made each other strong. Their souls reached higher when their hearts beat as one. I felt all of this, instantly, with their touch, and in their eyes reflecting one another.

And then I heard a crash. Thunder. I watched a bolt of lightning stretch across the sky, and I watched the air begin to darken. Clouds rolled in swiftly, the wind picking up and throwing the grass into erratic patterns. They held each other's hands tighter, gripping now, refusing to let go.

Their eyes showed fear. Both of them. All of them.

"Please," she begged, tears starting to fall before the rain did. "Please don't go."

"I have no choice," he whispered, pain drenching each word.

Thunder.

Lightning.

Rain.

Her hair was drenched now, and her tears were hidden amongst the storm. He started to pull away, one hand, and then the other which held on longer, their fingertips moving against one another's as long as they could. *I love you*, they mouthed over the noise of the rain. *I love you.*

And then, with another bolt of lightning, the screen split in two. There she stood, alone amongst a sea of wet grass, and there he was, weapon in hand, amongst a sea of soldiers and death.

I watched her there, making her way into a small cottage. Inside, there were three small children, two sisters and a brother. I saw no mother or father there. No sign of them at all except for an empty bed.

I watched him there, cloaked in the dark, hiding, fearing, holding a friend in his arms as blood ran down his cheeks.

I watched her there, holding a metal pitcher of water over her six-year-old sister's glass, until a blinding pain shot across her arm. The pitcher fell to the ground with a loud ding, and water splattered everywhere. She took her right hand and touched where the pain had been. Where it had come and then gone just as quickly.

I watched him there, a bullet approaching him seemingly in slow motion, making its way through clothing first, and then skin and muscle, tearing as it went, ripping through layers like they were wet cement. I watched him moan. I watched him take his right hand and place it over the wound. I watched him remove it and stare wide-eyed at the blood that then dripped from his palm.

And then, the view became one again. Just her. Just her in that field, sitting by the water's edge. I could make it out more clearly now. It was probably a mile in each direction. The sun settled upon it gently, moving with it, telling it where to go. She sat there, and she looked out at the horizon. She sat there and waited. I watched her sit there and wait, and I watched her age. Time was scattered. It didn't seem to matter. I don't know what happened before and what happened after, but I watched her sit there, over and over again, day after day. It moved quickly, like flashes, but I knew. I watched her sit there and hold her arm tight.

And then, as a part of one of these quick moving visions, I watched her eyes lighten. I watched her see something before she saw it. There, far off. A shadow. A man. Clearer and clearer as he approached.

She flooded with joy, her eyes overwhelming themselves with tears. I felt her bubbling up. I felt it. Really felt it. I wrung my hands together in my lap. I felt it but then I felt something else. I watched her eyes darken. I watched it.

Something was wrong. There he was, but something was wrong. I felt the dread.

He was stumbling. Struggling to reach her. She ran to him as he got closer, putting his right arm over her shoulder, leading him to the house. She laid him in her parent's bed. They both knew no one was using it. She laid him there and she kissed him, over and over again, and he kissed her back. Their tears mingled together now, all salt and sweat and love. The love flowed out of them again, more than ever. I felt it. I felt it all.

His arm. She removed his shirt and she saw it. It was awful, all dried blood and puss and ripping skin. I could see her, pretending to not be sickened by the smell. She tended to him. Days. Weeks. He laid there, loving her.

And then I saw her. I saw her there holding his hand. She was on her knees. Her hair was matted to her forehead. Her face was drenched in tears. His eyes were weak. They opened, and then they closed again, over and over. I saw him whisper something. I saw him whisper it again. We both could not hear him. Not me or the blonde-haired girl. We wanted him to say it again. We asked him to.

He coughed, and then he used all of his strength in a whisper.

"I will never leave you," he choked.

She held his hand in both of hers, gripping tightly, sobbing now.

"I will never leave you," he whispered. "Even when I am far away. Our love makes that promise. But it is time to let go…"

His eyes closed then, and we both watched him. We watched him, praying silently. But they didn't open again. They didn't open again.

She sobbed with her entire body. I watched grief wash over her like a tidal wave. She sobbed in screaming agony. She sobbed so loudly I could hear her from where I sat. Feel her, all these years later. She sobbed so loudly that I sobbed too, tears running down both our faces in harmony.

And then, I watched him, and I saw something she could not. She saw him die, and I saw him rise. I saw him rise above his body, a glowing symbol of himself, hovering there in the space above and watching her. Watching her with eyes of kindness and light. I watched him take this hand of mist and run it through her hair. I watched him linger there, instilling in her something beautiful. Something beyond what I could fully understand. And then I watched him leave. I watched her there, alone. I watched her alone.

And then, in fast-forward, I saw the rest of it. I saw her grow old. I saw her as a nurse, tending to the sick. I saw her save lives and watched her siblings grow old. I saw her kindness, never hardened by her pain. I saw her keep giving and never stop loving.

But every day, within this vision where time had new meaning, I saw her. Every day I saw her walk down to that lake, and watch the sun glisten upon it or snow fall across it. Every day I watched her go down to that lake, and let the tears fall. Every day until I watched her, too, rise up. Rise up to meet him.

And then it all went black again. I waited. I waited. There was nothing else to see then, but I heard a cracking sound. It was loud. It came from within, but also sounded in my ears. I opened my eyes.

There was the candle I had lit, dancing before me. Its single flame, in a crack of light, had become two. The fires danced together, mingling into one and then separating again, reaching high toward the heavens. I was drenched in sweat. My face was covered in salty tears. My hands were shaking violently. My heart pounded with love.

Our love makes that promise. But it is time to let go.

I let myself cry. I let myself cry for a long time. I sat there, unmoving, soaking in the moment that was all sadness and beauty and truth, and the flames that flickered brightly before me.

But it is time to let go…

We think we understand life. We think we understand it and then we are shown that we never did. The truth cannot be unseen. Once it shines on us, nothing can ever be the same.

28

Bear the pain of longing silently, my heart,
for this is the cure.
The ultimate sacrifice is to curb your desires
and surrender the ego.
—RUMI

  The next day was spent in quiet and somber contemplation, my soul aching with new wisdom. I moved about space unblinking until it was time to prepare for the evening. An evening I was in no way emotionally ready for.
  I walked into the restaurant and they all yelled in unison. "Surprise!" echoed across the walls and ricocheted in my rib cage. There were balloons and smiles and a bombarding blur of excitement.
  The people I loved were meshed together into a single mass of dazzling energy, faces alight with giddy satisfaction as I threw my hands over my wide-open mouth. Justin stood out and caught my eyes, watching them fill with quiet tears from across the room.
  The tables were lined with plates of my favorite dishes; pastas and steaming heaps of buttered vegetables and savory sauces. The bartender mixed up colorful cocktails, and people stood around sipping on them under low-lights, swaying to the music in the background and the hum of happy banter.
  Madeline walked over and handed me a glass of champagne.

"It was all Justin," she said. "He was determined to make this perfect for you."

I hugged her and didn't say a word. I was too choked up by it. By all of it. Emotions clunked around inside of me, colliding in their erratic rhythm. I blindly moved forward, greeting people with hugs and thank yous and nervous laughter that I did my best to steady. And then I turned toward Justin and he smiled and clanked a knife against his glass. Everyone looked up toward him.

"Thank you, everyone, for being here," said Justin. "It means so much to be able to celebrate Lena's birthday with the people that mean the most to her." He looked over at me. "Lena, we are so lucky that you are a part of our lives." He cleared his throat and extended a soft smile. "I love you with all my heart."

I clutched a napkin from a table nearby and dabbed the corners of my eyes. He stopped for a moment, watching me. Loving me. And then he looked up again.

"To life, to love, and to laughter. Thirty years of it, and many more to come."

My view was misty with tears, partially out of heart-opening gratitude, but mostly out of everything else that I kept tucked away. Everyone raised their glasses then, voices mingling in cheer and delight. I raised mine too, transfixed on Justin but looking somewhere beyond, overcome by emotions that lit up across the heart's spectrum. The low-lights caught the champagne in their kaleidoscope, and I watched the colors twinkling as people brought it to their mouths, tasting its gleaming sweetness.

I walked over to Justin and hugged him. I hugged him tight, and I stayed there, gripping at his back with my fingertips. He let me linger there, and I stayed there because I needed him to know. I needed him to know I was grateful. I needed him to feel the love that poured out of me, gushing from my chest to warm us. I was terrified of losing him, and I clung to him as guilt pounded at me, merging with all the rest of it. I kept my face to his chest to hide the tears that were flowing. I didn't want him to see them. They weren't pure.

I whispered in his ear then, hiding as best I could the shake in my voice.

"You are beautiful," I said.

He pulled back and kissed me softly on the lips.

"It's you," he said. "You light me up."

I hugged him again as tears flowed from me quietly, yet uncontrollably, and I whispered thank you once, and then again. When I finally let go, I turned toward the bathroom without looking up into his eyes.

I shut the door quickly and took a deep breath. The mirror reflected my puffy eyes, and I could see my stories written there. These people who loved me, they didn't know these stories. They wouldn't love me as much if they did. Justin wouldn't love me as much if he did. I grabbed two paper towels from the dispenser on the wall and dabbed my eyes, still breathing deeply so as to quell the tears. My whole life I wore a mask to protect myself, and to placate those around me. Now, it was becoming a cemented cast, hiding my darkness, aiding me in feigned benevolence. What kind of person was I, really?

I thought of Arun. I thought of that vision that hadn't left my mind for even a moment since the night before, but that I still hadn't properly processed. The vision that was wrought with beauty and devastation and wholly wrapped up in him. I thought of all I wanted to say. *What it is, is not good enough*, he had said. I pictured him speaking it and I felt the bubbling. I felt the familiar bubbling in my chest just then, so I looked at myself in the mirror and slapped myself across the face.

I felt that in my body, *that* excitement, more than any other. More than Justin's words, more than all of my family and friends standing outside of that door with champagne in their hands toasting to my life and to all they have done for me. More than the lights and the balloons and the songs of *happy birthday* that I was sure were to be sung. I realized this and I absolutely disgusted myself.

These feelings weren't without merit. They were real and they were there for a reason. But that didn't mean they were virtuous. I had seen too much to turn away from whatever truth was begging to be seen, but the overwhelming emotions whenever I thought of Arun had to be abstractions of reality. They were put into place to torture myself. A device used to create something negative even when things were perfectly good. They were tarnished versions of the truth. Things that needed to be washed away with one large crashing wave, bringing all of the sticky tar of their existence out to sea.

My left cheek was burning where my hand hit it. I welcomed the sting. I let myself feel its intricacies. I let it burn away at the abominable thoughts that shamefully resided inside of me. The light, after all this time, was still shining in my dark places. I cringed at the thought that I could have so many. That my mind was a cavernous maze of ungrateful musings.

I breathed deeply again, applied some lip gloss, and shook my fingers through my hair. At least I had done what was right. I had done what was right, told Arun I would not see him, and that was concrete. More concrete than my wandering thoughts. It was a small justification of goodness, but it was something to go on. I stood taller in the presence of it, walked outside, and consciously painted a smile back on my face.

I walked over to Justin's side and put my arm around his waist. I heard the song start and I squeezed him harder while a lump sat uncomfortably in my throat. Maybe it doesn't matter where it comes from—the candles are what lit us both up then.

29

This is a subtle truth:
whatever you love, you are.
—RUMI

"I don't know what to do with it all," I told Elora the next day, two days after experience that left me stunned. I ran through the stories and the emotions, reaching for whatever parts I could wrap into understanding. "And I tried so hard to be present last night. I really did. I was so grateful, and there would have been so much joy there. But I hadn't left that vision. I pushed it to the side as best I could, but I just couldn't leave it."

"Why do you think that is?" she asked.

"I don't know," I said. "But I'm wracked with guilt over it."

"What do you feel guilty for?"

"My feelings. My attentions. And, well..."

"Yes?" she prompted.

I sighed and looked down.

"And that I don't want to stop feeling them."

It was the first time I was honest about that with myself.

"I know I should, but I don't want to," I said. "I feel that this is bigger than me, you know?"

"How so?" she asked.

"He isn't just my opening," I said.

"What else is he?"

"I don't have a word for it," I said.

"Tell me what it means to you," she requested kindly.

"It was us in that vision," I said. "That girl and that boy. I'm sure of it. I don't know how to explain it. I just know it."

She shook her head slowly.

"Seeing that, feeling that...it was so powerful. I watched us. We were then, and we were now. And I just know we were everything in between. We are the same, and we are opposite. Like reflections, you know?"

"I do," she said.

"I watched him die. I watched him, and I was so afraid. I was grieving it all over again. It was traumatic for that girl. It never left her."

"And what about you? Has it ever left you?"

I was quiet for a moment. I let it settle in.

"No," I said. "It has never left me, either. I was always afraid of losing him, even when I was right next to him."

"Go on," she urged.

"I thought of it as a balance," I explained. "There was bliss, and there was fear. The deeper I got, the more he pulled away, and the more afraid I became."

She urged me on in silence.

"Maybe," I said slowly, "it was easier this way."

I hesitated.

"Maybe, it was easier to separate myself completely than to repeatedly experience the fear of loss. I couldn't lose what I didn't have."

We both sat quietly for a moment. She let it settle into me. I watched her eyes tell me I knew what to say next.

"And you know," I added, "maybe, it's not impossible that he did the same."

Fear. It'll control us stealthily until we see it. It really doesn't like to be seen.

"Do you think he was afraid, too?" she asked.

"I don't know. Maybe. He didn't seem afraid. That's the thing," I said. "He just seemed...detached. I wouldn't want to paint a false picture out of naivety. But, through his concrete confidence, I had a glimpse, you know? Of something... softer."

Elora spoke then. "When we are afraid, there is a tendency to imagine we are the only ones. Really, we are all afraid. All afraid of something, in our own way. It's a part of being human."

"Right," I agreed. "It keeps us grounded. Without it, we might trust when we shouldn't. Jump when we shouldn't. When it was unsafe."

"Yes. But what happens when there is too much of it? When it is something that we are carrying that isn't ours to hold any longer?"

"Then we don't jump, even when we should," I said. "Even when in the soaring, there may be something beautiful."

Her eyes were locked with mine. It was uncomfortable, so I stayed there.

"But what now?" I asked.

"What are your options?"

"I don't know," I said. "I really don't. Even if my soul wants to drop everything, would it even be possible? Even if I was to somehow find the strength to change my whole life for him, that in no way means he would do the same. Or would even want to. It's ridiculous to imagine that. He doesn't look at this the way I do. He isn't in the same place. I know we had something good. I know it wasn't one-sided. But I also know it was uneven. I would be ridiculous to think that this is possible now. That we are possible."

"What does physical union have to do with possibility? If this is on a soul level, aren't there different types of connection?"

I sighed again.

"I know," I said. "I know he doesn't have to be physically next to me for this to be truth. I know it is beyond that."

She stayed quiet.

"I just can't understand how that can be *right*. I can't comprehend the fact that we could be gifted the ultimate of all experiences in this life together, and we aren't taking it. It seems like such a waste. Such a waste to let life, to let anything, get in the way of it."

"I think we both know this is beyond right and wrong," she said. I nodded.

"It just makes me sad," I said. "And frustrated. When I imagine the potential that we are throwing away, it hurts. It hurts deeply. But the thought of throwing away the life and the love that I have now is heart-wrenching too."

"I understand your frustration. But no matter how you choose to move forward, you have within you the greatest cure for the pain."

"What do you mean?"

"You have love. It is within you. And, even if not from his physical self, Arun's soul is always filling you with it, also. There is no more beautiful energy to live this life in. There is none more powerful." She stopped for a moment. "You can use this, Selena. You can use this love for good."

I nodded. I considered this, my forehead wrinkling in deep thought.

She continued.

"You can connect with him from here, from anywhere, and use that energy to expand even further. Through that connection, you will indirectly help his light to expand, too. You can be the source of spiritual growth and support for the both of you. Loving him from a distance. And growing in it for the both of you, even when it hurts."

"That is pretty incredible," I said. "The opportunity to be that silent pillar of light."

"Valiant," she said.

I sighed and sat quietly for a few moments, and then spoke my musings aloud.

"To love anyway, near or far and through the pain until it isn't painful anymore. To rise above the pain of the separation and keep loving. Maybe it's another gift. The lesson. I just keep being taught in different ways. To accept. To flow. To open to possibilities I hadn't before imagined. Maybe if we were next to each other, it wouldn't be the same."

I took a deep breath, and looked down at the carpet.

"I need to let go. That was how the message ended. I need to let go."

She listened.

"I need to let go of what I thought this was. Of what I wanted it to be. Of what I hoped it would be. And I need to let it be what it is."

I thought about this as my chest contracted.

"What is it?" Elora asked, sensing my sudden tenseness.

"I just..." I said.

She waited. And so did I.

"There is something else," I said.

"What's that?" she asked.

"All of these choices—all of this—it's not only mine."

She shook her head in agreement.

"It's his too," I said.

I paused, wondering if I should speak the words, though really, I knew I had no choice.

"I want him to know."

"Know what?" she asked.

"All of it," I said. "I don't think I can truly let go until he does."

She waited again.

"Ok, I can. I know I can. But that part doesn't feel right. That part doesn't feel valiant. It feels cowardly. I know I am connected to him, no matter what. And I know I can find the strength to use that for good, and independently. But at the same time, shouldn't he have the opportunity to be privy to this information, no matter his reaction to it? We are living this life *right now*, and I've been striving to live it with balance. Bring the ethereal down to earth. To live these things not only in my head, but in my waking life. Why shouldn't this be one of those things? Why can't I let myself speak these words, even if he thinks I'm crazy? And why does it feel so immoral to share it with him, when really, it's made of something pure and good?"

I sat in the teetering consideration.

"This isn't mine alone to keep," I said. "It's not."

"Then talk to him," she said simply.

And just like that, I shook myself from it.

"Justin would be heartbroken," I said.

"Selena, I am the biggest advocate for truthful communication, transparency, and caring consideration in any relationship. There are some things, though, that are beyond black and white notions of right and wrong. Things that transcend the rest. Things that just have to be yours. Without these particular things, it may be difficult to feel whole, because in them, there lies truths that have been ignored. A path avoided."

I wrung my hands together.

"Does this feel like one of those things?" she asked. "Not from your head, but from your heart?"

I didn't have to think about it. "It is one of those things," I said.

Elora looked deep into my eyes then, and stayed there for a while, unblinking.

"I am not telling you which path to choose," she said. "I'm just reminding you to trust yourself."

∽

Our time ended when the sun was setting, a deep pink sky with the lingering warmth of a hot July day. I had been through so much on my journey, moments merging and breaking and undulating through time, but it seemed to all lead to this. I left without knowing what the next step would be. Simply wondering. Wondering what would follow.

I had always believed in the power of connectedness. I had always strived for a relationship that encompassed a spiritual foundation. But I never fully understood what that meant. What connects one person to another? What truly attracts us? It could be as primitive as biology. Hormones and neurotransmitters and enzymes mixing and reacting to each other in just the right way. It could be as provocative as lust, or something more safe and stable, like the ability to build a comfortable life and home together. It could also be intellect, the right words at the right time, or the proper meeting of emotional states.

If two people merge through some of these pieces, they can create something good. If two people mesh through all of them, they can create something great. But what about the idea of soul love? What about that layer? Is it the synthesizing of two souls, a merging of something higher, that creates true harmony? A love beyond what most of us can imagine? Or is this type of higher love void of all of those other things that we normally use to describe traditional relationships? Something completely separate?

My spirituality, unfolding through years of delving and uncovering and clarifying, reached in and tackled the primal forces that kept me from opening up to something higher. It excavated a lot of unnecessary apprehension and it spoke softly to my ego, helping me to feel safer and to better understand my place amongst both the earth and the sky. But perhaps this was what came next: uncovering at an even deeper level what love really means. A way to connect even further. Growth that wasn't just at an individual level.

Love is energy like everything else. Like we are. It would seem that in feeling love, we can temporarily become it. Perhaps there are certain souls that help to hold us there. That show us what it's like to live in a place of love. To show us what it's like to bring that to the world, allowing us to grow and see through its lens, and to help others do the same.

And maybe, just maybe, it goes even further than that.

Could it be that there is one soul in this Universe that is in fact the same as ours? In this vast Universe, that is filled with things that we don't yet understand, can this notion be one of them? Are we afraid to believe it because it is too grand? Too expansive? Too frightening in its power? I saw it before my own eyes in that vision, felt it running through my veins, watched it watching me with every ounce of truth in my soul screaming *YES, you've finally seen it!*

I arrived home and threw my shoes by the door. I didn't turn on the lights. The dusk was comforting. It mingled with the uncertainties and made me feel less alone.

I sat in meditation for a while, but for some reason, there were no answers there. My eyes did not want to stay shut. My muscles did not want to still. And, as darkness seeped in heavier, I again lit a candle and sat in the glow.

What would I do?

I thought about calling Aunt Athena. To talk toward answers with someone who knew more about life and love than I did. But it didn't feel right. Nothing did but the allowing of thoughts and fears and murkiness to dance through my throbbing heart while clarity poked at me from an intangible distance. Aunt Athena had answers, but maybe no one had all of mine.

And then, I remembered something.

Answers. Aunt Athena. That reading. I had been so distracted that I hadn't picked it up again. There was something that emerged from my subconscious and came to the surface of my thoughts. Maybe there was something there for me. Even if not an answer, an idea; something to urge me ahead past this narrow fork on a winding road.

With the lights still down, I hopped off the couch, and walked briskly over to my desk, shifting quickly from mental disarray to ebullient focus. The computer screen lit up my face with unnatural light as I pulled up the document and scrolled down from section to section until I found something that stood out with glaring essentiality. On page 5, there was a section labeled 'Your Twin Soul.' I read quickly, and then again.

> *A Twin Soul is your Soul's mirror. We all have one, though many of us are not incarnate (in physical body) at the same time as our Twin, and often, one is with us from their place beyond. Our Twin Soul is our ultimate connection. They are our perfect compliment. They are exactly like us, and they are the precise antithesis. They help us to grow through this dichotomy, for they have what we lack and they lack what we have. It is the ultimate balance. If you are to connect with your Twin Soul in the beyond, this interaction can be a spectacular source of growth—a guiding light. If you do happen to be incarnate at the same*

time, and you meet in this lifetime, you will know it. It is more powerful than any other interaction, and totally unique in its enchantment. If we are lucky enough to experience this type of interaction, it must be cherished, but we also must remember that this relationship is on the Soul level. It does not follow the rules of the ego, and can be fraught with difficulties along with its elation. A Twin Soul relationship unfolds most gracefully when ego's reactions become secondary, or more specifically, when there is conscious awareness of one's self and interactions. Often, only the most advanced souls are able to navigate this kind of relationship, meaning, a soul that has passed through many life-giving and perspective-growing experiences that enable the partial dissolution, or at least awareness, of conditioned ego reaction.

Your Twin Soul's reading would mirror yours perfectly across 25 criteria of which there are 7 to 15 possibilities each, leaving the odds so small, they are nearly void of coincidence. Your soul would be of the same age (on an eternal scale and across hundreds of lifetimes), you would balance as opposite of one another's personality and emotional determinants, and they would be identified in accordance to your core agreement in this lifetime.

Since your particular core agreement in this lifetime is of a lover of wisdom (a sage), your perfect mirror is a lover of intellect (a scholar).

I read it three more times, much more carefully. It sounded unbelievable. But, it also sounded true. Not from my head. From my heart. If this type of relationship existed, if it existed anywhere at any time and in any way, we were it.

My head wanted a say too, however, so my analytical mind kicked in to ease the elation. I could find out, couldn't I? I could get his reading too. If it is so miraculously void of coincidence, then it would be rather telling. But what about bias? What if this person who channeled his reading, either consciously or subconsciously, crafted it to be exactly what I wanted to see? I had to find a way to circumnavigate that possibility.

So, I ordered some readings.

I ordered one for my sister, one for my Uncle, and one for Jason. Each time, I ordered the reading and, three days later, the results were sent to me, and I'd send directly to their owner. It was perfect, since everyone enjoyed their gift and I got to test the field. We shared with each other, and it was interesting to compare, to read about our intricacies, where it claimed we were alike and what we could teach each other. Where we had supposedly been together in this vast and never-ending existence.

Then I ordered one for Justin. I was nervous about it. I was afraid it would tell me something I didn't want to know. Some glaring sign that I wasn't where I was supposed to be. But it didn't. Our Soul's histories blended together in a beautiful way. He, however, was not my Twin Soul, and neither were any of the rest of them, according to any of the readings, at least.

The process was so enjoyable, it would have seemed I had completely lost track my goal. But I hadn't. I just needed to wait until the right time. Arun's was up next.

I didn't have to provide too much information; just a full name, and a few other simple details. I filled out the order sheet and before I pressed 'Send,' I stopped.

There was something I had not considered.

Could I order Arun's reading without mentioning it to him? It felt impure, almost disingenuous, to receive it and never share it. To have all of those words, that were meant for him, as my own. Words he never told me I could see or agreed to wanting to see himself in the first place. I hadn't planned on having it sent to him. That would take explanation. I planned on having it sent directly to myself, where I could take it in, and react accordingly. But, this wasn't only mine. It really wasn't.

I stared at the blinking cursor until my periphery blackened.

I couldn't do it. Not that way. I was taking my mission to an absurd level, anyway. There were layers this time; steps involved in my pernicious research addiction. I didn't really need the proof. I know what I saw. I know what I felt. With all my reveries on truth and proof, I know I didn't need it.

I didn't need it, but I wanted it. I wanted it to help me make sense of it all.

Or maybe, I wanted it so that there was something concrete. A way *he* could understand.

I realized then two things I was most afraid of:

    1. That Arun was not my Twin Soul

    2. That he was, and he would not believe it.

I would have to talk to him.

30

Out beyond ideas of wrongdoing and rightdoing
there is a field.
I'll meet you there.

—RUMI

That night, I shut my computer, but the rest of me kept running. How would I broach this discussion? How much would I tell him? How would I explain myself without sounding completely unhinged? I undulated between full immersion in my truth, where this magical reality existed as the only thing that was, and wariness that I had become utterly misguided and psychologically unstable.

I woke up exhausted after tossing and turning all night, went to work begrudgingly, and plowed through my responsibilities as quickly as possible. I wanted to get out for my lunch break in time, so that I could sit with my phone and my words and him. When the time came, I took a ride back to the lake near my office. It reminded me of our chat months ago, and to another eons before. The sun was shining, so I got out of my car, and stood by the water's edge. The warmth rolled itself over everything and caressed my face.

I took out my phone, and scrolled down to Arun's name. The last messages were so empty, and had lingered there far too long.

I had to be bold about it, quick and resolute or I would lose my courage.

Hey.

There was silence for a while from his end. I listened instead to the water and to the birds, filling my time with their song.

Hey Lena, he said. *How's it going?*

Going, I said. *I have something I want to share with you.*

What is it? he asked.

Not yet. Not like this.

Something a little crazy, I said, and added, *but of the possibly life-changing variety.*

My favorite kind of something, he said. *Talk to me.*

It's too much to explain here, I responded.

So where can you explain it?

Can I call you later? I asked. The thought of hearing his voice reminded me of his ambrosia and what it did to my insides.

No.

My heart sank. Was he angry? He could be. But more likely, this obscurity, after our frustrating interchange last time, was simply irksome. Maybe he just couldn't be bothered.

No? I asked. And I waited. Minutes, perhaps. My chest was tight. I remembered the fear, and I grappled with it. It was telling me I wasn't ready to let go and I cursed it in response.

Tell me in person.

I stopped. My throat was dry, but my breath entered deep and exited slow. I closed my eyes and felt my heart beat. I asked it for help and then I asked the sky, looking up through my darkness, eyes still closed tight. My chest bubbled in that familiar way. I let it dance inside me for a moment, and then I opened my eyes.

Ok, I said.

Ok?

Perhaps he was as disbelieving as I was.

Yes. I'll tell you in person.

When? he asked.

Tomorrow night? After work?

Justin was working late the next night. The darkness reared its head. I hadn't decided if I would tell him or not yet, but either way, I wouldn't need to lie to him to avoid that dreaded interaction before embarking on my soulful mission.

Yes, he said simply. *That works.*

Where? I asked, attempting to solidify the ethereal. *I'll come to you. I can get in around 6:30.*

Meet me across from my office, he said. *We can have a drink outside and talk.*

Ok, I said again.

How about a hint? He asked. I could see his sideways smile in it.

You know what they say about patience, I responded.

Virtuousness is objective, he said.

Like most things, I said.

I put my phone away and plopped down in the grass. It plucked up around my edges and wafted its summertime aroma in billows around me. Its blades, in that moment, seemed improperly named, for they were soft and supple, leaning toward the sun with every small breath.

The sun. It is so far away. A ball of fire keeping its distance so that it won't burn us up, but still close enough to enlighten us, warming our skin whenever the clouds don't obscure it. I saw its light cascade over the earth, and I trusted it to stay with me awhile; to help me to see, to flood my eyes with light whenever I looked up toward the sky.

Tomorrow. The reality slowly sneaked in, mixing with the light and the warmth, blending together into a percolating excitement that I had not felt to any such degree in so long. It came to life in my belly and in my chest, tickling at my rib cage and filling my heart chakra. It fluttered with it, expanding and bubbling over again, needing more room for what it was filled by.

Tomorrow. To think I would see his face, smell his midnight-wide-awake, breathe and laugh with him in our rhythms; it was almost too grand to comprehend. I closed my eyes and let the sunlight hit the outside of my eyelids, barriers thin enough to let the warmth through.

I saw him behind them with orange hue. I saw his eyes glisten and his cheeks warm like mine.

Tomorrow. My mind was made up. There was no going back. I could find happiness without this, but there would always be a piece of my puzzle missing. A fragment that was far too vast and weighty to ignore. There would be a piece of me missing, and in turn, a piece missing in everything and everyone I touched. We are not all as separate as we think we are.

Even still, acknowledgement of my deceit pulled at me to be recognized. We can only dance so far from that tugging reality.

"I'm so sorry," I spoke aloud. "I'm so sorry, but I must."

∼

The next day, work inched by more slowly than it ever had. I was to catch the 5:33 train, and then make my way downtown to see the face I had not seen in almost three years. I wondered if he would look the same. I wondered if I did. Of course I didn't. Change can happen so gradually we don't notice it, but my life was shifting with each passing moment, transformation forming from every angle.

My hair was longer. Lighter. It did not have the sharp, black angles it used to. It flowed down to my shoulders now in soft waves of deep brown. I was thinner, but not sickly thin like I was before. Lean and angular, with slightly smaller breasts and slightly thinner cheeks. My nails weren't polished. They always were before. I wore very little makeup. I chose a pair of simple black sandals that clasped around my ankle, a pair of form fitting jeans and a black tank top. I wore a necklace of amethyst crystal that hung down past my chest on a thin linked chain.

At a bit past 5 o'clock, I went into the bathroom and examined myself in the mirror. I wore a floral cardigan sweater over my tank top in the office, which I removed and shoved into my bag. I ran my fingers through my hair toward my scalp and rustled it around. I applied some lotion that smelled like coconuts. I took a deep breath. It was time to go.

I got to the train station with time to spare, and walked all the way down to the last car, which was completely empty. The rush hour commute was headed away from the city, not toward it like me. I found a seat near the corner, put my things down, and got my ticket ready. I took another breath. This was it. I had waited so long for that moment, and there I was, sitting on that train again, the late day sun trickling in from every window and crevice around me. Time. In a flash of forever, there I was. Exactly where I was supposed to be, like none had passed at all.

I thought about Justin. I didn't want to lie to him. But telling him beforehand would tarnish the encounter, making it impossible for it to be purely what it needed to be—whatever that was. The surrounding intricacies of the situation were complicated enough. The rest needed to remain unruffled, at least for a while. I know how that sounds, but it was true. That was how it needed to be.

I could tell him tomorrow. Later. After. It may be more crushing, to tell him after the fact, but he deserved to know. If he called me later, I'd tell him I was with a friend, and it would be true. And when I told him the whole truth, I would accept the consequences.

Maybe.

Maybe it would hurt him too much. Maybe telling the truth in this situation was the thing that would ease my own guilt, but only cause pain to another. I didn't know yet. There wasn't enough space to think about it then.

I looked out the window as the train gave a small jolt and started creaking forward. It always rolled past the first stop slowly, as the second was only a few minutes away, giving the train no time to pick up speed. We glided past the water, and at that time of day, it was lazier. Quiet with the promise of evening.

With every moment that passed, our invisible thread shortened—that piece that connected us, that I could see and follow to him. I'd spent too much time denying its distinct presence. I'd forced it down. Away. But in that space, on my way to his world, it was almost tangible, pulling us willfully toward one another.

When I got to Penn Station, I dove headfirst into the rush hour crowd. I had been more grounded lately, my physical reactions to my new world easing into grace, but this was a particularly overwhelming clamor, and my head started to feel light like it used to. The intensity increased with every step. Maybe it wasn't the crowd that did it this time, but instead, where I was headed. Who I was headed to see.

I reach into my bag and pulled out the two pieces of hematite, my black polished stones that weighed heavy in my hand. I held them to steady myself. I held them so I could bask in my sky, but keep my feet on the ground. The ground I was to meet him on.

The traffic would be heavy through midtown at rush hour, so I decided to ride the packed commuter subway instead. I waited on the steaming hot platform of the F line, stones in hand, breathing as deeply as I could, and then stuffed myself into the train like a sardine. It was stifling, but for that time, it didn't matter. I closed my eyes and imagined walking up to him, smiling into his face for the first time in so long, and there was only open space.

I inhaled the beautiful evening when I got outside, its contrast obvious to the stuffy underground station. It was almost 7 o'clock. The sun dipped low in the sky. I put on my sunglasses and checked my phone. No messages, but no surprise. I didn't have service when I was underground. Past fears, though, they have a way of peaking their heads. *Not this time,* I thought. But still, I was holding my breath.

I started to walk. Slowly. I was glad I wasn't late, rushing from step to step instead of drinking in the moment. The almost-evening sky was soothing, cradling everything in its quiescence. It was the color of the pause; the space between the before and after. It carried with it both memories and promise.

When I rounded the first corner, my phone rang.

That familiar heat rushed through me, but this time, it was a luscious kind, filled with passionate anticipation and giddy nervousness. My mouth went dry as I brought it to my ear. I swallowed hard.

"Hello?"

"Hello there, Selena."

His voice, deep and otherworldly, spoke my name. His words always rolled off his tongue more eloquently than my memory allowed me to understand. My hands shook.

"How's it going?" I asked, my voice slightly tremulous.

"All is well. I have just arrived. What are your coordinates?"

"I'm just a block or two away," I said. "Walking over from the train."

"Perfect. I'll get us a seat outside."

He hung up.

The space between hearing his voice then and the moments that followed, the empty ones until I would hear it again, suddenly felt too long. How had I persevered through years of its silence? I couldn't understand. I couldn't understand it because in that moment, I could not possibly wait another instant.

I picked up my pace. Being in his presence became an imperative. The only thing that mattered. I needed to hear that voice again, and this time, I would see his lips moving with them. I would watch their subtle glisten in the setting sun as he sang his poetry.

I saw him first from a distance. He sat outside, facing away from the bar and looking out toward the street. I knew it was him. I could tell by the way he *was*. By the very way he sat in relation to the Universe around him. He looked up as I got closer, and for the first time in so long, our eyes met outside of my dreams. His smile was moments delayed, his body catching up to his soul. I watched his back straighten in his seat as he waited for me to approach, my heart pounding in my chest. I wondered if he could see it from where he sat.

Everything inside me was moving so quickly, its kinetic energy heating me from the inside out. I walked on stilts toward him, feeling my unsteadiness, worried that I would stumble. When I was mere feet away, he rose to his feet. He was sturdy. I felt us both exhale. We stood there for a moment, appreciating the relief.

"Lena," he sang. He came in to hug me. "You smell like coconuts."

I smiled. He always knew how to do that. To take my breath and then, just like that, make me breathe again.

"Observant as ever," I said, as I hugged him back. He smelled the same. The very same, as if I had never stopped inhaling him, not once, all this time.

I was shaking so much I was sure it was visible. The air between us was electric, vibrating with our unique rhythm, and it catapulted toward me, sending shock waves up my spine. I felt it in my bones and sparking against my soft skin. Alone, I could not hold it, so I looked up for a moment at the sky. And then, I looked down for something to hold on to.

"Come, sit." He directed me to a single wooden bench under a tree on the Manhattan sidewalk. "Let me get you a drink. What would you like?"

The bench was a welcomed savior from my mounting unsteadiness. I sat down quickly, and placed my hands over my knees.

"I'll have whatever you're having," I said. "Thank you."

A smile and a nod, and he walked away. I missed him when he did. He looked handsome. The same, but different. A bit more mature. A bit more worldly. He had a beard, cut very short, running up and down the sides of his cheek and jaw, and resting on his chin. He wore black jeans, similar to what I remembered, a black V-neck t-shirt, and black sunglasses, like mine. His smell lingered by me. I fixed my hair. Crossed and uncrossed my legs.

He came out carrying two glasses of Guinness. I looked forward to its ironic taste, silky and bitter. He handed me the glass and sat down. The bench was small, leaving little space between us. "Cheers," he said, and our glasses clanked.

"So," he said. "Before we get into the juicy details and all that, I would just like to say, you look beautiful."

I blushed. I couldn't help it. "Thank you. You look pretty dashing yourself."

"The thing about men that is important to know, Lena, is that we are like fine wines, or cheese. We only get better with age."

"I'd say you are most like a Cabernet. Or a gruyère."

"You've always known me so well," he grinned.

God, I'd missed him.

"So, what's new?" He asked. What a loaded question.

"Nothing. Everything. You know how it is."

"I do," he said. "Tell me some of the everythings."

Where in the world would I begin? Not yet. I wasn't ready yet. My legs were still learning to still.

"You first?"

"Me first. Well, let's see," he said. "I went overseas for a couple of months."

"Ah. For work or pleasure?"

"Pleasure. Needed a break. I went all over. Ireland, Italy, Spain, Hungary..."

"That's incredible. Favorite spot?"

"Hard to say." He thought for a moment. "Maybe Barcelona. Or, Budapest. The thermal baths."

"Thermal baths?"

"Budapest is rich in waters with healing qualities. They create these elaborate bath houses, and the hot springs fill them right from the earth. Combined with the warm lights and the falling snow...quite an experience."

"That sounds magical."

"As close to it as I've yet to see," he said.

He was more worldly after all. We both were. We took a sip of our drinks.

"What else?"

"You know, this and that. Working a lot, playing a lot."

"Single guy in New York?"

He laughed. "What a stupid label I made for myself. Sounds like the beginning of a dating profile."

I laughed too, more heartily than I meant to.

"And you?" he asked. "How's Justin?"

"He's well," I said, in truth. "Working a lot, too."

"He seems like a good man." He seemed to mean it.

"He is. A very good man."

"So, you're happy?" he asked, with a gentle sincerity that was obvious in the way his head tilted to the right.

I looked at the ground. I wasn't sure how to respond. It felt easier there though, in words, instead of on screen, where I could complement and augment my expression with something that could be otherwise lost in technological translation.

"I mean, I am..." I trailed off. "I am, but it's complicated."

"What makes it so complicated?" he asked. "Do you love him?"

"I do."

"Do you have fun with him?"

"Yes, sure."

"How's the conversation?"

"We get on well," I said.

"How's the sex?"

Some people may have choked on their drink then, at least a little bit. I didn't.

"It's good," I responded, succinctly.

"Good...?"

"It is. We love each other. It's good. Really good."

"But it's not..." He looked at me through his sunglasses. "It's not like, *you and me good*."

"Not much is," I admitted. He shook his head slowly, speaking understanding and agreement without words. It was a big thing for both of us to admit. We never spoke that before. Not even when his hips were pressed against my skin from behind.

"It's been a long time," I said quietly.

"A very long time," he said. "I've missed you."

He touched me then. I didn't know if it was his hand or the breeze or his eyes but no longer were those words caged behind rib. I watched them falling from his lashes and his fingertips. I was surprised he said them. I was surprised he let me know. I was even surprised that it was true, but I believed him, whatever it was worth.

"I've missed you too."

"Does Justin know that?" He said it without a stinging edge.

"I'm not sure," I said. "He has always been threatened by you. Not irrationally, though. For good reason."

"What do you mean?"

"Listen," I said. I took a deep breath.

"Wait." He cut me off. "Take off your sunglasses. I can't see you." I removed them, somewhat reluctantly. "Much better," he said, as he looked into my eyes.

Bare then, and tender, I felt the heat of his stare, drawing truth out of me.

"Me and you," I said, "we were different. Justin is amazing. In every way. He's one of the kindest people I have ever met. It makes sense, you know? Him and I. But there is something we don't have."

"What's that?"

I wasn't planning on saying all of this to him, but I couldn't stop myself. They were words begging to spoken.

"This." I took my hand and moved it back and forth in the space between us. "We don't have this."

He gave a small laugh and took a long sip, pushing bent legs into the ground with his other hand and sitting up straighter. I was worried that I had said too much. That even after all this time, it was laughable that I couldn't maintain lightness and composure around him even for minutes.

"Can I tell you something?" he asked.

"Of course."

"I've dated a lot of women. In these few years we haven't seen each other, Len, I'm not going to lie...a lot."

"A lot of women," I laughed. "Got it."

"Point is," he said, "I've also walked away from a lot of women. I've broken some hearts, you know? I've never meant to. I just don't want a relationship. I don't want to be tied to anything."

I nodded. I always hated hearing that. It sounded so final. So hard. I understood it, but I also knew him, maybe in some ways better than he knew himself. I knew how much he had to give, and how little he let himself.

"I've never been affected by it much. I feel a bit guilty to admit it, but I've never really cared. I've cared, of course, if anyone was hurting, but I didn't regret any of those decisions to walk away."

I listened intently, head cocked slightly to the side.

"That is, I didn't regret any of it," he said, "but you."

My brain couldn't calibrate around what he was saying. If I was hearing something hurtful or beautiful. I let myself breathe through it as he continued.

"Losing you was the only regret I carried." He paused for a moment, looked away, and then looked back. "You, Selena, are the one that got away."

The sun was dipping quickly toward the horizon now. It fell across the city shapes, unconcerned with its sharp corners and cold concrete. Its hue was deep orange, almost red, and the sky was turning royal and indigo. I realized I had stopped breathing.

We sat there, quiet for a moment while his truth seeped out of him and the shock washed over me.

"You had to have known that," he said.

"No," I said. "I didn't."

"Huh," he said.

"What?"

"I mean, I thought you knew that. I thought it was obvious, even though I couldn't give you much then. But you left. You met someone else. I had to accept that."

Everything I thought I understood was transforming in front of my eyes like shifting tides in a kaleidoscope, rearranging and trying to make sense of itself.

"I had to protect myself," I said.

"From what?"

"From you," I said, with gentle honesty.

"I know I was distant," he said. "I know."

He looked down, examining the pattern of our wooden seat. I watched his long blonde eyelashes flutter toward it.

"And," he added, "I know I hurt you that night."

I looked down then also, old sadness making its way to my surface and reminding me that some emotions like to stick around deeper and longer than they are welcomed.

"As distant as I had become, I still didn't like the idea of you getting close to someone else," he said. "I admit that. And those emotions came out in all the wrong ways. I blamed it on false beliefs of your dependency and skewed intentions because it was easier that way."

I let my head fall slightly, old sadness trying to hold on to its grip but quickly losing footing.

"Easier than what?"

"Fear, I guess." He shrugged. "Of not being good enough. Of not having control. Whatever it was, I am truly sorry."

I sighed heavy, an emotional combination of empathy and understanding, compassion and relief, and then found his eyes again.

"Even then, I knew you didn't mean to cause me pain," I said. "I've come to believe that even our tumultuous times were, in the grand scheme of things, necessary. Avenues toward our growth. They shook me out. They helped me to see parts of myself through a different lens. And, they made me stronger."

His eyes narrowed. "But," he said, "it was ultimately the thing that made you want to walk away."

"Walking away was not what I wanted." He looked back up at me when I said it. "Of course it wasn't. It was one of the hardest things I have ever done."

He exhaled audibly.

"I don't even know exactly what it was, Len. I was so focused on work and a break-up and all of these things and I just wasn't ready for it.

I just wasn't ready. I know you wanted more than I could give. I couldn't have a girlfriend. It scared the hell out of me, the whole relationship thing. And you—we—had this intensity that I didn't understand. I met you and it threw me off my center. I didn't want to mess it up. I just didn't expect you to be gone so quickly."

"I get it. I do." I fumbled with a loose thread hanging off of my jeans. "We just handled the intensity in different ways. I was holding onto it too tightly, and it wasn't mine," I said. "You weren't mine to hold. And eventually, I had to come to terms with that. I had to move forward. I had to open up to something else. Something that was good for me. Something that let me heal."

"I get that, too," he said. "Of course I do. I guess timing is a big part of it, you know?"

"I've thought about that a lot," I said. "About timing. About us being ready."

I had thought about it all so much that I didn't know how to explain it without stumbling on for hours. It went somewhere beyond words, our timing, that seemed unfortunate but was actually just as perfect as the rest of it.

"We both weren't ready, but for different reasons," I said. "We both had a lot of growing to do. I don't think we could have done that type of growing together."

"What type?"

"Experience. Different types for each of us. We both had healing to do. Things to understand."

"What did you need to understand?" he asked.

I took another deep breath. There would be no better time than that moment.

"I needed to grow through my spirituality."

"Elaborate," he said.

"I feel nervous," I breathed.

"Don't."

"It's hard to explain concisely," I said, "but I'll try."

And I told him about my unfolding. My delving, searching, uncovering, and expanding. I told him that I woke up, that I saw the world differently than I ever had before. I tried to explain the process, what it felt like, what it looked like. I tried to explain that I listened not only to my head now, but to my Spirit as well, to my very soul whenever I could hear it.

He listened intently. He asked questions, but not many. He allowed himself to not understand fully and be ok with that, and I allowed myself to be ok with being partially understood. I felt the relief in my shoulders. I pulled out a folded piece of paper from my bag.

"I'm telling you all of this for a few reasons. Firstly, I—I just needed to share it with you. I needed to share it because-" I stopped. I felt afraid.

"Why, Lena? It's ok..."

"Because I think you were the reason for it," I said, surprising myself with my bluntness.

"Reason for what?"

"For, well, all of it."

"I don't understand."

I looked up for a moment, and then back down to him, where his eyes were.

"I believe you were my opening. You were the thing, the person, the soul that inspired me to see beyond the limited perspective of which I had lived my life up until that point. The night I met you, the moment I met you, was one of the most amazingly powerful moments of my life. Did you feel that too? Did you feel that it was something unique?"

"Of course I did," he responded without pause. "I was blindsided by you since the moment I first saw you."

He placed his empty glass on the floor next to our seat.

We were quiet for a moment.

"So, you think I inspired all of this for you. How? Why?"

"I think..." I choked on my words a little, and cleared my throat. My heart was pounding in my chest now. "I think we are very connected," I said, "and that connection, that soul connection, is what made me see."

"Tell me more," he said.

I sat for a moment, wondering how I would put it into words. I looked into his eyes. Through them, I could see someplace that was beyond my dreams. Someplace that I was wide awake. He removed the smoky illusion. He left to me, in moments, a lens that was clear though tinted by love's warm hue.

"I believe our souls mirror one another's, Arun. I believe we are the same and perfectly different. I believe, when I saw you for the first time, I recognized you. Maybe not from this lifetime, from this here and now, but maybe even from someplace more vast."

He sat listening without words.

"This might sound crazy. I know. But I want to tell you everything I've seen. I want to share it with you because it's not only mine."

My chest bubbled over and I savored the tingling aftershocks with a moment of grateful awareness, then continued.

"When you sound like you are speaking as if you are from another time, I think it's because I knew you then. I don't know how else to explain it. It's like we have been singing this song since long before we knew the words."

The sky was turning dimmer then, his eyes contrasting against it with their brightness. He reached into his pocket and removed a box of toothpicks and placed one between his teeth.

"Wow." It was all he said for a moment. "I just...this is a lot."

"I know," I said. "I'm sorry. I know it's a lot and I know how crazy it must sound."

"It's just new to me." He paused. "I want to hear this. I want to hear everything."

I push my hair behind my ear. "Tell me one thing before I go on," I requested.

"Of course."

"Without conceptualizing anything further, and aside from the mutually experienced intensity when we met, was there any aspect of it that felt *bigger* to you?" I asked. "If this is one-sided, it doesn't mean much. If it's just me, then it is nothing."

"Bigger, as in, possible that you are and I are connected someplace beyond what any of us are used to?" he asked.

"Yes," I shook my head.

"Listen," he said. "I'm a scientist. This is a lot for me to take in."

"I know," I said, swallowing hard. "I'm sorry..."

"There is no need to be sorry," he said, both boldly and benevolently. "I wasn't done."

I listened.

"If there is any chance in this vast Universe, a Universe we don't understand even a fraction of yet, that this type of connection exists, then yes, we would be it. Of course we would be."

I exhaled heavily. He smiled. "Now relax," he said. "What's with the paper?"

"Right," I said. "This," I unfolded it as I spoke, "this is a reading my Aunt gave me."

"This just keeps getting more and more interesting," he smiled again.

"At least I'm not boring," I said, lightening the moment's weight.

"Far from it, Moon."

I opened the folded pieces of paper and explained the reading to him. What it meant, and how I felt about it. How it perhaps appeared cockamamie, yet felt totally grounded in an obscure and lovely truth. And then I let him read the part about Twin Souls.

"You think this is us?"

"Well, yes. I'm...curious, to say the least." I told him about how I had been testing the system, so to speak.

"What I want from you," I said, "the reason I am here-" and then I stopped. I had initially held that as the reason, but in reality, it was simply peripheral. "*Part* of the reason I am here, is to ask your permission. I'd like to have your reading done, too"

He did not hesitate. "Yes. Sure. How do I do it?"

"I'll take care of it. A gift," I said. "But I just wanted to be sure you understood, and wanted it, before I took it upon myself."

"I do. I do want it. If you want me to have it, then I want it."

I folded up the paper, and he fell quiet. I felt the shift. A heaviness.

"What's the matter?" I asked.

"It's just...I don't know," he hesitated.

"Arun, if you think this is all so crazy and you want no part of it, just say so. I know how..."

"Lena, seriously, stop apologizing. It does sound a little nuts, I admit, but I'm interested." And then he painted on his face the sideways smile. "And, I don't know if you'll believe this, but you happen to be one of the least crazy people I know."

"That's saying something," I laughed. "So, what's the problem?"

He paused for just a moment.

"What if," he said, and he looked me straight in the eye. "What if this thing tells us we are *not*?"

I shrugged sadly.

I knew it shouldn't matter. But it did.

31

There is a sun within every person.

—RUMI

When I got up to go, Arun hugged me goodbye. I lingered there, with my arms around him too, a bit longer than I would have for most goodbyes, and far shorter than I would have liked to.

He asked me if he would see me again. I said I didn't know. He asked when. I said I didn't know.

And then he let go.

"Wait," he said.

The sun had dropped below the skyline by then. We were sitting in the summer twilight under a black-purple sky. There was a chill in the air and we had gotten too close to each other on that bench, justified by the need for warmth. His hand had been laying across my thigh. It still burned where he had touched me, even minutes later.

"Can you stay just a little bit longer? I want to show you something."

I thought for a moment.

"It won't take long."

I shook my head. He took me by the hand.

"You have to trust me, ok?"

I nodded.

We walked up the block and Arun turned quickly, dipping us both into a high-framed doorway, which opened into a golden hotel lobby. There were ornate designs chiseled over door frames and delicately arranged atop sprawling carpets.

"Follow me. And play it cool."

He directed me toward the elevator, and pressed the button that led *up*. A man in a tailored suit and polished shoes waited beside us, and a woman with deep red stilettos and matching lipstick floated by with a Louis Vuitton on her arm. I shifted in my skinny jeans, ripped at the knee, and looked down.

The doors opened into an elevator with leather-lined walls. We leaned against them silently. Arun looked straight ahead and solemnly most of the way, and then turned around and gave me a small devious smile when no one was looking. The elevator stopped at the 7th floor, and the man in the suit got off.

"How are we doing? Fitting right in?"

I laughed nervously. "Not quite."

He pressed the button that shut the doors more quickly, and then up we went. Eight, nine, ten, eleven. The ride was smooth, as if we were hardly moving at all, ascending rapidly but in that space, unable to feel the stinging momentum. The doors opened at floor 39 to a white-walled hallway, much less elaborate that the lobby. Empty, almost, aside from boxes stacked along the walls housing supplies that looked like table linens and folding chairs.

"Come on," he said, directing me to a door to the right.

It was a stairwell. Dingy and dark, the concrete floors stained with wear and the railings creaking with lack of upkeep. This was obviously not a passageway for guests. We climbed.

"Ok?"

I breathed with nervous excitement, but I was ok. More than ok. My every move was coated in a thick layer of trust.

"Good," I said, curiosity seeping out of my wide eyes as I watched him climb story after story ahead of me.

We came to a door then, and Arun tried to open it, but it was locked.

"Damn it," he said. "This way."

We climbed and we weaved until we found escape by way of an old door with a crash bar. It opened into a pristine hallway. The floors were made of marble and the walls were made of stone, and it led to a large, empty room with massive chandeliers. There was a low-light leading our way, blue-hued and entrancing. The space looked covered in full moon.

At the far end of the room was another door. This time, a double. The handles were made of oak, heavy and smooth. We each took one in our grasp, and they opened to one more staircase, carpeted also in ornate design and rolling from top to bottom, urging us ahead.

"Are you ready?" he asked.

"Ready," I said, for what, I did not know. But I was ready.

"No pictures," he said. "This is ours. Keep in in here." He tapped his skull twice as he opened the final door, the height of our ascent.

And there it was. The rooftop of a 45-story building, completely empty except for us and the lights of the sky. The view wrapped completely around us, all 360-degrees of light and sound to be seen from our place above.

I walked out slowly, mouth and eyes agape. I felt him watching me, seemingly appreciating my reaction even more than the view that caused it. My hands rose slowly from my side, and made their way to the top of my head. I held myself there.

"This is one of the most beautiful things I have ever seen."

The city skyline sprawled toward the horizon. It seemed to have no end. A million lights shone and reflected in our eyes. Every piece looked so small from up there, but when combined, it was an expansive masterpiece, magnificent in its immensity. Vast. Grand. Absolutely breathtaking.

"Really something, isn't it?" he marveled. "It's everything, all at once, but it is so quiet from here. There's something about that. Something about being far enough away that we can view it without touching it, but still be here, right in the center, a part of it all."

And then I was there again. He made me remember. The lights moved in a twinkling symphony and the air danced to its rhythm.

"We never have to lose this," I whispered, eyes floating from earth to sky.

"Lose what, Lena?"

I was quiet for moments as I opened. As my heart expanded with my vision and the breeze ran through my hair. I looked straight ahead. We both faced the horizon.

"The climb, the crescendo, the knowing. We never have to lose it. Our journey is all of it, and it's all right here. It's ours, whenever we remember."

Arun took my hand in his as we stood there, sharing breath with each other and the wind. I heard his voice in it.

It is time to let go…

"Is this it?" The moon drenched his face in its pure, blue-white light. It was such a perfect contrast to his fire and I whispered, so as not to disturb it.

"Sometimes goodbye is only the beginning."

32

This being human is a guest house. Every morning is a new arrival. A joy, a depression, a meanness, some momentary awareness comes as an unexpected visitor...Welcome and entertain them all. Treat each guest honorably. The dark thought, the shame, the malice, meet them at the door laughing, and invite them in. Be grateful for whoever comes, because each has been sent as a guide from beyond.

—RUMI

When we got back to ground level, I walked away, and then turned around to watch him do the same. I watched him until I could not see him anymore. And then I closed my eyes so I could see him again. I felt full of him, and still, so empty once I could no longer smell his skin. I pressed my nose into the sleeve of my jacket. There was still some of him there.

I missed him instantly and beyond that. I felt the strong and incessant pull. The unceasing desire. The need to just be next to him again in that moment, and always.

I was never truly separate from him, but still, I wanted to be near him when I was. Paradox. He was teaching me that it is a lovely act of faith.

I ordered his reading that night, and prepared myself for three days of waiting. I envisioned the possibilities as a tree diagram. There were two directions this could go at the top, and then countless tributaries branching off in exponential numbers, speaking of what could come next. In a few days, our suspicions would be confirmed or negated. Then for each option, we could choose to agree or to disagree, to give it worth or to deem it meaningless. What came after that I could not tell. I tried to remind myself that truly, the results didn't matter. After delving into so many mystical experiences, learning to trust my intuition and the sky, learning to speak to the beyond, to feel safe and cradled in the arms of the unseen, I had learned a new language that was beyond both concrete notions and unsubstantiated spiritual fluff. But still, for some reason, the importance of this tangibility lingered.

Perhaps its importance fell beyond logic. In following my intuition, this was just another tugging sensation that spoke somehow of truth. It didn't feel unhealthy, untrusting or unclear, but somehow necessary. Another step in my coming unfolding. But what was it about these silly pieces of paper that magnetized me so? That were the only things powerful enough to bring me to Arun again? To smell his skin and look into his endless crystal blue eyes?

Arun grounded me in science, and I expanded him in magic. I couldn't tell him yet about all of the details; the things I saw behind closed eyes, or what I dreamed about at night, and that I spoke to him across the ethers when our words were too far from each other to hear. It would be too much. But this? It was the nearest thing to quantitative we could get. If all of these criteria matched up, even if it meant nothing beyond the exquisite nature of chance, it would be some kind of miracle. I'd seen so many of them. I breathed them in for the both of us. Maybe it was time to see one together.

Whatever it was, whatever brought me to this point, I was aware of its pivotal nature. I was aware that something had shifted. That years of separation just gave way to something else. That walls had crumbled. That misunderstandings had started to vanish before my eyes, and new stories were being written. But what did that mean?

When I looked around, everything appeared the same. Madeline put on a pair of heels and walked over the wood floor before work that morning, jacket and coffee in hand. I threw a yogurt in my purse, grabbed my keys, and jumped into the car to make the same trip I always made, to the same place I always went, with the same people I was always there with. Justin called me when he got to the office, just to say hello. Just like he did every other morning. And in order to not cause any glaring psychological effects of guilt and anxiety in relation to the enormity of the night before, I did what I could to minimize it. *This was important, we did nothing wrong. I would tell Justin, it would be fine, we would be fine.* But when words stopped forming in my head, and I only heard my heart beating, I knew everything had changed.

I had wondered how it would be—to see Arun again. What I found was not surprising. Sometimes, when we don't see someone for a long time, our minds skew the memories. We aggrandize the relationship, focusing on what made it work, forgetting what made it hurt, and imagine that there will be only magic again when, instead, there are only cobwebs in its place. A thing of the past, tarnished by time and experience. This wasn't that. What made us work was momentous, and what made it hurt was just as important. Both part of the path that brought us higher, together, because of each other. The difference was that even when it burned, we rose in its warmth, and shook off the charring.

We felt like an exception. Maybe that was because we *were*. Because we found all that is, even if in finding it, we had to live it apart. By defying that perfection, we were perfect—whole, flawed, and intricately ourselves. A leaf could not grow without some darkness. It would wither under the monotony of light.

I sat so close to him on that bench, and I only wanted to be closer. To say that my feelings were purely platonic would be a laughable farce. The air between us was so charged I could feel it pressing against my skin. Whenever his lips moved, I wanted them to move on me. I watched his hands gripping his glass and wished they were grabbing at my skin instead, his breath heavy in my ear.

I felt inflamed by sexual energy when I left him, and it only got more powerful as the hours went on. My space had been touched by him again. I was alight with his burning warmth. Even if my mind tried to push him back, my body would not let me forget him. Every inch of me longed for him, perhaps even more then, as I sat in my new knowing. A knowing that all along, he too, in his own way, longed for me.

It was hard to believe, after all those years, that the reality I had built around our circumstances was skewed. I knew he cared, to a certain degree, but I didn't think it ran as deeply as he had finally admitted to me. It comforted me, filled me with exuberance, and then stabbed at me. What had we done? I knew, from a grander perspective, in the greater story, we needed this time. I knew we did. But the realization of what we had thrown away out of pride, ignorance and fear—it was almost too much to hold.

Now what?

Aside from the variety of grand-sweeping realizations that the past weeks, days, and hours had brought to the surface, what effect did any of this new knowledge have on circumstance? I was still in a relationship with another man that I loved, and Arun still didn't want one at all, with me, or with anyone. Could it really be that simple? We felt so much beyond the social mores of a relationship space, Arun and I. It felt like none of those rules applied, but even if that were the case, there were still rules everywhere else. My relationship with Justin had rules. Plenty of them. And I had broken quite a few already.

Justin. I was supposed to see him that night. Would I be able to do it? I wanted to avoid him. I wanted to hide away, to sit for three days and wait to receive the email that would say so much, to contemplate what the night before had done to my perspective on almost every facet of my life. But I knew I couldn't hide. Being in Justin's presence might be renewing. It might help to remind me what I had, and what I would risk losing for a reality that was as enigmatic, transitory, unpredictable, and intangible as the wind.

I went to Justin's apartment that night, freshly showered and feeling unclean. My contemptible actions sat in my chest, heavy and unyielding. I planned on telling him. I planned on not telling him. I went back and forth like a ping pong ball, smacking into one side and then hurtling toward the other, over and over again.

When I arrived, he was sitting on the couch, smelling as fresh as ever, and smiling his kind and genuine smile. There were two empty plates and silverware laid in front of him, two glasses of sparkling water, and cartons of take-out ready to be opened. I walked over to him, hiding the rupturing emotions behind my eyes. He hugged me, tight and warm. It felt good to have those arms around me. It felt wholesome.

It frustrated me to admit to myself how good it felt. All of this would have been easier if I didn't care about him. If I didn't love him so damn much. If I could picture my life without him. But he had become such an integral part of my existence that the very thought of eradicating our relationship from my life, eradicating him from my life, brought upon me an instant and intense sense of angst. As much as I longed for Arun, felt him pulsing in my bones, I knew that in our connection, he was never that far away. Being without Justin, however, was terrifying. It was final. It was a shifting of our tectonic plates.

We watched a movie and ate Chinese food under a thin blanket, my legs curled over him. There was comfort there. A fleeting relief from some of the tense emotions and running thoughts of the last few days. I didn't feel I deserved it, but I sunk into it anyway. I had no choice.

How could I tell him then? How could I break his peace, even if I thought I deserved to break my own? I waited. *When dinner is done*, I thought. *When the movie is over. When our eyes start to become heavy with sleep. Then I will tell him. Then I will let him know.* I imagined speaking in a higher pitched voice than usual, nervousness cracking my words. My heart started to move faster. He yawned.

"Want to head in, my love?"

"Yes," I said, feeling nervous, time running out. "Yes, I'm just going to go wash up."

"Is something wrong?"

"No. No," I stammered. "I'm tired."

He looked me in the eyes then.

"Are you sure?" he asked.

I paused.

"Yes. There is something I want to talk about, though."

"What's up?"

"I'll be right in, ok? We'll talk in bed."

I made my way to the bathroom and flicked on the light. It washed over my face and showed me my reflection. In that quiet, I could feel every emotion tugging at my insides. Longing, fear, loss, excitement, wonder, guilt—I was swimming in a sea of it. I had to tell him. There was no other way. Whatever the outcome, he had to know. Fear, then. My old friend.

I shut off the light, and made my way back softly. I was afraid to step too hard; afraid to do anything that was not treading lightly. The lights were still on. Justin sat on the side of the bed, wearing all of the same clothes, his watch still fastened around his wrist. He didn't look up at me when I walked in. He looked straight ahead, his face blank, his muscles stiff and unmoving.

"Justin?" I said it quietly. Gently. I tiptoed over as if I was afraid to shatter him.

"Something is wrong," he said, gutturally, not moving anything but his mouth.

My heart instantly pounded against my chest. I tried to keep my breathing even, my words steady, but I started to shake all over.

"Talk to me," I said. "What's going on?"

"You talk to me, Selena. Tell me. Right now."

"What are you talking about? What happened?" I stammered.

"I feel it, I know it. Something happened."

I couldn't play dumb without minimizing his part in it, his strong emotions that were in fact with merit, any longer than I had.

"Yes."

He gave a quick and repugnant laugh. A chill ran through my body, from head to toe.

"Take a deep breath," I said. "Please. Everything is ok."

He turned to me then. He looked into my eyes with his, begging me for answers. I sat there, immobilized. Frozen. Unable to speak.

"Did you speak to him again?"

"Yes."

"Why?"

"I had to."

"Why?" he demanded.

"It's hard to explain."

"You'd better try."

His words were even and monotonous in their darkness.

"Arun and I, you know, we have history..." I said. I was careful. Slow. "...and I had some questions for him."

He listened without speaking.

"I had been intrigued by those readings, you know, and I just wanted to talk to him about it."

"Jesus Christ..."

He shook his head. He took a deep breath.

"I know, Lena, I know you guys had this *thing* that I can't understand," he said, mockingly. "But do you know how fucking difficult this is for me, all the time? Will this ever stop?"

"I'm so sorry," I whispered, looking at the ground. "I just needed to talk to him. I should have told you."

"Yes, you should have. Is there anything else you'd like to tell me?"

I froze again.

"No."

"Nothing?"

I was silent.

"Let's go to bed," he said. "I can't think about this right now."

He pulled off his jeans and his watch and he got under the covers. I went to turn off the light and undressed in the dark. He was turned away from me. I heard him breathing. I could feel his open eyes, but he was not speaking. I got into bed, weighing the mattress down slightly on my side, and curled up next to him without touching him. We laid that way for minutes; the seconds trudged by painfully.

Suddenly, without warning, he spun around. It scared me, and I gave a small gasp.

"Last night," he said. "Where were you?"

I was frozen in space. I felt myself icing over first in my chest, and it expanded from my center, encasing all of me in its cold.

"Selena, where were you last night?"

I didn't answer. I couldn't. I didn't know how. I felt like a child, small, afraid and guilty, clutching onto a hope that if I closed my eyes, no one could see me. The dark room started to blur around us. Nothing was stable. Fear covered us like a heavy blanket. He ripped the other blanket off of him. It was too warm with both of them on. He jumped out of bed and started to pace the floor, violently.

"You saw him last night, didn't you? Didn't you!"

He was furious. I could tell he was furious but it was masking the rest. He was terrified, also. I could see it in his eyes. He was absolutely terrified, and so was I.

"Answer me," he growled.

"Yes," I whispered in a very small, shaking voice through threatening tears. "I saw him last night."

"How could you, Selena?" he exclaimed. "How could you hide this from me? How could you deceive me this way? You lied. You promised. You promised you would always be honest with me." The ground shook with his thundering emotion. "I told you what my breaking point was! You walked all over it. You walked all over me."

He went on this way, berating me, loudly and with vigorous emotion. I let him stab me, again relishing the pain that I had learned was a relief from treachery. A treachery that ran well beyond last night. I had been lying to the both of us, to myself and to him, all along, even through my drapes of honesty and valor.

I was crying now. Sobbing, really. My face was buried in the bed. Tears formed a growing pool in the sheets where my eyes crashed against them.

"I'm sorry," I said. "I'm sorry."

My tears became a roar. I heard his footsteps, fast and heavy, trekking back and forth across the carpet.

"I'm sorry, I'm sorry, I'm sorry." My yells were muffled by the sheets and my tears.

I couldn't stop. There were no other words. The only ones I had poured out of me. There was no plea for atonement. Just a torrent of echoing apology.

"I'm sorry, I'm sorry, I'm sorry."

I was a broken machine. A record skipping over the same note, its needle stuck in slashed plastic.

Eventually, my words stopped, and so did his. I sobbed heavily into the bed for what felt like a long time, until my tears were gentler from exhaustion, and his steps were lighter with the same. I heard him walk over to me. And then, he stopped. He stood over me for minutes, wordless and dry, until he draped his body over mine. I felt his weight on me, pushing me into the mattress. His heart beat across my shoulders.

We fell asleep that way, beating together, merging in what was still love and the pain it can bring.

33

Yesterday the nightingale was singing,
a beautiful song by the stream:
'You could make a rose out of rubies, emeralds and gold,
but would it have a scent?'

—RUMI

Tenacity, passion, and commitment. These are qualities we respect. We are coded to honor these characteristics. We are taught in school to keep trying until we get it right. We are taught by our parents to never give up. We are taught by our steel-plated society that the toughest will survive. That those who are strong enough to push through, no matter the obstacles, will be the ones reaping the rewards.

Don't give up. Don't loosen your grip. Don't let your defenses down, for even an instant.

There is a certain honor in such resolution. A certain inspiration in such devotion. Its potency, though, does not leave room for much else. Audacity and courage are not one in the same. The former is often a short-sighted honor; one of armored defense, roughness and insolence.

We see such power in the incessant push and pull, and such weak surrender in releasing our grip. Fear is the motivator. We are afraid of our reality, so we convince ourselves that we can change it. We trudge uphill, against our teachers, the flow of water, the path of the fallen leaf. We ignore the grace of the truth that was sitting right beside us on the grass below.

Grace is truth. Grace is the path. When we fight the flow, things get uncomfortable. When we grip too hard, either we get stuck, or things break.

Grace does not always mean we have exactly what we want, but that we have it exactly as we should.

The next morning, Justin and I said goodbye with grace. When the hateful and guilt-ridden emotions ran dry, we knew there was no other way. We said goodbye the way we were when we were together—filled with love and gentleness. And amidst it all, there was the sadness. It coated everything in its wise ascendancy.

Tears flowed from me like they never had before as I walked out that door. It was grief. It shook my shoulders and wailed heartily from my throat. I was reminded of Amelia. I thanked her for teaching me. Without her, it may have been too much. I may not have been able to bare it.

We would have created a beautiful life together. That we were sure of. But we finally realized a truth we had fearfully denied: the beautiful life that we would have created was not ours to live.

That night, I hugged my pillow, pain wrenching at my chest with veracity. As I had learned to do many times before, I let it take me. Something so beautiful deserved this painful reverie. I knew I would never stop loving him, and that comforted me. I knew I would never stop loving either of them. But neither of them were mine to hold. They weren't. Only the love was.

I let go of everything that night. I let the pain burn every edge, exhausting me with its fiery truth. I let go of what I hoped everything would be, and allowed everything to be as it was. I let go of Justin. Our life. Our moments of warm laughter and our vision of a future. Of forcing a beautiful epic love that wasn't meant to be more than a chapter of our reality. I let go of Arun. Of everything I wanted us to be. Of the incendiary hold he had on my every waking thought that was filled to the brim with yearning. Of my vision of us in a relationship that the world told me was right or usual. Of the prayer doused in desire that he would want me again, the way I wanted him. Of any notion that kept us in that box. Any notion that was not grace.

I let go of the loves I had created, and instead, sat in love's creation. I was alone. Alone with my tears and with my pillow and in my future's vision, but I didn't feel lonely. I felt the warmth of love surrounding me. I felt it cushion my blow. I let it make its way through my body like trickling water, fitting and moving through fissures until they were filled. I let it remind me of truth.

I let myself feel every bit of elegant destruction and let love open me up to everything that was.

There was strength there, but it hurt like hell.

34

Gamble everything for love, if you are a true human being.
If not, leave this gathering.
Half-heartedness doesn't reach into majesty.

—RUMI

Letting go is a truth opening.

It is not failing, not surrendering, not succumbing, but instead, a great fortitude.

It took all of my courage to shift from gripping to accepting, from tenseness to release, and say goodbye to my constriction. In that shift, what changed was the pain. There was less of it. I was the one who was causing it all along. Creating pain under the heavy fog of illusion.

Letting go is part of the path. It is the ebb and the flow, and the gentle release. When our minds are screaming at us to push further, our hearts whisper something softer. If we listen closely, we can find the strength to trust, and when we finally let go of our grip, we can see clearly again. The answers lie somewhere beyond tight muscles and obstinate ideas.

Letting go, truly letting go, and feeling all of its enormity, pain, and release, is of paramount importance when it comes to growth. It's not about letting go with intent of a certain outcome. It's about letting go because sometimes, in love, it is the only way. Truth's path. In its purity, in its gentle strength, we can begin to flow again in what is true—leaving behind ideas of *right* and *wrong*, the *should* and the *what if*, the *why* and the *how*. We have to go within to find it, deep, past the ego's veil. Beyond the voice that begs us to hold on to its scripted ideas, and in toward the one that gives the strength not to.

We all have it in us. Sometimes the truth is a gentle nudging. A faint whisper of intuitive knowing that reminds us that we have someplace to be. Someplace important. A place of honor. A place of respect. For ourselves, and for our path.

Sometimes, we are flooded by truth with the force of a raging river. It takes us up in its current and drives us down our path with effortless abandon. It soaks us in moonlight and seeps into our cells, leaving us transformed. Determined.

Either way, gently or with urgent force, its insistent trust won't let us forget this glimmering view of a purpose. Our eyes might not be able to always see it, but our soul knows. We are here for a reason.

When it is time, the stirring will rouse us from deep within. It may bubble up when we watch the ocean, moving with a force that looks outside of us but feels familiar. It may happen when we look toward the sky and the colors mesh in a bold kaleidoscope of colors that were chosen without restraint, and in the swirling and ebbing of the clouds we *know* those colors exist beyond our place on the pavement.

We don't want a love that is ordinary. We want a love that blurs our corners, tears away at our gritty masks, shatters our hearts open and then soothes it all in an instant with its touch of unconditional softness. We want a love that leaves us pure, filled to bursting with that same beauty that we see glimmering in the sky. The same beauty that seems out of reach but is really all that we are. We may walk through the world with our feet on the ground, but our hearts? They are amongst the stars.

When the email finally came with the results of the reading, I opened it peacefully. I let the truth fall over me, singing a melody I already knew but for a time of which I had forgotten the words. Over and over again, Arun and Selena matched up perfectly across 25 criteria, each with all its possibility and logic begging against odds. We were written in the same hand, telling the story of two souls entwined like roots, sending branches up toward the heavens.

I waited a few days to tell Arun. I waited while my dust settled. I let myself assimilate all that had changed. I thought of Justin. I took time to grieve. I let my tears fall, heavy and hard. There was no rushing this. No making it anything that it wasn't meant to be. Justin was deep in the trenches of pain's stifling grasp, but he was safe. I wished I could take it from him, the pain, but he needed his process too. It wasn't mine to hold, and as much as it hurt to know his pain was coming from my truth, I knew it was, in a way, right for the *both* of us. That this was an important step in our unfolding. I was sure his path was to be lined with gold. I was sure that, once he made it past the hurt, once he let go, he would soar higher than he ever could with me. If anyone in this world soars from solely being deserving of it, he would fly amongst the highest.

I wondered about Arun. I wondered how he would react, but I wasn't afraid of it anymore. It felt peaceful to know I could watch the truth unfold in him, and be whatever he needed it to be. I loved him even more then. Without the gripping in the way, without the fear and the push and the pull, there was so much more room for love. It was lovely in that space. It was a purity I had never known. No matter how he responded, I loved him. No matter what he believed, I loved him. No matter where it took us, and the pain that I felt, I only loved him, more and more.

No matter.

This phase of awakening was a lesson in unconditionality.

I liked it there.

It was the eleventh night of the second warm month of summer. It was the night that I called him. Dampness careened from the sky in sheaths, absolving us of all that was. I sat in my home with my candle that smelled like peace. Its flame was still this time. It was tranquil in its wisdom, for it didn't need to teach me then. It only needed to sit by me in truth's warm glow.

"I have been waiting for you," he said.

His words draped me in their silk. I burned like the candle, but from the inside.

We were quiet for a moment. A comfortable silence filled with reverence. I curled my feet under me, and settled myself into the cushions behind, feeling the elaborate softness I was enveloped in.

"The results," I said, facetiously nonchalant, "are in."

He took a deep breath. I noticed what it was filled with. His apprehension merged nicely with the moment, one filled with grandeur and substance.

"Speak to me."

His words were the same in their gentle command, but unique in their tenor. They hummed with their weight.

"It's you," I said, my eyes filling with misty recognition. "It's you and I, but as an always."

He went quiet again. We let the knowing seep into our skin. I continued.

"Everything. All of it. Perfectly mirrored," I said.

He was quiet still. I felt nervous, but fearless. It was a new irony in my emotional repertoire.

"I will show you," I said. "It's fascinating."

"I'd like to see," he said. "This is a lot for me to take in."

"I know," I said. And it was ok. It was wholly ok. I could sense his skepticism, but it coalesced with something else. Something gentle. Something vast.

"It's like…" He stopped for a moment before letting the rest come. "You know what it's like?"

"Tell me," I said.

"It's like the new moon."

"How so?" I asked.

"You can't see it with your eyes, but that doesn't mean it isn't there."

And I was wholly flooded by his beauty. By his words that were shining with the seeds of an opening. I opened too, with an expanding heart. The light of every new beginning was within us, starting with that trust in an invisible moon.

The misty emotion accumulated in my eyes and made their way down my face, cleansing me as they rolled over my skin and my stories. I knew that if the entire world went dark, I'd see him as the one thing that still shines.

"That is very beautiful," I said, my voice again humming from somewhere far away, sending its echoes into his ears.

"So," he said. "What now?"

He didn't know about my last few days, or about Justin, or about how I had let go of it all. Let go of it all and the person that I created, and that I only grew in love. There would be time to tell him.

"We can make it through the dark alone," I said. "We always have."

He sighed. It was so soft, I could barely hear it, but I felt its air in my chest. The next words I would be gentle with, but it was time to say them.

"But," I said, "I know we can see further together."

He inhaled then, and my chest rose too.

"I thought the other night—I thought it was the end," he said.

"Maybe it kind of was," I said.

The rain stopped then. I walked to the window, to look out at the sky. It was so still, wiped clean and as pure as a new beginning.

"When can I see you again?" he asked.

35

This is love:
to fly toward a secret sky,
to cause a hundred veils to fall each moment.
First to let go of life.
Finally, to take a step without feet.
—RUMI

    I have seen miracles. Would you know, just from looking at me, that I have seen miracles? At night, my dreams cascade over my soul with memories of magic from this life that feels like a part of so much more. I have flown above the clouds while my feet were on the ground. It's true. I have been one with the sky.

    I have seen hurt. Would you know, when you look at the lines that pull from my smile, that they can tell stories of a darker place? I have seen the abyss and I have let it take me and I have learned of my life through the touch of its outstretched hand. It's true. I have grown from dark earth.

    I have seen purpose. Would you know, from simply the curves of my face, that I am drawn by my truth with the force of an ocean? I am here for something. Something bigger than myself. My passion bubbles over and drives me beyond reason. It's true. I have been inflamed by truth.

And then, there is the love. Would you know, just from looking at me, how much love is in my heart? I am surrounded by it in form and formlessness. It is a part of me and it is all around me. I have been held by love and I have held it too. Sometimes, when I see something beautiful, I remember; my heart opens, right there in my chest. It's true. I have been bathed in love.

We are destined for greatness. All of us. Can we see it in each other's eyes? Sometimes, I wonder if it matters. I have seen miracles and torment and love. Is that not enough to feel complete?

Purpose and truth are relentless. They teach us something that is drenched in paradox. They teach us to embrace where we are, to be grateful for our experiences that put us together and build us up, while simultaneously striving for more. They push us. They get inside us and they rouse our Spirits, urging us ahead into a great unknown that uses all that we are to become all that we can be.

Purpose and truth won't let us settle, but at the same time, let us settle into our greatness. They are forces not to be reckoned with, but to trust. We are great. We are all great, exactly as we are, right now, in this moment. We need nothing more. We do not need to *do* anything to be spectacular. But still, sometimes, with just a little push, we can touch people. We can write that story or sing that song or find that bit of light that we can share with the world—that thing that can bring our greatness forward and recalibrate the Universe around its light, ever so slightly.

Arun didn't give me greatness. He *was* my greatness. He was an integral part of it all. He was my purpose and I was his. In his eyes, I saw God. And somewhere, deep down, I must have trusted it all along. Trusted that each step took me closer to him. I smiled through cascading hurts, humming my soul's song, unaware that his background music was my melody. Once the fire was lit, it could not burn out; we only had to caress the burning embers with patient delicacy.

I had to leave for a while to find the magic. To find myself. I had to start the healing process so that I could become strong enough to hold him, and strong enough to hold myself. And all that time I was away, all that time I swam through those dark waters of the unknown, I knew I really only wanted to get lost in him. All those years, without even realizing it, I was taking in air for the both of us. Whenever Arun held his breath, I could be his inhale. As sure as the sun forever kisses the trees, I would never stop breathing for him.

The first time I saw him again, I knew I was home. He opened the door and stood there, eyes wide open and again reflecting mine. I wrapped my arms around him and we were like we were before—two souls entwined in perfect song. To me, he shone so brightly that every bit of darkness was illuminated by his Divinity. Alight with such power that even shadows crumbled in his grace.

I loved him. I loved him with all of myself. The joy that I had felt the night we met seemed flawless, but somehow, this new joy reached higher. It took me up in its arms, allowing my heart to greet the sky and float there amongst the clouds.

We knew it would not always be easy. Once alight with each other, we could never again be able to ignore the pull of our souls. We also knew that it would be worth it. In navigating this world together, we would be strong enough for whatever was to come. It was time to stop running. From each other, from ourselves, from our pain. It was time to let love take us. Teach us. Unlock layers of our infinite selves that were begging to be seen. I made a promise to myself that when love oozed out of every pore, I would use it as both our rapture and our salve.

We walked gradually into love's warm waters with patience, and with trust. The words didn't have to be spoken. Not yet. I knew that he was still afraid. But there would be time for that. Plenty of time in our eternity. And though he may have viewed things through his own lens of life and experience—unsure of how the magic tied us together, but still, aware that the magic existed, one way or another—I learned that it didn't really matter. Our souls know of the beauty of all that we are. And when it comes to this type of beauty, how our feet hit the ground is irrelevant.

36

We come spinning out of nothingness,
scattering stars like dust.

—RUMI

The labyrinth stretched before me. It was an uncomplicated but elegant maze, subtle in size but massive in its magnificence. The cobblestone path unfolded, etched on the edges by small manicured bushes and fresh mounds of earth, swirling toward the center in a graceful spiral. There was a clearing there, where we would soon be, right in the center of its harmonious vortex.

I felt grateful to finally be standing before this space. Its sacredness was apparent even from the outside, inspiring an opening of my chest that warmed to my extremities. The sky was grey and the clouds were moving quickly, the wind bringing with it the dampness that was not yet rain, but of which hung in the air with promise. I wrapped my sweater closer to my body while my long skirt whipped around my ankles. The entire scene, from forefront to periphery, surrounded by a group of powerfully spiritual women and all of the heavens, looked otherworldly. Like a dream. I closed my eyes for a moment, letting the air caress my face and my thoughts wander.

They got lost in Arun, as they often did:

"Wake up," I said, shaking him softly. "I have to go soon."

I kissed him on the forehead and on the cheek and on the neck until he started to rouse.

"Don't leave," he said. "Not yet."

He opened his eyes wide and grabbed me by the torso, turning me onto my back and sitting across my hips.

"Try me," he said.

I couldn't budge and I didn't want to. The morning light shone through his bedroom window, draping over the white bedsheets and his skin, and reflecting off of the four pieces of magnetic hematite stacked on his bedside table.

"Only two days. And then Sunday night is ours."

He sighed with partial concession, but without lifting off of me.

I loved what he looked like upon waking, when he was somewhere between here and there, his eyes still hazy with otherworldliness. He leaned toward me and kissed me softly on the lips. Like breeze to willow. Like dusk against the sky. There was a time that I believed that you learned the way someone's lips felt against yours. I was wrong. Every time he kissed me was new and softer than the last. I lingered against him and brought him closer.

He leaned his forehead to mine when our lips parted. We weren't afraid to keep our eyes open there, so close to each other, where our souls could speak. Now and then mingled in our eternity when we looked into each other's eyes, immersing ourselves slowly in the warm water of our reunion. It was our patient and blissful blip in eternity, and sometimes, I could have sworn I saw him as I saw him then, back before these bodies and right into his core.

"Do you think the particles of two people's skin can vibrate the same?" he asked, as he rubbed his hand up and down my arm. "Maybe that would explain it."

I laughed as he attempted to gauge our frequency. He was always trying to quantify our miracle—but that didn't make it any less of one. I wondered what frequency he felt from us then. I hadn't been keeping count. I just knew that when we vibrated together, we caressed the rhythm of everything we touched.

"Maybe I won't go," I whispered.

He took his hand and ran it over my hair. I could feel its gentle spark, bringing all my nerve-endings to life.

"You have to go," he said. "You've been looking forward to this retreat for months."

He flipped off of me then and fit his arms around me from the side. "Maybe, you'll just be a little late." I pressed my cheek against his and wrapped my legs tightly around his waist, skin to skin and exhaling contentedly.

It flooded me then, as it often did. The aligning of mind, body and souls.

"The labyrinth walk is an ancient practice," Elora said, shaking me from my reverie. "It is said to help us to find balance, impart a sense of wholeness, instill a sense of peace, and promote healing. It is a meditative place. It allows us to bring ourselves from the outside world and deeply into the center of our spirituality. And then, it brings us back into the world again, allowing us to take with us what we have learned."

We listened intently. Seriously and with reverence, breathing softly, eyes pointed toward the earth and toward the sky. We were still. No one wanted to disturb the earth beneath our feet.

"We will walk quietly around the maze," Elora said. "Slowly. Use it as time to connect. To truly feel this powerful energy of which you will soon be a part of. Once we are in the center, we will join hands. I invite you all to call on someone then. A guide from beyond. I invite you to ask them to speak to you. To give you whatever message they feel you may need."

I took a deep breath, and sensed everyone around me do the same. They were all adorned in ceremonious garments, matching my long skirt and warm sweater in their own unique patterns and ways. I was the youngest one there, but I didn't feel separate. They taught me, and I shared my love's wisdom with them. There, I was able to do so without question.

Elora raised her eyes and started to walk. We bowed our heads and followed. Slowly and silently, our feet touching the ground with delicacy and veneration. As soon as I crossed the threshold of the labyrinth, I felt its power. The energy was strong. So strong it opened my heart and made my head swim in that now-familiar way. I was not afraid of that feeling anymore. It meant I was there. It meant I was immersed in love's magic.

We made our way around the circle, balancing over cobblestone on our swirling path toward wholeness. I thought of Arun again as I inched myself rhythmically toward its center, flooded by that space and its magic and him. He was this energy and this energy was him. I was a part of both and all of it at once. I longed for him to be next to me, walking the path too, though at the same time, I knew he was. He was there with me, his heart glowing like mine did, with every step I took.

Tears began to stream down my face. They ran heavy down my cheeks and splashed against the cobblestone ground. The power of the energy was increasing as I made my way inside. Deeper, deeper. I was overcome with emotion—beautiful emotion that soaked into my skin and squeezed itself into my crevices.

When we got to the center, we took each other's hands and let wet tears run unreservedly down our cheeks. We looked toward the center and then closed our eyes.

"Invite your guide from beyond," Elora whispered. "A loving request."

For a moment, I stood there in black silence. It crackled softly in my ears. The intensity built to this moment, and in its crescendo, I felt peace. I let it come.

There, in my mind's eye, in the center of this labyrinth, there appeared a figure. She was floating there, all weightlessness and light. She was nearly formless, but making way to shape with nebulous movement. Her mystical light flowed in the wind, touching the clouds and looking toward me.

I spoke to her from the inside.

Thank you for coming.

Thank you for having me, she said playfully. I sensed her soft voice and it blanketed me in indescribable safety.

What is your name? I asked.

Amelia, she sang. *My name is Amelia.*

It coursed through me, pure and ecstatic. *Amelia.*

Her amorphous light started to take on a more obvious form then. She didn't have to. She did it for me. She looked just like she had when I had known her, but draped in peaceful perfection. Her eyes shone like two beacons of tender enchantment.

How are you? I asked. *Please, tell me, how are you? I've missed you with all of my heart.*

I am perfect. It is perfect here, Selena. That is all it is. An endless dance of peace and joy.

She spun around, dancing in the sky.

And flying.

I laughed aloud. A joyous laugh coated in joyful tears.

You are very beautiful, I said.

As beautiful as you are, she said.

I could make out her features. Every bit of her was shining in the essence of purity. That's what she looked like where pain did not exist. That's what she looked like when she was only light. I inhaled and I could almost smell her popcorn paws. Her eyes were deep and round.

Can I tell you something about the moon? she asked.

She was quiet for a moment, and it happened again. Life spun around me. I stood firmly. I was ready.

Please, I said from my heart.

When the moon is full from your vantage point on earth, something beautiful happens. The moon and sun align, and the earth sits between, flooded in both warm and cool light.

I smiled. She continued.

The sun sets, the moon rises. All balanced. All perfect.

Perfect, I thought. *Balance and the effortless way nature finds it.*

But you found it too, Lena, she said, reading my hearts words. *You just needed to fill up enough first. Do you see? You needed to fill up enough to rise, and to find balance there. To drift back into the space you belong.*

I saw. I saw it glowing inside of me and everywhere else. I remembered the single wildflower Arun put into my hand, in that field, so long ago. The one that I held and then gave to my heart to keep me warm while he was gone.

My moon, you are so delicate. With the fiery Sun, you find purpose. You shine brighter when you are one. There is nothing that is out of your reach. You reflect all that you are given and it cascades over all that you touch. In turn, you are warmed. He warms you and everything that lets his light in.

The tears came in rolling waves then, washing over me, purifying me with their clear waters. Love and gratitude exploded out of me, encircling me in a light so bright it touched the heavens.

Together, you will light up the world, she said. *Together, you will touch this world and its beyond, vibrating faster and faster toward a center where you will match each other's light and raise everything around you in its glow. You will help to show the world what love is, just as all eternal lovers do.*

Her words were vast. I let them move inside of me, feeling the enormity of my part in this earth's heightened consciousness. Our part in raising it.

Amelia, was he my gift? Was he my gift from you?

Life is a road that led you to him, Selena. All of it. The messy and the beautiful, the difficult and the lovely, the winding and the shining and the darkness, too. Every detail, Every moment. Slippery slopes that nudged you on icy path toward his warm glow, or peaceful garden trails, calling you ahead toward love's deep sea.

Through it all, you have had choices, and beyond it all, you are safe in love's arms. With trust, faith, and love, all unfolds in elegant perfection. Arun was my gift to you. He was a gift from me and from everything else. I watch you love him from here. I watch you love just like I have always felt you love. Do not hesitate anymore. Do not falter. Go to your love, now and always. Embrace it all. It isn't only perfect here, where I am. It is perfect there, too. Where you can touch it. Where you can take that love in your hands and hold it. *Don't let anyone ever tell you there can't be heaven on earth.*

I love you, Amelia. It repeated in my heart so that she could hear it. *With every bit of my soul and then even more than that.*

She smiled brightly. *Love... there is always enough, and there is never enough. We mustn't be afraid of a little paradox.*

She winked and I giggled in the knowing that she had been watching me, all along.

Whenever you are in doubt, whenever things get tough, whenever you are angry or afraid: just love more.

I took that and held it close, nodding my head and crying joyously.

Just love more, she repeated.

And suddenly, I felt the breeze on my neck again. I didn't want to go, but I knew I had to.

Let me leave you with this, she said. *Your purpose is everything you understand it to be right now, and simultaneously it lies somewhere beyond. Trust in it, Selena. In not only in the Moon and the Sun, but in the lush soils of this Earth. In life itself. Trust in it, always.*

My heart wanted to ask her questions, but just as soon as she said it, she started to fade away. She watched me while she did, leaving the place I was and heading toward somewhere beyond, but I wasn't afraid. I did not grieve, for I knew she was not going anywhere, really. She was in the breeze, and in my heart. My precious, wise Amelia. I knew I would see her again.

We walked back into life then. We made our way out of the maze, and out of the cold. The chilling haze lifted with each step forward, unraveling the circle out toward the earth we were used to. My feet touched the grass again, and as I stood with my feet more solidly upon the ground, I could feel its softness cradling me, urging me ahead. The world looked clearer, more pristine, and the sky was wide open—reminding me of moments before, telling me of moments to come, and holding me in the present. Each nothing short of a miracle. I walked with my back gratefully toward my past, and my heart facing lovingly toward the future. Our future.

We had seen each other die a thousand deaths, but it was living then that we were learning how to do. Reflected in the sky and dancing in the soil, I saw our Souls. They were the full and the new, cascading over plant and pavement. The rise and the set, painting the sky with the soft and the vivid. The lights amongst the deepest shadows.

It was time to go home to him now.

The space between my thoughts and cells. My bridge between earth and sky. Connecting me to everything.

Acknowledgements

We are surrounded by phenomenal humans.

Thank you—to those who were a part of the book-making process—and to those who were there through all the moments of my life that inspired a story in the first place.

To my grandmother, Bertha Gaetano, my very first reader, and someone whose smile alone has this way of teaching someone what this life is truly about. To my Aunt, Alison Shields, a soulmate of epic proportions, always helping me to understand how vast and miraculous this life truly is. To my mother, and best friend, Christine Breitfeller, whose kindness is truly superhuman. Everything I am in this life has a piece of her in it. To our Shirley, who may not be of this world anymore but who will never, ever stop teaching my heart. To my sister, Erika Breitfeller, for her friendship and endless encouragement. To my father, Richard Breitfeller for his tireless support and feedback.

To my editor, Fran Rittman, who dedicated her talents to this project with unique caring and consideration. To my therapist, Fayina Cohen, and my mentor and teacher, Christine Agro, who have been unparalleled sources of loving support and inspiration throughout every stage of an unfolding journey.

And, to you, my love. You aren't just a partner in this life. You are my heart's purpose. I adore you. I absolutely adore you.

www.ingramcontent.com/pod-product-compliance
Lightning Source LLC
Chambersburg PA
CBHW022110040426
42450CB00006B/649